THE BURDEN OF GIRLHOOD

A GLOBAL INQUIRY INTO THE STATUS OF GIRLS

For Andrey

THE BURDEN OF GIRLHOOD
A GLOBAL INQUIRY INTO THE STATUS OF GIRLS

NEERA KUCKREJA SOHONI, PH.D.

Affiliated Scholar
Institute for Research on Women and Gender
Stanford University, Palo Alto, California, U.S.A.

In friendship

NK Sohoni

May 29, 1996

THIRD PARTY PUBLISHING COMPANY
Oakland, California, U.S.A.

THE BURDEN OF GIRLHOOD:
A GLOBAL INQUIRY INTO THE STATUS OF GIRLS

International Standard Book Number 0-89914-040-8
Library of Congress Number 95-060679
Published in 1995

Printed in the United States of America
Third Party Publishing Company
A Division of Third Party Associates, Inc.
P.O. Box 13306, Montclair Station
Oakland, California 94661-0306, U.S.A.
Telephone: 510/339-2323
Fax: 510/339-6729

Managing Editor: Paul R. Mico
Electronic composition by Patrick Kammermeyer
Editing: Mary Bem, Alison Biggar, and Jana Coman

TABLE OF CONTENTS

DEDICATION

I dedicate this book to my three children—
Aparna, Sharmila, and Aparajita—all daughters,
through whom I daily discover the expanded
horizons of girlhood, even though unmistakably
inhibited by gender.

PREFACE

In a formal sense, this inquiry into the status of girls began as a result of brief consultancies with the Indian government (1988) and UNICEF (1990). But as a woman, I, like millions of women, have been an unresolved subject of this inquiry. The girl in every woman precedes and shapes the woman in her. And to the extent to which girlhood is denied, liberated, and fostered, womanhood perishes or prospers. My inroad into the status of girls thus began not with recent consultancies but with my girlhood.

I was born in India, a country with the unique negative distinction of having fewer females than males, and where the number of females has declined from a ratio of 972 per 1,000 males at the turn of the century to 927 per 1,000 males in 1991. And, as with others in the development discipline, I have only recently begun to sense the connection between women's continued diluted socio-demographic presence and the treatment of girlhood. After three or more decades of harping on the status of women and working to integrate them in the processes of human development, it is now clear to theoreticians and practitioners of development that rational gender equations are difficult to achieve in the adult world. More importantly, it is clear that strategic corrective and preemptive actions need to begin with girls.

Gender discrimination is not a consciously practiced science or discipline. Yet it surrounds us. No one family, society, culture, or government deliberately decides to deny food, care, knowledge, and life's opportunities to girls, but the fact remains that she is the lesser gender and the lesser presence in the theory and practice of childhood. Proof of this fact derives from the widely accepted disparate status of the woman, as compared to the man. When the woman is unequal to the man, the girl is unequal to the boy as well.

The thrust of the discourse that follows is that the girl is the cross-bearer of gender discrimination, but can, given appropriate moral and material support, become the standard-bearer of gender equity and parity.

Childhood is politically mute and girlhood is culturally mute, as well. It is this veil of silence that needs to be lifted if any corrective affirmative action is to occur. At the end of three U.N. Development Decades, women continue not to benefit equitably from development's positive outcomes. This inequity is first lived out by girls. Girls bear the greater burden of discriminatory treatment. In poorer countries, privation and denial begin early for children. But for the female child, it is not only poverty but also her gender which are suspected to form the basis for her lack of fulfillment. Even where choices between genders are not related to basic issues of survival, the spirit and essence of girlhood are still diminished. In contemporary times, no culture, country, or people can truly assert that, among them, girlhood stands tall, proud, and free.

National constitutions in all regions of the world affirm the equality of women and men. Global commitments embodied in the Charter of the United Nations, the Universal Declaration of Human Rights, and the Convention on the Elimination of All Forms of Discrimination Against Women re-affirm that equality. But custom, law, and practice continue to perpetuate women's inequality. Many of the disadvantages women face begin in childhood.

Apartheid and racism are still rampant in many parts of the world. Sexism is silent but no less abrasive or pervasive. It is also a continuum, one in which the female child and the adult experience discrimination and disparities in tandem. What the woman will experience at 21 years of age obviously does not begin then but rather at the time of her birth, and even prior to that as a fetus: conception marks the inauguration of the discriminatory discourse, especially in traditional cultures. Fetal prejudice against the female child appears in the almost universal parental aspiration to have a male child, and in the sense of disappointment that must then accompany the birth of a female. In many societies, even when a male child is already born, a girl may be welcome as a rearing curiosity or alternative, occasionally for her doll-like charm and "dress-up" potential, and in rare contexts as a source of potential income. Hardly ever are girls welcome as a singular compulsive need, such as that which fosters the parental desire for a male child.

Anthropological and sociological literature from more than one developing region of the world amplifies parental reluctance to have a baby girl; cultural homilies manifesting cynical attitudes toward the girl abound. Biases against conceiving a female fetus are now encouraged by legal and illegally practiced sex-selective devices—amniocentesis being the key reliable, effective tool for calculated gender selection. Abortion is widely suspected to have replaced female infanticide in certain cultures.

The status of girls, judged purely from their thinner global demographic presence[1] compared to boys and women, suggests that they are being victimized on account of their age as well as their gender. In that sense, their loss is incomparable and the urgency for addressing the problems of girlhood is thus greater. Compensations gained by addressing the girl's problems are also unique because they restore her to function effectively not only as a child, but also as future woman and mother. Her gain is truly intergenerational and intertemporal. By protecting and nurturing her, we are ensuring a healthier present and future humankind.

But the case for the girl rests independently of her link to future womanhood and motherhood. There is her intrinsic right to be a child and be valued for both her childhood and her gender.

This book is about girls and their right to childhood. It is in pursuit of a gender-blind, or gender-fair, childhood. It seeks to apprise academicians and feminists, along with makers and practitioners of development policies everywhere, of the status and constraints currently experienced by girls in such key development sectors as acculturation, health and survival, nutrition, education, and employment. It points out the strategic shifts necessary to overcome those constraints and work toward a more gender-just childhood. The broader issue of individual and institutional violence against girls is also addressed. While the text is focused mainly on the developing world, a comparative perspective has been attempted which should evoke interest among advocates of greater equity for girls globally.

To attain an equitable childhood, the current ethos for girls has to alter radically. Beginning with parents, the task of transforming the girl's environment from one of neglect and inequity to that of equal entitlement and opportunity must engage the attention of development's strategists, scholars, and practitioners at all levels. Only the calculated, concerted, courageous, and sustained action of parents, cultures, religions, nations, and multi-national bodies will make a difference in the present and future of girlhood, globally.

It is important to point out what this book is not. It is not a treatise, offering feminist, historical, or anthropological analyses of why and how girls have come to be what they are; rather it is a transparent lens into their current status and reality.

Absence or inaccessibility of separate data on girls is a major limitation to any analysis. Whereas, WID (women in development) sources—national and global—have grown exponentially in recent years, girls have endured an invisibility similar to that which women experienced in development projects approximately two decades ago. A handful of existing sources have been drawn upon extensively. Among others, those that come to mind are Newland (1979), Ware (1981), Ravindran (1986), and a collection of articles edited by Richardson/Taylor, entitled Feminist Frontiers II (1989). UNICEF reports and documents are ever invaluable for studying children, although disaggregated sources there, too, are relatively recent. I am grateful for a 1990 consultancy with UNICEF that enabled me to draw upon the more recent country-level and international girl-specific sources. A summary based on a short report which I prepared was published by UNICEF in 1990, under the title, The Girl Child: An Investment in the Future. The imprints of that report are unmistakable in this book. Unusually candid reports relating to girls began to appear in developing countries toward the late 1980s (for example, Chatterjee, Mimeo; Government of India, 1989; Oppong, 1987). Ground-breaking reports from the American Association of University Women, in the United States (1992, 1993) and the works of such other scholars as Gilligan, Lyons, and Hanmer (1990), Lees (1993), and Lott (1994) have added richly to the discourse on girls. Many of their insights are reflected or shared here in the belief that combining relevant voices gives momentum and accessibility to a theme. If the synergy thus created crystallizes and facilitates the task of fitting "development" to girls' needs, this book will have served its modest purpose.

Neera Kuckreja Sohoni, Ph.D.
Atherton, California, U.S.A.
April, 1995

Endnote

[1] In 1990, the world had 954 girls (aged 0–19) per 1,000 boys, compared to 1,011 women (aged 20-plus) per 1,000 men. In total, there were 987 females per 1,000 males of all ages.

Quotes

I was born in a small hospital in Tokyo.
Mamma says she remembers two things:
A mouse running across the floor,
which she took as a sign of good luck.
A nurse bending down and whispering apologetically:
"I'm afraid it's a girl.
Would you prefer to inform your husband yourself?"

Liv Ullman
Ambassador for UNICEF
(from UNICEF exhibition on "Girls and Girlhood: A Perilous Path")

As the river of a girl's life flows into the sea of Western culture,
she is in danger of drowning or disappearing.
To take on the problem of appearance,
which is the problem of her development,
and to connect her life with history on a cultural scale,
she must enter—and by entering disrupt—
a tradition in which "human" has for the most part meant male.
Thus a struggle often breaks out in girls' lives at the edge of adolescence,
and the fate of this struggle
becomes key to girls' development and to Western civilization.

Carol Gilligan
in Gilligan, Lyons, and Hanmer (eds.)
Making Connections:
The Relational Worlds of Adolescent Girls at Emma Willard School
Harvard University Press, Cambridge, MA 1990, p. 4

Equality should be a criterion of the rights and care of every child;
nourishment, physical and emotional,
and the way in which children are inducted into their societies
should not depend on their gender.

United Nations,
1989 World Survey on the
Role of Women in Development,
New York, 1989, p. 381

I

GIRLS IN DEVELOPMENT

One significant lesson of the U.N.-sponsored development decades has been that the development phenomenon is neither uniform nor egalitarian— it is sexist. Development strategies and planning have been male-centric, consigning women and children to a subordinate position. Inevitably, girls have received the fewest benefits from development planners and processes on account of both their age and gender. They are twice denied and in a worse position than even women.

DEFINING GIRLHOOD

If development processes were gender even and just, there would be no need to isolate girlhood from childhood. For analytical purposes, defining the girl is useful. The dictionary's (Webster's, 1988:571) reference to girl, inter alia, as "female child; a young, unmarried woman; a female servant; a sweetheart," is out of step with the reality of a considerable proportion of the world's girls, many of whom are young, yet married. Of the definition's three parameters, the first is a valid biological fact; the second, a sad comment on the subtle semantic bias against girls or their labor; and the last is too frivolous to deserve comment or explanation. But the substantive and thematic parameters of the girl child's status are more or less laid out by the dictionary interpretation of "girl."[1]

The age parameters of girlhood are ambiguous—girlhood ranges from age 0 to a flexible ceiling extending to age 20—depending on various cultural, legal, political, civil, or religious dictates. Often in the same country, a girl is

---

[1]All "footnotes" will be placed at the end of chapters as "endnotes."

considered a minor on the basis of one law but an adult according to another. Her adult status entitles her to vote or to run for public office, and may commence at a different age than her lawful maturity in terms of her right to inheritance or property ownership; her right to work; right to marry; right to choose abortion; or even her right to drive a motorized vehicle. Then again, the confusion may be compounded by varying age limits in each piece of legislation with respect to girls and boys. There is a need in law, culture, and religion to establish a common definition of "girlhood," as well as to correct any disparities in relation to "boyhood," to achieve legal uniformity. But it is pragmatic to accept the "girl" broadly as ranging from age 0 to age 19, and for each country and culture to determine its own age ceiling. Upper age differences do not significantly alter either the existing or prospective limitations experienced by the girl, or the scope of interventions necessary to help her overcome those. For purposes pertinent to child development, it is useful to view the girl in terms of these sub-age groups: below 0, 0–1, 2–5, 6–10, 11–14, and 15–19. The pre-birth and other age groupings mark a departure from standard child age groups, but they reflect the years of the girl's greatest vulnerability and risks to her survival. The upper age perspective is developmental, as it seeks to encompass unmarried and married girls, and girls who are mothers.

WHAT IS DEVELOPMENT?

Development implies change, movement, progress, growth, and the achievement of potential. The Concise Oxford Dictionary (1964:281) defines development as a "gradual unfolding; fuller working out; growth; stage of advancement." To "develop" means to "unfold, reveal, bring or come from latent to active or visible state; make or become known; make progress; mature." In documents from the United Nations and other sources, development is described as "the process by which distributive equality is achieved. . .Equitable allocation of access and benefit is intrinsic to true development." (U.N. World Survey, 1989:360)

The philosophical basis of all development is that it seeks to equalize access to, and benefits derived from, opportunities to improve one's level of life and capabilities. Development implies a continuous, never-ending process. One can never say that one is "developed" but only that one is "developing." In that sense, the term "developed countries" is a misnomer. It presumes a state of completion or perfection. The term "developing country" is likewise open to questioning. It is interpreted by the dictionary (Concise Oxford, 1964:281) as a "poor or primitive country that is developing better economic and social conditions." This definition implies a simplistic, condescending, and arbitrary approach to determining just what constitutes "primitive" or "better" conditions. Development has several parameters and should have several yardsticks against which to measure it. There is social as against economic development. There is spiritual as against material development. There is development in a historical and cultural sense which is associated with such countries as China, Egypt, and India, whose historical presence and wealth go back several centuries, as against such countries as the United States, which, although industrially and technologically advanced, are still in their comparative infancy.

There is also a state of mind or consciousness reflected in the culture of a society which makes it more or less "developed." Some societies and people are more introspective, philosophical, and seasoned, or more mature than others. Each of these parameters needs to be measured equally in order to justly decide which country is developed. Unfortunately, this has been the major failing of the development discipline and fraternity. The most obvious yardstick—the economic, and to a limited extent social, performance of countries—has been the more accepted way to judge a country's level of "development."[2] Yet, development's scholars need to distinguish between economic, social, and emotional poverty or affluence. A country, like an individual, can be economically wealthy but emotionally poor and socially deviant. Another can be economically poor but socially rich and emotionally stable. When we think of "Third World" countries as "poor," we have to be more cautious about which type of "poverty" we are speaking.

The concept of "Third World" is demeaning, historically inaccurate, exclusionary, and negativistic. Just as in the period before the French Revolution, the Third Estate or *Tiers Etat* was defined negatively as all the common people who, unlike the nobility and the clergy, had no privilege. The term "Third World" refers to "all those areas of the world that did not become, during the historical process of the establishment of the present World Order, industrialized and wealthy." (Sabri-Abdalla in Zachariah, 1992:551) Apart from its unsavory exclusionary connotation, the term "Third World" suffers from a serious conceptual limitation. First World defines European or Euro-borne countries with privatized, capitalist economies. "Second World" refers to countries with state-controlled economies. Third World is an umbrella term applied indiscriminately, without regard to ideology or methodology, to the aggregate of countries including Africa, Asia, Latin America, and Oceania (usually refers to Southern Pacific Islands, as a group) that emerged or re-emerged after World War II. Their emergence marked the demise of colonialism and their embarkation on a path of planned economic growth. As Zachariah observes (552), "The phrase carries too heavy a load: over one hundred countries on three continents as well as on many islands; it encompasses people of astonishingly diverse ethnic origins and cultural histories."

DEVELOPMENT AND GENDER DISCRIMINATION

The concept of equality is vitally linked to development. Equality is theoretical. In reality, there are inherited attitudes, prejudices, resources, facilities, conditions, and aptitudes which make for differences between people, communities, countries, and cultures. Wealth and poverty are unequally shared not only by nations but also by men and women, adults and children. Everywhere in the world, women and children experience the unequal apportionment of the benefits and opportunities of human evolution and development. In all societies and countries, gender is the dividing line not only between men and women, and boys and girls, but also between development and the lack of it. Gender is a more consistent constraint than race, color, creed, or poverty in the equitable development of people. When any of these other variables combine with gender, the resultant disability and inequality are matchless. Whatever the socioeconomic or intellectual level of countries, a poor woman anywhere is likely to be poorer than a poor man.

The more frustrating aspect of the above contention is that it applies, albeit in differing measure, to capitalistic, socialistic or quasi-socialistic countries. It points to patriarchy, rather than "underdevelopment," as the true constraint on women and their integration in development.

Fortunately, the discourse on development seems less definitive than the context of patriarchy in which it is formulated. There appears to be a certain "moving target" quality to development which is refreshing as well as promising, notwithstanding its hitherto divisive and uneven outcomes for class, race, regions, countries, gender, and age. Whereas it is not strictly within the scope of this book to delve into the on-going debate over the *raison d'être* and scope of development, it is useful to briefly recapture its evolutionary history.

Nations desirous of psychological healing or economic rebuilding in the years following World War II and the break-up of colonial imperialism saw it fit to promote international cooperative endeavors. This served either to assuage their conscience or to subtly protect their access to cheap raw materials and labor, as well as to protect their access to gullible, profitable markets. The U.N. First Development Decade began, consequently, with a great aspiration for economic success, relying principally on accelerated growth rates of national economies to move their citizenry forward. By the end of the 1960s, the stark reality of world poverty and growing economic disparity had caused sufficient skepticism and disenchantment with "growth only" to turn the development discourse over to advocates of social justice. Growth with justice was thus adopted as the *leit motif,* and amelioration of poverty was incorporated into the Second Development Decade's strategy. Poverty eradication became "iconized" through basic needs approaches, which focused on employment generation and improvement in the health, nutrition, and education, or the population's collective level of living through such improved public amenities as housing, sanitation, water supply, and primary schools. Rather than abstract monetary indices of rise or decline in per capita Gross National Product (GNP), the new approach afforded development a visibility and a tactile quality. Importantly, it linked economic and social parameters in judging levels of development. Included in the Second Development Decade's strategy document was a historic reference to integrating "women fully in the development effort."

The 1970s marked the watershed in the history of women in development. The adoption of 1975 as International Women's Year by the United Nations, followed by the mid-decade global Conference on Women (1975), placed women as an issue on the global agenda for the first time and led to the U.N. Decade for Women (1976–85). But as subsequently established, merely placing women there did not accomplish their integration into the development process. It was left to women advocates, scholars, and development practitioners, including male sympathizers, to identify and devise ways of effectively incorporating women into the beneficent world of development.

Enforcing the basic needs approach brought forth clearly for the first time the structural problems involved in reaching women and men equally, bringing out the resultant greater vulnerability of women. As concerned women became more vocal about their lack of rights and resources in various countries, the principle of gender equity was introduced in the perspective of developmental strategy.

The process of subsuming women in development was certain to be debatable and divisive. Women, like any broad category of people, are neither monolithic nor homogenized, and hardly prototypical. *There is no all-encompassing woman.* Depending on where they come from, who they are, what they do and feel, how they are treated by their men and children, the world of women differs and development processes must recognize those differences. At the same time, they need to address the commonalty of women's oppression, subordination, and exclusion, which are rooted in patriarchy.

At the beginning of the Third Development Decade in the 1980s, pressure built to question the values and validity of development theory and practice. Feminist and non-feminist advocates of women—from the developing world particularly—spoke freely of the negative experience of women with the forces of "marketing," which, like colonization, had exacerbated inequities not only between classes and races but also between genders. Women's vulnerability was demonstrated as being upheld and accentuated by the male-dominated institutions of religion, culture, politics, education, science, government, and family. Women visionaries of developing countries presented a new perspective from which to view development—that of the poorest women. Recalling that different protagonists had shaped development in the last three decades, Sen and Grown (1987) used women from the poorest, most oppressed sections of all societies as the new protagonists. In their "alternative vision," poor women constitute a legitimate vantage point from where to view the gains and shortfalls of development. Other scholars (*inter alia*, Young, 1988; Dwyer and Bruce, 1988; Buvinic and Yudelman, 1989; Boserup, 1970, 1990) funneled their efforts into optimizing the value of women's non-valorized labor. Women's inability to gain from development was traced by these analysts to the dichotomy between valorized and non-valorized categories of labor and its institution along gender lines.

Of the feminist criticisms of the preceding Development Decades, in particular the Women's Decade (1976–1985), the most disheartening was that they did little to change the valuation or distribution of household labor, or to enhance women's share of valorized roles, resources, and labor. From the perspective of this book, even more disturbing was the recognition that many of the Decades' projects had "increased children's labor (especially that of daughters) who took on a share of the additional workload created by their mother's participation in the project." (Sen and Grown: 43) Also accentuated was the probability of school drop-out among young girls "forced to substitute for older women in home tasks or. . . drawn into putting-out work or sweatshops in order to supplement the family's real income." (63) Uneven outcomes for girls surfaced also in other studies from countries as developmentally disparate as India and the United States. (Government of India, 1989; American Association of University Women, 1992)

Based on past experiences as well as existing literature, it can be contended that the burden of "development"—in so far as it is presumed and shown to fall on people individually (rather than the abstract collectivity represented in the term "nation")—may weigh more heavily on the younger female. Sex-based disability may also be accentuated when gender combines with age.

LINKING GIRLS TO WOMEN'S DEVELOPMENT

At the end of three development decades, and midway through the fourth, as women continue to be marginalized from development's positive outcomes, it is likely that the key to women's disability and its amelioration lies in girlhood.

Many of the disadvantages women face begin in childhood. Anthropological and sociological evidence from cultures and countries around the world corroborates a parental reluctance to have girls. Family provisions in terms of food, labor, and health care distribution, as well as access to schooling and other life's opportunities, benefit boys more than girls. Rearing and socialization processes flatter and reinforce the male child's self-worth and status, while consigning the girl to a confining or even a negative self-image. Due to historical, cultural, and economic reasons, there are expected differences among countries and cultures, but in all societies girls face certain disadvantages compared to boys. Moreover, the demographic (specifically numerical) status of girls does not appear to be linked to women, or to the countries' level of development. Both in developed and developing regions of the world, girls are found to be proportionally fewer than boys, as well as women.

Unlike apartheid and racism, gender prejudice is not acknowledged as a formally articulated behavioral precept or doctrine. But it clearly exists and has an impact on the female life-cycle. Yet, even as childhood is more vulnerable than adulthood, the female as a *girl* is far more susceptible to the disabling consequences of gender prejudice than as *adult*. To address her disabilities as a girl is more logical and fruitful than to wait for them to turn into permanent handicaps and traits of her adulthood. The development discipline has only recently begun to sense this payoff. As the connection between women's continued diluted presence in development and the treatment of girlhood becomes clear, more and more of development's theorists and practitioners will accept that rational gender equations are difficult to achieve in the adult world. As the world prepares for the Fourth U.N. World Conference on Women (Beijing, September 4–15, 1995), development practitioners will need to move away from the past tendency to perceive gender equity as an adult requirement that has left girls and their entitlements out of the development and gender discourse.

Even though it may have been unconscious, the feminist movement and international development strategies generally have not sufficiently addressed the issue of sexism in childhood. The conceptual and operational oversight of girls is perhaps traceable to the widespread and simplistic view that it is through the gains adult women make that girls can find their own liberation. A false complacency exists among development's planners and feminists that women's gains will automatically percolate down to younger females. In fact, the trickle-down theory has not worked in female development, just as it has not worked in economic development. It is becoming increasingly apparent that changes in the adult world cannot make as significant a dent on gender inequality as can childhood interventions. This is because the culture of patriarchy is imbibed during childhood and is only more aggressively manifested and articulated during adulthood. The message needed for women's development to emerge from the 1995 World Conference will be less than *inclusive* or *just* if it carries forth the unconscious but overwhelming bias toward women in international advocacy for gender equality. The steady participation by girls in the feminist and development discourse is necessary, especially at Beijing-type international conferences, in order for a change to occur in their position in all societies.

THE DEVELOPMENT STATUS OF GIRLS

Today, viewed globally, women's development status is far from commensurate with that of men—and in some key respects, including survival, women have experienced retrogression. For girls who bear the brunt of sexism, the costs of gender-disparate development have probably been higher—pushing investment in their protection and preparation further down the scale. To measure their development status, gender-specific data are necessary. Unfortunately, not much has been available until recently. Following the Women's Decade of 1976 to 1985, when data on women began to be categorized separately from men, children continued to be profiled as a collective entity, with the exception of data on schooling. Therefore, while it is difficult to accurately define the status of the girl compared to the boy, some broad contours of her socio-demographic profile can be briefly presented:

1. *Girls, more than women, are a numerical minority in the world.* Widely quoted U.N. sources (1989:4–33) indicate that in 1990 there were 987 females for every 1,000 males in the world. A closer look reveals that there were only 954 girls (aged 0–19) per 1,000 boys compared to 1,011 women (aged 20 and above) per 1,000 men. The total number of girls in 1990 was estimated to be 1.09 billion, compared to 1.14 billion boys. As in the case of women, the sex ratio among girls experienced a decline between 1970 and 1990. Negative sex ratios are more universal among girls than among women. Among women, adverse sex ratios are specific to Asia, rather than being universal. (See Table 1, next page)

2. *The median age for women in the developing regions,* which was 18–19 years in 1970, *has increased to 22–23 years in 1990* in all regions except Africa. The estimated (1990) proportion of girls (aged 0–19) is approximately 55 percent of the female population in Africa, 43 percent in Asia, and 46 percent in Latin America. *In all three regions, as well as in the developed world, the proportion of boys is slightly higher than of girls.*

3. While marriage age has increased worldwide, *girls married by age 15 are estimated to account for 18 percent of marriages in Asia, 16 percent in Africa, and 8 percent in Latin America.* On the average, marriage currently occurs earliest in Africa (at 19.7 years) and latest in Latin America (at 21.9 years). *Boys, on the other hand, marry when they are considerably older,* as is evident from the comparative marital-status data of several countries ranging from Bangladesh and Brazil to Ethiopia, Indonesia, Senegal, Sudan, Turkey, United Arab Emirates, and the United States. (See Table 2, page 11)

Table 1
Females per 1,000 Males, 1970,* 1990

	All Ages	0–19	20-plus
World, 1990	987	954	1,011
	(996)	(957)	(1,032)
More Developed, 1990	1,061	952	1,108
	(1,075)	(959)	(1,144)
Less Developed, 1990	966	954	976
	(966)	(956)	(977)
Africa, 1990	1,012	987	1,044
	(1,020)	(991)	(977)
Asia, 1990	954	942	963
	(957)	(947)	(967)
Latin America, 1990	1,002	976	1,025
	(966)	(977)	(1,019)

Percent Decline in Number of Females per 1,000 Males
Between 1970 and 1990

	More Developed Regions %	Less Developed Regions %
0-19	0.7	0.2
20-plus	3.2	0.1
All Ages	1.3	0.0

Source: Derived from United Nations, *Global Estimates and Projections of Population by Sex and Age,* The 1988 Revision, New York, 1989, pp. 4–33

*Note: 1970 figures are bracketed

Decimal figures .05 and above are rounded to .1

4. *Although more educated today than before, girls are less educated than boys.* Approximately 60 million girls have no access to primary schooling, compared to 40 million boys. In the developing regions, fewer girls enroll in school and far more drop out than boys. Gross enrollment ratios (1970–1986) at all three levels of education in the developing regions continue to show considerable disparities in favor of male children. (See Table 3, next page)

5. Whereas 40 percent or more of the world's children are born in poverty and face the consequences of limited nutritional intake, the *intra-household distribution of food* in many developing countries is *skewed in favor of the earning adult male and the boy child* (as potential earner), with women and girls getting the lesser share, both in terms of quantity and quality. Differentials in the nutritional status of girls have been observed in several countries, among them Bangladesh, Bolivia, Colombia, Egypt, India, Iran, Jordan, Nepal, Pakistan, Saudi Arabia, and Syria. (Ravindran, 1986:6) Discriminatory breast feeding, weaning, and dietary practices begin

---

Table 2
Sex-wise Marital Status of 15–19 Year Olds for Selected Countries

Country	Year	Female % Married	Male % Married
Sudan	1973	41.0	4.2
Bangladesh	1974	71.8	7.4
United Arab Emirates	1975	55.0	8.4
Senegal	1976	33.2	1.1
Brazil	1980	16.0	2.3
Indonesia	1980	27.3	3.3
Turkey	1980	21.4	8.0
United States	1980	8.2	2.7
Ethiopia	1982	53.2	5.2

Source: Derived from United Nations, *Compendium of Statistics and Indicators on the Situation of Women,* 1986, pp. 88–110

early (in the affected countries) and continue through adolescence, accounting for lower heights and weights, and making a lifelong difference.

6. *Reproductive and productive burdens are shared inequitably by the girl.* Girls marry at younger ages than boys and also take on parenting responsibilities at earlier ages. Early marriage leads to *children bearing*

Table 3
Difference Between Male and Female Gross Enrollment Ratios
(Percentage Points)

Region	First Level		Second Level		Third Level	
	1970	1986	1970	1986	1970	1986
World	15	15	9	10	4	3
Developed Countries	1	1	2	-	8	-1
Developing Countries	19	18	11	14	3	4
Africa	22	18	8	17	2	4
Latin America and the Caribbean	2	5	2	-4	4	3
North America	1	2	-2	-	15	-9
Asia	20	20	12	14	3	4
Europe and USSR	1	1	2	-10	5	1
Oceania	4	4	3	-	8	0
(Arab States)	32	22	16	17	5	7

Note: In interpreting the figures in this table, it should be kept in mind that figures for different levels of education are not strictly comparable due to the different values of enrollment ratios and the different age ranges used in the calculation of enrollment ratios at each level of education

Source: UNESCO, *A Review of Education in the World: A Statistical Analysis.* ED/BIE/CONFINTED 41/Ref. 1, Paris, October, 1988, p. 6

children. Maternity and its demands on younger girls further constrain their capability for survival, life expectancy, health, nutrition, education, and employment. The burden of mortality in many regions and countries is borne unequally by female infants, children, and young mothers.

7. The productive burden shouldered by the girl continues to be a gray area. Current yardsticks to measure labor (with and without monetary value) are inadequate and inequitable, and do not honor the real-life work situations of girls or women. *Time-use studies in Africa (Berio, 1988) and Asia (Acharya, Bennet, 1979) show that the female child bears a heavier burden of household activities and siblings care than the male child.* Girls aged 10–14 put in seven or more hours of labor per day in household and other domestic work. Greater engagement of girls in domestic and unpaid labor also occurs in such developed countries as Australia, Italy, and the United States. The economic value of the girl's *unenumerated, unremunerated* work stands outside the calculations of GNP. Moreover, it gives little added value to the girl, reinforcing parental perception of her as a liability. The under-enumerated labor of the girl and its exploitation parallel the labor patterns and female invisibility in the adult world.

8. *The real gender differential is attitudinal and, as with racism, its damage is immeasurable.* Like color, gender is an accident of birth, but its entitlements are man made. A different and discriminatory set of values and expectations are applied to the girl, and to her preservation and development. Boys, like men, command greater space and value: that differential is sustained through a process of covert or overt neglect of the girl.

Universally, more boys are born than girls (Miller, 1983; Newland, 1979; Ravindran, 1986; Sen, 1990; U.N., 1991). Yet nature miraculously adjusts and compensates for survival risks. Even though fewer girls are born than boys, the female is believed to be capable, given an equal chance, of outliving the male. When this biological fact is not reinforced or reflected in national or global statistics, serious, incipient discrimination against the girl is suspected. In countries or cultures where the intrinsic biological safeguard provided to girls is respected in demographic terms, but disparities are allowed to exist in all other respects, there is a gender-divisive context that needs to be acknowledged. It should be the commitment of everyone who seeks to advocate or promote the cause of childhood, and of equitable gender development, to assess the bases and forms of such disparity and to identify and launch effective countervailing responses and strategies.

Endnotes

1. In a curious etymological reference, the Dictionary traces the origin of girl to "girlie" or "gurle" in Middle English, meaning perhaps "youngster of either sex." The irony in this uncertain but gender-neutral interpretation of the linguistic beginning of girlhood is poignant.

2. Since 1991, the U. N. Development Program has started using a gender-sensitive Human Development Index (HDI), but so far only thirty-three countries, of which barely a dozen are developing nations, have the requisite gender-based data to qualify for inclusion in the Index. The Index relies on three indicators: life expectancy; educational attainment (as expressed through adult literacy and mean years of schooling); and national income.

II

CULTURE, SOCIALIZATION, AND GIRLS

Culture refers to a set of shared ideas, beliefs, values, and practices about what is right and wrong, good and evil, desirable and undesirable. Acculturation begins with birth, as a person learns the rules, relationships, roles, expectations, and entitlements of the culture into which she or he is born.

One of the earliest ideas that a child picks up, and one that is intrinsic to its socialization, is the notion of gender. As scholars have noted, name choice, clothing, nursery environment, bed linen color, toys, and the length and content of feeding and weaning, all set the mode for girlhood or boyhood. Parental and societal behavioral expectations, and patterns fostered in support of these, reinforce a person's gender identity. If a girl plays with dolls and kitchen utensils, and a boy with guns, toy trucks, and bows and arrows, or if a girl is meek and a boy aggressive, they are behaving in a manner appropriate to their gender. If they cross "toy lines," and transgress other behavioral expectations, they are confusing gender lines and sex behavioral codes. "We raise in effect, two different kinds of children: boys and girls. . .Even if parents monitor their actions in the hope of preventing sexism from affecting their child, their endeavors will not succeed, because other socializing influences bear down on the child." (Richardson/Taylor, *Feminist Frontiers II* 1989:1)[1]

Learning About Sex Roles

Psychologists generally agree that by age 3, children have an "irreversible conception of what gender is." (Kohlberg, 1966 in FFII:46) There is also agreement that gender is not a biologically but a culturally determined identity, shaped by and adopted through interface with mother, father, or other caregiver. Gender-specific role training and learning take place by interacting with the world outside the family. Boys remain "children'" while girls become "little women." (Aries, 1962:61 in FFII:48): Girlhood becomes a preparation and informal training ground for motherhood. But boyhood is not necessarily a preface to fatherhood. In most societies, boys spend their childhood without having to take on adult roles. (Chodorow in FFII, 1989:49–50; Jay, 1969; Barry, Bacon, and Child, 1957) They spend their time either alone or with peer groups—and remain more or less unconnected with the adult world of work and activity, or the familial world. Girls, beginning at or before age 5, start helping their mothers with their work, and spend time in the company of mothers or other female relatives. This leads to different gender characteristics.

The evolution from being a biological female to becoming a culturally defined girl begins early. At a very young age girls begin to understand and imbibe the culture of meekness, subservience, conformity, domesticity, and circumscription. They accept by rote and their mothers' examples, the five-fold role of 1) mother, 2) wife, 3) housewife or homemaker, 4) household emotional connector, and 5) producer/manager of household economy. In addition, the *extended* rather than *nuclear* nature of African (Obbo, 1990) and Asian families compels women to live with multi-household mechanisms. They have to learn to operate within what MacFarlane (1978:118 in Obbo, 1990) designates as the "corporate rights of the kin group."

It has also been established that the sex-role training of girls in and outside the home fosters dependency in Western societies. "Competence, independence, objectivity, logical thinking, will-assertiveness, and self-confidence all are stereotypically attributed to and reinforced in males, while emotional expressiveness, sensitivity to others, as well as incompetence, dependency, subjectivity, poor logic, submissiveness, and lack of self-confidence are stereotypically attributed to and reinforced in females." (Levy, 1972 in Gersoni-Stavn, 1974:50) In most societies, as Chodorow points out (1989:50), the socialization of boys is oriented toward aggressiveness, achievement, and self-reliance, and that of girls toward docility, nurturance, and responsibility. Girls are pressured to be involved with, and connected to, others; boys to bypass, deny, or ignore this involvement and connection.

Throughout the developing world, "children are taught very early in life about distributive justice in terms of differences in gender and age. When some get more food on their plate and others less, when some are sent to school, and others are not, children can see, in dramatic ways, what the differences are between boys and girls in their societies." (Papanek in Tinker, 1990:163) Furthermore, from an early age, girls understand the inevitability of hard work and the risks and public contempt associated with being lazy. Laziness and leisure are the male child's prerogatives. "Lazy" girls (expanding to Asia what Obbo, 1990, has noted in respect of East Africa) are threatened with "no suitors," "failed marriage," "spinsterhood," or "having to live and earn one's keep like a prostitute." The successful and respect-worthy female is the perpetual doer—the uncomplaining, multipurpose, omnipresent worker—a modern configuration of the slave, serving the household and its male.

The sex-role development of girls in modern society is also complex. "On the one hand, they go to school to prepare for life in a technologically and socially complex society. On the other, there is a sense in which this schooling is a pseudo-training. It is not meant to interfere with the much more important training to be "feminine" and a wife and mother, which is embedded in the girl's unconscious development. . .(Chodorow, 1989:49) One obvious consequence of this socialization is that women in most societies are "defined relationally (as someone's wife, mother, daughter, daughter-in-law; even a nun becomes the bride of Christ"). Independent status normally comes only with age, when women become mothers-in-law and grandmothers. In the hierarchy of patriarchy and kinship, age is eventually allowed some stature but it is almost always at the expense of the younger female. (Boserup, 1970; Obbo, 1990)

The origin of the word woman indicates that the female's right to social existence was valued in terms of her secondary relationship to the male. The word *woman* was originally "wifman" or wife man; that is, the wife of a man, and it was only in the Fourteenth Century that the letter "f" was dropped and the word became "wiman," and later "woman." (Montagu, 1968:49). Drawing on earlier evidence, from Homer through the end of Greek literature, there were no ordinary words with the specific meanings "husband" and "wife"—wives were ordinarily referred to as "bed mates." (Stivers, 1993:92)

This female personality subversion and dependence on the male identity accounts for the sense of powerlessness among girls—even more so than among women. It affects their self-esteem, self-awareness, and life options. A recent study (Lees, 1993:27-28) of a sample of adolescent girls in the United

Kingdom notes that they are already locked into a life centered around domesticity, subservience, subordination, and motherhood; any career aspirations, personal ambition, or freedom hold second place to the ideal of finding the man of their dreams. And even worse, the study shows that many accept the differences between girls and boys as biological.

As status typically depends on how one perceives oneself, as well as how one is perceived by others, the status of girls is very clearly dictated by their gender. Given that everyone is born into a culture with pre-set notions about males and females, and about what is appropriate for males and females, the traditional sex roles and the different "values" given to genders within the family and society prove to be the most significant stumbling blocks on the road to gender parity.

SON PREFERENCE AND DAUGHTER NEGLECT

The girl's devalued status as the "lesser" child is directly traceable to *generic* and *chronic* sexism in the family. Even where there is no special preference for sons, very few cultures actively prefer daughters. In her worldwide survey, Williamson (1976) found only five small groups of aboriginal populations in Assam (India), Australia, California (U.S.A.), New Guinea, and Peru where fathers would rather have daughters than sons. In all the other cultures studied, parents either preferred to have a clear majority of sons or wanted an equal balance of the sexes." (Ware, 1981:120) Daughter preference was found in only two out of nearly forty countries included in the 1983 World Fertility Survey. (See Table 4)

Son preference, however, is not unique to developing countries. Wanting a son for a first or only child is well-documented in the United States. (Lott, 1994:18) Furthermore, American studies of adults in the United States reveal that females and males both think it is preferable to be male and to have male children. Drawing from earlier researchers, Levi (in Gersoni-Stavn, 1974:50) establishes how, as they age, both boys and girls develop a progressively poorer opinion of girls, and by the age of 5 to 6 learn to attribute greater power and prestige to the male role. Further, calling on the work by Pohlman (1969), Levi asserts (50) that "a mass of evidence demonstrates that American parents tend to prefer boys. More mothers of girls have postpartum depression than do mothers of boys; pregnant women dream twice as often about male babies; mothers who have only daughters are happier about a new pregnancy than are

Table 4
Preference for the Sex of Children

Country	Index of Son Preference*	Country	Index of Son Preference•
Strong Son Preference			
Pakistan	4.9	**Equal Preference**	
Nepal	4.0	Guyana	1.1
Bangladesh	3.3	Indonesia	1.1
Korea	3.3	Kenya	1.1
Syria	2.3	Peru	1.1
Jordan	1.9	Trinidad & Tabago	1.1
		Colombia	1.0
Moderate Son Preference		Costa Rica	1.0
Egypt	1.5	Ghana	1.0
Lesotho	1.5	Panama	1.0
Senegal	1.5	Paraguay	1.0
Sri Lanka	1.5	Portugal	1.0
Sudan	1.5	Haiti	0.9
Thailand	1.4	Philippines	0.9
Turkey	1.4		
Fiji	1.3	**Daughter Preference**	
Nigeria	1.3	Venezuela	0.8
Tunisia	1.3	Jamaica	0.7
Yemen A.R.	1.3		
Cameroon	1.2		
Dominican Republic	1.2		
Ivory Coast	1.2		
Malaysia	1.2		
Mexico	1.2		
Morocco	1.2		

*Index of Son Preference = Ratio of the number of mothers who prefer the next child to be male as compared to the number of mothers who prefer the next child to be female

Source: *World Fertility Survey, Cross-National Summaries*, Number 27, October 1983, and First Country Reports
Table appears in Ravindran, WHO/UNICEF/FHE 86.2, WHO, Geneva, 1986, p. 5

mothers of sons; if the first child is a boy the interval before a second child is conceived is longer than if the first child is a girl; and the likelihood of having a third child is greater if the first two children are both girls than if they are both boys." It is likely that Pohlman and Levi, while speaking of U.S. parents, speak to the experience of parents almost universally.

It is a natural phenomenon that for every 100 girls, approximately 105 boys are born. (Newland, 1979:177) Yet, parental preferences are far removed from this natural norm. According to Newland (177), in most places the ideal sex ratio (boys per 100 girls) is higher than the natural one. The preferred sex ratio in India and North Africa, for example, is 3 to 6 sons for every daughter. In Korea, a 1971 nationwide survey of 2,000 wives showed that the average ideal number of children was 3.6 while the ideal number of sons was 2.2 (Chung et al., 1972). "This would yield a sex ratio at birth of 160 males to 100 females in a perfect gender predetermined reproductive context in Korea." (Ware, 1981:125)

A daughter's neglect begins at birth, or in the fetal stage. The desire for sons is so strong that parents, especially in traditional cultures, follow strict guidelines for nutrition and intercourse to facilitate the conception of a male child. Astrologers are consulted to detect the most propitious time for the conception of a male. Women in India pray to certain gods and observe fasts on given days to maximize their probability of conceiving a male fetus.[2] There is anecdotal evidence that the same motivation drives women in Western countries to use vinegar douches, baking powder, and Epsom salts. (Lott, 1994:18)

Special treatment also awaits the birth of the male child. In several cultures, elaborate rituals prepare for and herald the coming of the male child, while the female child is ignored, abandoned, starved, or killed.

Customs in many countries manifest the pride with which the male child is welcomed, and the shadow of gloom cast by the coming of a baby girl. Baum, Hyman, and Michel (1975:10 in Lott 1994:18) note that among orthodox Jews in Eastern Europe the birth of a boy was time for rejoicing, while the birth of a girl was a time for stoic acceptance. Siring a female child was a shameful act for which Hassidic Jews occasionally flogged young fathers. The British spend more time and money celebrating the birth of a son—traditionally, a prince was given a twenty-one-gun salute, a princess only ten.

Popular sayings from a variety of cultures provide solid evidence of the girl's devalued status. An English saying from the Eighteenth Century suggests: "Daughters and dead fish are no keeping wares." A Dutch proverb declares: "A house full of daughters is like a cellar full of sour beer." Daughters are referred to as "water spilled on the ground," in Taiwan, and as "only a prostitute" who will be exchanged for cattle at the time of marriage among the Iteso in Uganda. An old Chinese saying asserts: "girls are maggots in the rice...when fishing for treasures in the flood, be careful not to pull in girls." Among Zulus, the girl is "merely a weed." To be called the "father of daughters" is an insult in Arabic. An unexpected silence or conversational gap in an assembly invites the Arabic expression, "Khilqat bint," or "Why the silence? Has a girl been born?" A Korean saying warns: "A girl lets you down twice, once at birth and the second time when she marries." (Ravindran, 1986:14–15; Sohoni in *Ms* magazine, July/August, 1994:96) Girls thus represent the parental feeling of being let down, cheated, or burdened.

Lack of enthusiasm for female babies is not confined to developing countries. Although American parents do not selectively discard female infants nor ridicule parents of girls, female babies continue to be seen as second-best. Sadly, a study of 236 American parents who had experienced the death of a child found that boys had been grieved far more than girls. (Lott 1994:18–19)

The reasons for strong son preference where it prevails are well recognized. (See Box 1, next page, on "Sons in Demand in Nigeria, Korea, and Bangladesh") The son is a potential and permanent source of income. In societies without the protective cover of social security and pensioner provision, the son is the only protection parents have against poverty during old age, or other disabling circumstances. The male child also derives his favored status from being his father's "genetic imprint" and lineage carrier. In such countries as India and Korea, where the son alone is vested with the right to perform post-death rituals that assure peace and salvation to the departed soul, the son becomes a conduit of both the material and spiritual aspirations of the parent. The daughter offers no such gains. Where she is desired, the underlying reasons are the expectation of her loyalty ("A son is a son till he gets a wife; a daughter is a daughter all her life"); her help as a nurturer and caretaker in the home; her value in providing additional labor in the family farm and business; her doll-like cuteness and "dress-up" potential; and, in rare cultures, her material worth in the marriage market. In such cultures, the girl commands a price which the bridegroom is expected to pay to the parent. That practice also makes her a commodity.

In traditional cultures especially, the fact that the girl is a temporary boarder or transient passenger in her natal home also weighs heavily against her. Any material or other investment in her is considered wasteful, amounting, as an Indian proverb cruelly puts it, to "watering a plant in a neighbor's garden." The girl's share in her natal family's resources is directly linked to her transitory presence. The expectation that she will and must marry makes her dispensable, and her dispensability determines what and how much are given to her. She ends up with fewer investments and rights but with greater liabilities and duties in the natal home. Parental frugality toward the girl child is well illustrated by an old Taiwanese woman's explanation of why she gave up her infant girls in adoption: "Think of all the rice I saved!" (in Wolf, 1972)

Box 1
Sons in Demand in Nigeria, Korea, and Bangladesh

The presence of at least one male child in the family is regarded as absolutely necessary in most **Nigerian** communities. (Orubuloye, in Oppong 1987:87–89) It is important to have sons for economic support, continuity of the family name, and their permanent residence near the ancestral home.

In **Korea**, custom and economics combine to generate a preference for sons that is among the strongest and most persistent found anywhere. According to tradition, only a son can perform the crucial rites of ancestor worship. South Korean law still affords the eldest son head-of-household status and he is favored in inheritance laws so that he may fulfill his duties, while a woman's status is closely tied to her ability to produce sons. (Newland, 1979:179–180)

Remuneration to local midwives, if the baby is a boy, can increase up to 66 percent, according to one **Bangladesh** study. (Elahi, in Momsen and Kinnaird, 1993:90)

The girl also "causes" distinct limitations and disadvantages for the family. Greater care and responsibility are required in raising girls to prevent their getting pregnant or undermining their eligibility for marriage. Thus, although the girl has indispensable societal value as a potential breeder, that reproductive function has done little to enhance her status in the family or society. Girls also represent a lower earning capability than boys. This is largely due to inherited work patterns between genders, and the fact that no economic value is given to the work which girls do at home as surrogate mothers and caregivers, or what they contribute through their labor to the domestic and farm economy. Marriage represents the gravest handicap in assessing the worth of a girl. In most cultures, marriage is expensive and in some it can entail a costly dowry. Unfortunately, this marriage incentive further reinforces the perception of the girl as an economic liability. Another source of ire against the girl is the loss of lineage which she represents. Families in which only daughters are born face the bleak prospect of their name being wiped out. Finally, there is a psychological basis for rejecting girls. The lack of autonomy and the continued female subjection which the girl represents, both to and for her parents in society (by way of the in-laws), is a source of considerable misgiving against the girl child. (Newland, 1979:179)

In more male-centric cultures, the birth of a female infant lowers the status of the parents, particularly the mother. Recurrent female births in such cultures lead to separation, divorce, suicide, or murder of the mother, and often, to the killing or abandoning of the female child. The desperate mother is also forced to agree to the option of bigamy. In Korea, for instance, "Economics and customs lead to strong and persistent son preference. Around one-fourth of urban and two-thirds of rural women would agree to husbands taking a concubine to produce a son." (Newland, 1979:179)

ELIMINATING DAUGHTERS

Predatory behavior by parents against female children has been an ongoing theme of human evolution. For centuries, the preference for sons has led parents to find informal solutions to eliminating female babies. When genetic techniques for sex determination were not known or widely available, parents sought to influence the gender composition of their family by neglecting to feed, nurture, and protect the female child; by investing fewer resources on preparing for her productive and healthy adulthood: and by abandonment, or infanticide. Female infanticide has been widely practiced in many cultures throughout history. In Ancient Greece and Rome, "exposing" girls, a euphemism for letting them die through neglect, was practiced. In contemporary times, science has made it possible for parents to abort female fetuses. Research evidence from several developing countries shows a parental willingness to resort to any one of these ways to minimize the probability of conceiving, delivering, and rearing a female child.

1. Sex bias in health care has been documented in several recent analyses in Asia, Africa, and the Middle East. The findings show that:
    - More male children are immunized and treated by hospitals;
    - Girls have a higher rate of death from measles, diarrhea, and respiratory infections;
    - Girls are weaned earlier; boys are breast-fed longer;
    - Girls are usually brought to the hospital in a worse condition than boys;
    - Milk products and protein foods are fed more to boys than girls in several South and East Asian countries, and girls receive a more diluted weaning diet than boys;
    - Stunting (low height for weight) and wasting (low weight for height) are higher among 6–7-month-old female infants than male infants in some countries, such as Bangladesh. (Sohoni, 1990 and UNICEF, 1990)

2. A strong, persistent son preference in China accounts for daughters being put up for adoption or sale, abandoned, or killed. (Ware, 1981:122 and FFII:21) (See Box 2, on "Aborting of Female Fetuses and Killing of Newborn Girls in China")

3. Parental preference surveys in Bangladesh and Nigeria reveal a majority of parents aspiring for a son. (Sohoni, 1990:8)

4. Birth intervals after sons in India are likely to be longer than after daughters (Halder and Bhattacharya, 1970 in Ware, 1981:122)

5. A 1986 report prepared for WHO and UNICEF found that there was "a very significant excess of female child deaths, and that every sixth death of a female infant in India, Pakistan, and Bangladesh was due to neglect and discrimination." (UNICEF, 1990:13–14)

6. In thirty developing countries, "death rates for girls between the ages of 1 and 4 were found to be higher than or equal to the death rates for boys. This contrasts with the industrialized countries, where

Box 2
Aborting of Female Fetuses and Killing of Newborn Girls in China

According to official publications and press reports, Chinese peasants are killing newborn girls at such a high rate the nation's balance between males and females is being affected. Female babies are drowned or abandoned at such a rate that in twenty years Chinese men may have trouble finding women to marry. In a study of rural communes, a *China Youth News* report said that three out of every five babies were boys. Because of reports of widespread killing and abandonment of unwanted female babies, the male to female ratio could be artificially damaged, it said. China's tough birth-control policy allows only one child per couple in urban areas and a maximum of two in the countryside without the risk of economic penalties, and in extreme cases, forced abortions.

The Chinese traditionally believe a son can provide more labor as he grows up, take better care of his parents when they retire, and carry on the family name. A daughter is often viewed as a financial burden who eventually would change her name once married and care for her in-laws first.

Recently, ultrasound testing to determine the sex of unborn babies has become widespread in China, with the result that many female fetuses are being aborted. A Chinese newspaper reported that in one province, residents used ultrasound to determine the sex of 2,316 fetuses; of those, 1,006 female fetuses were aborted. The report said the practice is just as common in cities, contrary to the popular belief that less traditional city residents are not as desperate for boys. Boys accounted for 74.8 percent of all births in one city last year, the highest percentage ever in modern China. The report said sources disclosed that the reason was ultrasound testing.

Census figures show that China had 36.2 million more males than females in 1990, and for every 100 girls born in China in 1990, 113.8 boys were born. The government has repeatedly ordered a halt to the use of ultrasound to determine sex, but many hospitals continue to provide the lucrative service. Private businessmen have gotten into the act. The newspaper said a man earned $6,631 a year—more than 12 times the average urban-worker's salary—from disclosing the sex of unborn babies.

The report warned that repeated abortions may damage a woman's health.

Source: Derived from Richardson/Taylor, Eds, *Feminist Frontiers II*, 1989:21, *San Francisco Chronicle*, June 22, 1993:A-1, A-13

death rates of boys are generally higher than those of girls."
(UNICEF, 1990:13)

SEX SELECTION

The use of sex-determination and selection techniques have contributed to
the reprehensible practice of preventing female fetuses from being born.
Evidence from several countries points to calculated sexist birthing practices,
as noted below:

1. In one Chinese experiment in which sex determination and abortion
   were offered to one hundred couples, twenty-nine of the thirty who
   chose abortion opted to abort female fetuses; (a 1975 study
   conducted in Tietung Hospital, in Ware, 1981:123)
2. In a hospital sample of seven hundred women in India, all who were
   told that they would have sons opted to continue their pregnancy,
   while 96 percent of the women expecting daughters had abortions.
   Seriously defective male fetuses were accepted while almost all
   healthy female fetuses were rejected. (Ramanamma and Bambawale,
   1980 in Ware, 1981:124) In another hospital-based study of
   amniocentesis in India, among parents who knew the gender of the
   fetus, only one out of eight thousand aborted fetuses was male;
   (UNICEF, 1990:14)
3. In Singapore, in a clinic-based sex-selection program, only 6 percent
   of the women attending the clinic were actively seeking daughters;
   (Ware, 1981:125)
4. The use of sex-determining techniques in a Chicago clinic revealed
   an overwhelming preference for male babies in a sample of American
   women. (Lott, 1994:18)

The desire to have sons, overwhelming as it is, has a close bearing on
reproductive behavior as is evident in several Asian, Arab, and African
nations. "Boy preference would still appear to be a major obstacle in the way
of achieving the two-child family ideal and reduced fertility levels." (Ware,
1981:122) In Korea, for instance, 58 percent of couples with two sons
practiced family planning, compared to 31 percent of couples with two
daughters. (Newland, 1979:180) Son preference is a major birth-rate
enhancer in such countries as Bangladesh, China, Hong Kong, India, Korea,

and Singapore. In recent years, many of these countries have adopted a policy of discouraging son preference and motivating parents not to discriminate against girls. Yet, in most countries—particularly in the most populous ones, such as China, India, Bangladesh, and Pakistan—parental violence and neglect continue to pose a major threat to the survival of female fetuses and babies.

IMPACT OF NEGLECT ON GIRLS

Traditionally, demographers and planners have confined their concerns to the desire for sons and its impact on fertility levels. But the impact of sex preference on the unwanted sex has not been given much attention. (Ware, 1981:120) As pointed out in the previous chapter, the outcome for girls of the absence of an ethos of care is disturbing and lasting. Apart from danger to her immediate survival, what the girl experiences is a disabling nutritional, health, and educational environment, and a lack of adequate preparation for the same opportunities afforded to boys. In countries where son preference persists, girls that survive the fetal and infant stages may still succumb to later neglect. Adolescence, in particular, brings additional traumas due to the unhealthy connotations and sexual overtones associated with it. In many cultures, menarche begins a process of emotional and physical isolation as well as nutritional and other types of denial that are demeaning to girlhood. In such cultures, menarche becomes the dividing line between freedom and incarceration, leading to her isolation, and, in some cultures, to her cauterization. Female circumcision or similar practices are observed in at least twenty-five countries in Africa, Asia, and the Arab regions. The number of girls affected by these practices is estimated at about one hundred million, with another two million added each year. (UNICEF, 1994)

Survival is not the only risk girls are confronted with. Perhaps even more damaging to girls is the callous flouting of their "right to childhood." In that sense, it is hardly a boon for surviving girls to be forced to experience the hardships associated with adult life. In several recent studies, there is considerable evidence that girls are not only neglected in terms of their nutritional and health care needs, but are also overworked. The greater share of work within the family is reserved for girls. In Java, for instance, "most young girls spend at least 33 percent more hours per day working at home and in the market as boys of the same age. Malaysian girls aged 5 to 6 work 75 percent more hours per week than boys of the same age. In the Ivory

Coast, 10–14-year-old girls work three to five hours per day in household chores, while their male counterparts work only two hours. In Nepal, girls spend more time in fetching water, collecting fuel, processing food, and agriculture than boys in the same age group." (UNICEF, 1990:21-22) Even in developed countries, disparities surface between the workloads and the nature of work of girls and boys. Time-use studies of agricultural households in Italy reveal that girls put in four-and-a-half and five hours daily on paid and unpaid work as compared to slightly over seven and two hours respectively put in by boys. (INSTRAW, 1990:17-28) In Australia, sons do only two-thirds of the unpaid work that daughters do. Wage differentials among children reflect the discriminatory adult world in which they live. (WIN *News*, 17-4, Autumn 1991:63) Girls received lower wages than did boys of the same age in a study of four thousand rural households in India. (Chatterjee, 1988:75) Evidence from a U. S. study points out that parents are more likely to pay boys than girls for the work they do inside the home. This pattern holds for work outside the house as well, so that girls earn less in general. Moreover, boys are encouraged and observed to work for "pay" and girls to work "out of love." (Lott, 1994:71)

Irrespective of the length and hardship of their work, the work that girls do is invisible, not only to the larger society and economy but also to their parents. Parental perceptions continue to underrate the economic value of the girl. A study of the value and cost of children among six hundred rural wives and husbands in Nigeria revealed that the majority of parents believed boys were more productive than girls of the same age. Both men and women also thought that parents should invest more in their male children, particularly on their feeding and education. Such parental attitudes explain why boys often receive greater opportunities to learn economically valuable skills than girls. (UNICEF, 1990:22) Similar parental perceptions keep parents from sending girls to school or allowing them to continue their schooling. Gender stereotyping in school textbooks and curricula reinforces the belief in the limited potential of girls, and in the questionable value of educating and investing in them. In turn, the lack of education and formal or informal employable skills compels girls to be consigned, as adults, either to unemployment or to low-skill, low-pay, and low-status occupations.

The price of girlhood is vulnerability, and its solution and safeguard is early marriage, which, in more traditional cultures, inevitably becomes the only "development" option offered to the girl. Yet her marriage itself becomes a constraining factor, restricting her mobility and her access to routine child-related services and entitlements. Where tradition expects the girl to be materially endowed by way of a dowry as a condition of her marriage, it adds to the perception of the girl as an economic liability.

In many developing countries, marriage further devalues the girl's status. In the marital home, she is rarely accepted as an insider; often even her dowry or personal wealth does not buy her improved status or autonomy. Her intrinsic status in such contexts depends on her own biological (reproductive) resources. Offspring become the sole emotional, psychological, and material anchor of the woman, hence the compulsive need to procreate. When a son or sons come her way, her reward is substantial.

Her perception of feeling rewarded through giving birth to sons forms the basis of sexism and of her denial of further generations of girls, consigning them, in turn, to being children without childhood. The cycle of disadvantage and gender-dictated development is thus complete.

To break the cycle, countervailing strategies are required, the most important of which has to do with parental persuasion. As facts about girls' earning and care-giving functions, and their "monetary" value are highlighted, more parents will be convinced of their value. Instances of positive attitudes toward girls appear in some traditional societies. Married women in Thailand, for instance, show only a slight preference for boys and also desire children of both sexes. Among Thai men, son preference is much stronger, but even they appreciate one daughter per family, recognizing that girls and women work for wages as well as help at home. (Newland, 1979:179)

Where son preference declines or does not exist originally, it is almost always due to a demonstrated economic contribution women make to the agricultural and trading economy. The same impact is associated with female entry into the cash-paid labor force as a result of urbanization and industrialization. "Programs designed to reduce sex preference will have some impact if they increase the visible economic contribution of women relative to men. Certainly, moral arguments alone will not be sufficient." (Ware, 1981:122-23)

Endnotes

1. Hereafter referred to as FFII and without specifying the two editors.

2. Earlier, pregnant mothers who had previously delivered daughters were known to resort to many purely superstitious practices "to convert the unborn child into a boy, if unhappily it be a girl." Important among such practices were: procuring and praying with rosaries used by mothers of sons; swallowing herbs and roots that are popularly trusted for their ability to generate a male fetus; and worshipping trees and son-giving gods. There was also the custom of carrying out a ceremonial sacrament in the third or fourth month of pregnancy for the purpose of converting the embryo into a boy. (Srinivasan and Kanitkar in Gopalan and Kaur, 1989:39) Many of these practices and beliefs continue to be followed in modern-day India.

III

EARLY MARRIAGE
AND ITS IMPACT ON GIRLS

Marriage age and its prevalence are crucial to determining the status of females. In most developing countries, a pattern of early and universal marriage prevails. Among traditional cultures, being married is highly prized as an "essential prerequisite for attainment of full adult status." (Ware, 1981:88) In those cultures, adolescence as a stage in the life-cycle is non-existent, and often has no special name. Individuals move from childhood directly into adulthood. Although among boys in such societies the changeover is formally acknowledged through male initiation ceremonies or rituals, there are no equivalent rites for girls, barring that which occasionally marks menstruation. Evidently, marriage and motherhood serve that purpose.

In developed countries, marriage is occurring later in life. A significant proportion of women in these countries are also choosing to remain single. For instance, the average age at first marriage in the United States rose by at least two years between 1970 and 1988 for all but the lowest educational group, according to figures released by the National Center for Health Statistics. (*San Francisco Chronicle*, 5 Sept. 1991:B-5) The reported data showed single female high school graduates marrying at 23.4 years and their male counterparts at age 25.2 years. There was also a 0.3 percent decline in the number of marriages in 1988, marking the fourth consecutive year in which the rate has declined. A U.N. report (1991:13) shows that most women in developed regions marry between the ages of 20 and 27—on average at age 23—and very young marriages are exceptional. The marriage age for women in Latin America and the Caribbean is 22; in Asia, 21; and in Africa, 20. Averages, however, are not representative of countries and populations at either end of the spectrum. The average marriage age of girls in Bangladesh, for instance, is estimated by UNFPA to be 11.6 years. (See Box 3, on "Early Marriage of Girls")

Where girls marry before or soon after the onset of menses, there exists the problem of children becoming pregnant and bearing children. (Ware, 1981:191) The purpose of early marriage is to ensure that the girl does not lose her virginity or conceive, either of which would be a source of great

---

Box 3
Early Marriage of Girls

---

1. In **Sierra Leone**, "Girls are married shortly after puberty. As a result, 60 percent of women (but only 2 percent of men) are married before age 19. Incentive for early marriage is partly economic. Once married, the daughter no longer relies on the family's resources; the family benefits also from the dowry."

2. In **Nigeria**, "The traditional and cultural practices that affect the position of women continue to influence age at marriage: one-quarter (24.5 percent) of all marriages took place before the age of 13, over one-third (37 percent) by the age of 14, and (51.8 percent) by the age of 15. More than 80 percent marry before reaching the age of 20 years.

3. In **India**, "Child marriage, though prohibited by law is still prevalent. Parents, anxious to wash their hands of their burden, marry their daughters young. In families where there are two daughters, they may be married off together to save the expense of two separate ceremonies, even if the younger one is well below the legal age of marriage." Further, "In two Indian villages, the average age of marriage for girls is just 14.3 years."

4. In eleven countries in Africa, eight in Asia (East and South Asia), and one in Latin America, the average age at first marriage for women is still below 20 years.

Sources: Item 1, UNICEF, *The Children and Women of Sierra Leone*, 1989:55; item 2, UNICEF, *Children and Women in Nigeria, A Situation Analysis*, 1989: Para 31; item 3, *The Lesser Child: The Girl in India*, monograph produced by Government of India with assistance from UNICEF, New Delhi, p. 14; and UNFPA, *1988 Report*, 1988:20; and item 4, U. N., *The World's Women, Trends and Statistics 1970-1990*, 1991:14

family shame in traditional cultures. Early marriage also takes advantage of the greater malleability of the young girl to adapt herself to the ways of her husband and his family. In other words, early marriage ensures that "women have no experience of independent adulthood prior to becoming (wives or) parents themselves." (Madan, 1965 in Ware, 1981:191)

Because virginity is prized, marriage is arranged early and often, as in African, Asian, and Arab countries where the bride is married as a young child but is formally handed over to the in-laws only at, or just before, menarche. Even after she moves in with her in-laws, conjugal life for her may not begin until one or several years later. Until then, she may live with, and under the supervisory care of, her mother-in-law. As a Moroccan woman noted during an interview about early marriage: "I stayed with my husband until I had my first period. . .I had no breasts then, nothing. I was like a boy. . .He never approached me until after a whole year. . .I was living with my mother-in-law (in her room). She used to treat me like a child of hers." (Kenza in Mernissi, 1985:73)

In this way, early marriage is perceived as an easy method for bonding the child-bride to her husband and his family. At the same time, it minimizes the risk of pre-marital sex. But it also encourages greater fertility, with consequent risks to the survival and health capability of both the young bride and her offspring. Among the harmful consequences of early marriage are the resulting long marital and tedious reproductive spans for the female. Researchers have established that "while Latin American and European women spend about 60 percent of their reproductive lives in formal marriages, women in tropical Africa spend fully 85 percent of the time available in marriage." (Ware, 1981:88) In India, where only 0.5 percent of women never marry, and widowhood is almost the only acceptable way for a marriage to be terminated, women's marital and reproductive span is probably even longer. The reproductive span for African, Asian, and Latin American women is estimated to be around eighteen years, compared to about seven years for women in developed countries. (U.N., 1991:13) Inevitably, longer reproductive spans account for maternal health depletion and high levels of infant, child and maternal mortality and illness. Early child-bearing also is related to low school enrollment and its attendant economic and social costs.

One of the clearest indicators of the modernization of family structure and a key indicator of the improved status of girls is a rise in the female marriage

age. The marriage age rises when, as has been observed in such countries as Hong Kong and India, parents appreciate the earning capability of girls, or when, as in India, parents are unable to afford a dowry and the other costs of arranging a marriage. Where girls have access to life outside the home and can mix freely with members of the opposite sex, some postponement occurs in the marriage age. In China, the upward age movement occurred in response to a wider social change campaign associated with the "new democratic family" and the official encouragement given to "free choice marriages" rather than those arranged by parents.

Literacy is expected to shape and change people's attitude and behavior. However, with respect to early marriage, based on a study of eight Asian countries, "female literacy by itself may not always make a difference. Reduced difference between male and female literacy is observed to be more important in determining the female mean age at marriage." (Sundaram, 1977 in Ware, 1981:89)

The impact of increased marriage age on female fertility is well-documented. It has certainly paid off in Kerala, India, which has the lowest infant and overall mortality rate, the highest expectation of life at birth, and the lowest birth rate, along with the highest average marriage age of women in the country. (Government of India, 1985:14) In Malaysia, "two-thirds of the fertility decline prior to 1970 was the direct result of declines in the proportions married." (Jones, 1980 in Ware, 1981:88) Even as far back as 1960, "the age of brides in the Philippines, Hong Kong, Sri Lanka, and Thailand was as high as that of brides in the United Kingdom or Belgium." (Dixon, 1978 in Ware, 1981:88)

EARLY SEXUAL ACTIVITY OUTSIDE OF MARRIAGE

Delayed marriage reduces fertility in marriage but not necessarily out of wedlock. Where virginity is prized and protected, as well as enforced through religious and social control, the risk of promiscuity and early sexual activity is less. But as Ware notes, "in Coastal West Africa, for instance, with much less emphasis on virginity, abortion among school girls becomes a significant problem." (92) In developed countries, contemporary social revolution has caused increased teenage sexual activity and teen pregnancy. (See Box 4, on "Adolescent Sexuality: The Global Facts") In the United States, for instance, adolescents are found to be sexually active at younger ages. The U.S. Centers for Disease Control and Prevention (CDC) reports that 70 percent of American girls now have sex by their high school graduation day, and that 25.6 percent of girls reported having had sex at age 15, in 1988, compared to just 4.6 percent in 1970. The pregnancy rate for teenagers younger than 15 has increased from 15.9 per 1,000 such girls in 1980 to 18.6 per 1,000 in 1987, and teen births account for one-fifth of all births. Pregnancy among

---

Box 4
Adolescent Sexuality: The Global Facts

1. More than 15 million girls aged 15–19 give birth every year, and another 5 million may have abortions.

2. In Central America, 18 percent of all births are to adolescents, and in some parts of Africa the proportion reaches 23 percent.

3. In the United States there are nearly 1 million adolescent pregnancies, of which more than 450,000 end in abortion.

4. Figures on the number of adolescents in developing countries having abortions are very hard to obtain; estimates range between 1 million and 4.4 million. Many of these procedures are illegal and performed under unsafe conditions.

5. It is estimated that globally there are some 50 million girls aged 15–19 who undergo induced abortions annually.

6. A recent survey in Costa Rica found that only 10 percent of sexually active teenagers (17 and under) used any form of birth control at first intercourse. A study in Kenya showed that 89 percent of sexually active teenagers never used any method of birth control. Fewer than 30 percent of married adolescents in developing countries use modern family planning methods.

7. One out of twenty teenagers contracts a sexually transmitted disease annually. About half of all HIV infections to date have occurred in people under 25. Since the pandemic began, more that 6 million youth have been infected with HIV.

Sources for Facts: Items 1–3, International Planned Parenthood Federation (IPPF); items 4–6, Population Action International (PAI); and item 7, Center for Population Options and Population Reference Bureau (CPO/PRB)

Source: UNICEF, *First Call for Children,* July–September 1994:15

United States girls aged 15–19 is also highest among the ten top industrial nations. More than one million girls between the ages of 12 and 19 become pregnant annually. (*San Francisco Chronicle*, October 14, 1994:A-4)

Promiscuity among girls is also on the rise, causing a higher rate of extra-marital fertility. Almost two-thirds of all births in 1990 to American teenagers were to unmarried girls, compared with fewer than one-third in 1970. A 1988 UNFPA study notes that three-fourths of teenage births in Denmark and Sweden were out of wedlock. Approximately 40 to 50 percent of children in Paraguay, Peru, and Venezuela, and 32 percent in Ecuador were found to be out-of-wedlock children. (Newland, 1979:193)

Although unintended births among unmarried adolescents grew from 79 percent in the late 1970s and early 1980s to 87 percent from 1985 to 1989 (Hechinger:6), a growing trend among teen mothers in America is to take their pregnancies to full term rather than undergo abortion. Recent findings show that more American girls aged 15 and younger are getting pregnant and more of them are keeping their babies. According to the CDC, abortions among women below 20 years of age accounted for 29 percent in 1980, compared to 25 percent in 1988. (*San Francisco Chronicle*, October 14, 1994)

Therefore, though marriage rates may have declined in the United States and other countries, sexuality and fertility are not necessarily declining among younger females.[1] On the contrary, younger-age girls are being trapped into the similar burdens of marriage and motherhood, which are culturally mandated for young girls in traditional societies. Largely as a result of the economic, educational, and health disadvantages which early sexuality and marriage pose for the young female, fertility and other needs of adolescence are drawing wider attention. In more traditional countries, laws are being formulated or tightened to help raise and enforce girl's minimum marriage age.

But laws alone are not enough to make a significant behavioral change among sexually active teenagers in developed countries or among parents determined to marry off their girls in conventional cultures. Better, more rigorous sex education, greater societal sensitivity to, and investment in, the health and status of girls, and more vigilant and efficient enforcement of minimum-age-at-marriage laws will enable girls to overcome the risks to their health and life chances from early conjugal life or sexual cohabitation. Above all, the girl's economic, emotional, and social autonomy has to be restored to her. As the eminent Indian leader, Jawaharlal Nehru, put it: "The habit of looking upon marriage as a profession almost and as the sole economic refuge for women will have to go, before women can have any freedom."

Endnote

1. More recently, it is encouraging to note the first decline in six years in teen birthrates in America. After rising 24 percent between 1986 and 1991, birthrates for 15–19-year-old females showed a 2 percent decline between 1991 and 1992. (*San Francisco Chronicle*, October 26, 1994:A-4)

IV

DEMOGRAPHY OF GIRLS

The universal demographic disparity between girls and boys has remained invisible, mainly because demographic studies of the status of women have not focused separately on girls. Only recently have analysts attempted to correlate the weaker demographic status of women globally to discrimination against girls. This is particularly true in such South Asia countries as Bangladesh, India, Nepal, and Pakistan. Scholars have detected conclusive evidence of unequal food disbursement between sons and daughters in Oceania (Southern Pacific Islands), East, West, and South Asia. (Ravindran 1986:5–6) Nutritional biases, mortality, and incidence of disease differentials between genders have been established by various scholars. (Chen et al., 1981: Newland, 1979; Ravindran 1986; Sen 1989; Waldron 1987; Ware 1981) More recent inquiries have extended the onus of discriminatory gender development to a wider range of such countries as Egypt, Ethiopia, Malawi, Peru, the Sudan, and Uganda. (Sohoni, 1990) Sohoni found that girls between 0–19 years of age, while representing a fifth of the world's population, are denied their requisite share of the benefits of development. Furthermore, unlike women, the less favorable demographic status of girls is not confined just to developing countries.

In most existing socio-demographic studies, the primary concern has been with the female as a woman. Evidently, the growth process continuum between girlhood and womanhood is not adequately reflected in human development strategies. Most treat the unequal socioeconomic status of the adult female compared to the male, rather than protect womanhood from the preventable consequences of neglected girlhood.

The concern of this chapter is to deal with the quantitative limitations on girls, and some of the myths and realities that govern the female's numerical presence:

1. Myth: Although fewer females than males are conceived and born, the female overtakes the male population rather quickly. Reality: There is slim evidence that females overtake males in a population "rather quickly"; indeed, positive ratios occur in many countries much later in adult life than current demographic literature suggests.

2. Myth: An improved female/male sex ratio is consistent with developed countries, or with the more developed among the developing countries. Reality: There is no consistent pattern of improved female sex ratios in countries at various levels of development; in fact, improvement in the demographic presence of females (as manifest through the female/male sex ratio) is not as impressive or consistent even in the developed world as one is led to expect.

3. Myth: Where adult females enjoy a favorable sex ratio, one could expect that favorable level to begin making an impact even during girlhood. Reality: Where women show an improved ratio, it does not follow that girls experience the same positive outcome. In fact, there is no significant correlation between the age at which the female component in the population overtakes the male and the development status of women or countries.

The principal objective of the discussion that follows is to establish that if the demographic analyses and concerns of gender scholars are confined to women, they cannot expect to catch or treat the greater vulnerability of girls to discrimination. A related objective is to establish the need to expand the inquiry into female's (women's and girls') disparate demographic status from its present concentration on South and West Asia to all regions of the world.

I. This section deals with current demographic perspective and perceptions regarding sex ratio;

II. this examines existing data on the demographic presence of women compared to men, and girls compared to boys and women. Sex-ratio comparisons are presented for different age groups and regions of the world in 1970 and 1990;

III. this focuses on a group of twenty-one countries selected to represent various stages of development, and regions of the world. It analyzes the correlation between the age at which the female population exceeded the male population, and other indicators of women's status and development; and

IV. this section presents conclusions.

I

Development strategists, scholars, and demographers need to understand the developmental implications of the differences between the male and female population. As a result of the last three development decades, the assumption that development works alike for everyone has been largely eroded. The development discipline is now showing greater concern for making development more relevant and responsive to various socioeconomic, regional, and ethnic groups. Gender and age are also becoming widely accepted as the criteria for measuring development's impact and efficacy. Gender-by-age analysis as a means of measuring the outcomes of development, however, needs to be more systematically deployed in order to catch development's varying impact not only on (i) male versus female adults and (ii) adults versus children, but also on (iii) female versus male children and (iv) female and male children versus female and male adults.

The sexist bias in demography must also be eliminated. The study of fertility, mortality, migration, marriage, education, income, health, and nutrition has to focus equally on women and men, and on girls as well as boys. Currently, "more than three-quarters of fertility studies are restricted to female population and even greater proportion consider women to bear a greater responsibility for fertility levels than men. In contrast, studies of migration or labor force participation are frequently restricted to male migration or male labor force participation. . .This is despite the fact that the majority of all migration around the world is still undertaken by women moving to their husbands' communities at marriage." (Ware 1981:5) In mortality statistics, the focus has been "on deaths during the first year of life, when boys are at a marked biological advantage. There is no equivalent simple term (such as infant mortality) for, or special interest in, mortality at ages 1–4. Yet it is at this age group that, if there is any social discrimination against girls or relative neglect of females, it will become most apparent in the mortality statistics. Developing countries strive to produce infant-mortality statistics to monitor the progress of development but assign a much lower priority to childhood-mortality statistics. . .The result has been an actual decline in information on sex differentials in mortality at young ages in developing countries." (Ware 1981:6)

Fertility and marriage, as sub-fields of study within demography, further demonstrate the inequitable preoccupation with the adult female and the virtual neglect not only of the adult male but also of the girl, 0–19. Studies of fertility behavior and contraception research, development, education, knowledge, and practice are widely observed as having been geared primarily toward women. Although current estimates indicate that "around 30 percent of Latin American women are married by the age of 18," and "40 percent of all 14-year-old girls alive today will have been pregnant at least once by the time they are 20, worldwide, three-quarters of girls under 15 and half of those 16 or over, have no access to family planning information," which continue to be targeted to older women. (UNFPA 1988:13, 21–22)

The United Nations Women's Decade (1976–1985) caused development scholars, for the first time, to explore the status of women. International data and country studies undertaken to examine the status of women as part of a global celebration of International Women's Year (1975) uncovered, among other things, disturbing demographic differences between the health and survival capability of the female, compared to the male population. In certain countries, such as India, it was discovered that the female/male ratio (F/MR) had declined in 1971 from what it was at the beginning of the century. Women's life expectancy in such countries as Bangladesh, India, Iran, Iraq, Liberia, Nepal, and Pakistan was found to be less than that of men (Bangladesh, Bhutan, Maldives, and Nepal continue to show lower life expectancy for females than males, even in 1991). (U.N., 1991:55)

Fifteen years later, the situation has changed positively for many countries but the global situation is not as promising. A recent global analysis by the United Nations reveals that "there were 996 women per 1,000 men in 1970 compared to 987 women per 1,000 men in 1990." (U.N., 1990) In the report, the disparity between the two years was attributed to Asia, where the F/MR was found to be 91.1 per 100. South Asia, in particular, and Asia, in general, emerge as areas of concern in United Nations and other analyses. There is a universal trend noted in all regions of the world, with the exception of Asia, for females to experience a more favorable sex ratio, usually for women above 20 years of age. Persistent and pervasive societal biases against the female, during childhood and adulthood, are suspected to be responsible for the continued demographic disadvantage of the female in that region.

In existing socio-demographic literature, it is commonly assumed that approximately 105 male births occur for every 100 female births. (Miller 1983; Sen 1989) Because more male infants die than female,[1] given an equal chance, both genders are expected to quickly reach parity. Another assumption is that under normal conditions, women outlive men, thus achieving a favorable sex ratio. According to Bernard (1981:123–25), "Females are born into the world with numerically minority status: they constitute only about 49 percent of all infants at birth. It is estimated that only about two-thirds as many females as males are conceived but that the greater viability of females [more male fetuses abort than female] increases their proportion from conception throughout life. . .The greater viability of females thus allows them to lessen the disparity in numbers between the sexes at conception and to equal the number of males in the early 20s."

Other scholars who support the biological or environmental viability of the female, at least in the context of developed, industrialized societies, include Kingsley Davis (1979:37–64) and Sheila Ryan Johansson: (1977:163–81 in Bernard 1981) Davis referred to "the advantage of females in mortality" appearing "at all ages" and predicted that the "mortality gap may continue to increase giving rise to sex ratios still more distorted than observed today." (57) Johansson, while rejecting the strictly biological approach to understanding the emergence or existence of a female mortality advantage, suggested that socioeconomic factors are important as well, and "today they are making it more and more deadly to be male." (181)

Many of those perceptions are now debatable in the light of subsequent demographic evidence. There is less concrete basis for assuming that parity occurs between genders when women are in their early 20s. Nor are sex ratios as progressively favorable to women as some of the earlier scholars had predicted. Globally, there were fewer women per 1,000 men in 1990 than twenty years ago. Increasingly, women are experiencing many of the environmental stresses that two decades ago were making it "deadly to be male," thus narrowing the survival edge they may have had over the male. On the other hand, the reproductive as well as contraception-related stresses on women's health and survival capability seem to be a persistent disadvantage to women even in developed countries.

The perception that it is natural to expect an early balancing of gender ratios in a population on account of either the biological or the environmental resilience of the female needs to have further debate and statistical substantiation. When that biological or natural process of gender parity does not occur in national or global situations, socio-demographers think that it points to a serious, incipient discrimination between genders that deserves a careful understanding and redressive affirmative action. "Females have a genetic and biological advantage over males which they lose only under strongly adverse social and cultural circumstances." (Morris, 1979 in Ware 1981:13) According to this perspective, the inferiority of woman's status presumably decides the numbers and timing of female deaths.

Subscribing to the above view, analysts have concluded that gender-demographic disparity is an outcome of disparate mortality rates—concentrated in countries with a high preference for sons, and a subordination of female health and nutritional needs to those of the male. A 1987 WHO study, using 1983 World Fertility Survey data for twenty-seven countries on son preference, clearly noted that results support the hypothesis that a stronger preference for sons contributes to higher mortality for females. Increased sex discrimination in nutrition and health care, which increases the girl's vulnerability to infectious diseases, presumably causes the increased mortality rate. (Waldron 1987:207) Risks to females in those countries are acute and the basis for the risk is a preference for sons. Other recent studies of children in Bangladesh, Egypt, India, Jordan, and Pakistan all point to the greater mortality and disease incidence among girls, and their lesser nutritional intake and health care in those countries. (UNICEF, 1990)

Whereas son preference and daughter neglect are well-documented social behavior patterns in many if not most developing countries, they do not help to explain the continued gender disparity, particularly among younger females, in developed countries. Nor is there adequate explanation for why women surpass men in numbers so late in life, even in developed countries.

II

In the tables and text to follow, sex ratios are examined globally, regionally, and, for some countries, selectively. Macro analysis of the demographic status of girls compared to boys and women for 1970 and 1990 shows disturbing trends. Table 5 presents the gender ratios in the world's population in 1970 and 1990. With the exception of Latin America, the ratio of males to females between 1970–1990 increased in all regions of the world. However, in the 0–19 population, the male's position improved universally, as seen in Table 5. For girls (age 0–19) as well as women (all ages), the gain in male proportional presence is much more for developed than for developing countries over the period of 1970–1990. In the three developing regions, the maximum gain by

0–19-year-old males in 1990 over 1970 is evident in Asia (0.6 percent), followed by Africa (0.4 percent), and Latin America (0.1 percent). For men of all ages, the percent change in the same period is greater in Africa (0.8 percent) than in Asia (0.3 percent). In Latin America, there is a 0.6 percent decline in the male presence. Those figures contrast with the male increase in developed countries of 0.8 percent for 0–19-year-olds, and 1.3 percent for men of all ages; and 0.2 percent and 0.1 percent, respectively, in developing countries.

Table 6 (next page) constitutes the mirror image of Table 5 and presents the number of females per 1,000 males in the world and in each of its regions, in 1970 and 1990. It affirms that there is a greater decline in female population per 1,000 males in the developed than in the developing regions, among all ages.

Females of all ages show more than parity levels in developed regions and in Africa, 1970 and 1990, and in Latin America in 1990, but girls remain below parity in both years in all regions. It is noteworthy that the negative girl/boy ratios for developed and developing countries are similar. In fact, both Africa and Latin America show better girl/boy ratios in both years than

Table 5
Number of Males per 1,000 Females: 1970, 1990

Region	All Ages		0–19 Age Group	
	1970	1990	1970	1990
More Developed Regions	930	942	1,043	1,050
Less Developed Regions	1,035	1,036	1,046	1,048
Africa	981	989	1,009	1,013
Asia	1,045	1,048	1,056	1,062
Latin America	1,004	998	1,024	1,025
World	1,004	1,014	1,045	1,049

Source: Based on United Nations, *Global Estimates and Projections of Population by Sex and Age, The 1988 Revision,* New York, 1989, pp. 4–33
Note: 1970 figures are estimates, and 1990 figures are medium variant projections
Decimal figures .05 and above are rounded to .1

Table 6
Female/Male Ratios 1970, 1990
(Number of Females per 100 Males)

Regions	1970 Estimates		1990 (medium variant) Projections	
	0–19	All Ages	0–19	All Ages
World	957	996	954	987
More Developed Regions	959	1,075	952	1,061
Less Developed Regions	956	966	954	966
Africa	991	1,020	987	1,012
Asia	947	957	942	954
Latin America	977	996	976	1,002

World: Total Population, Millions (rounded) 1970, 1990

	1970			1990		
	Male	Female	Total	Male	Female	Total
Ages 0–19	895.3	856.7	1,752	1,141.8	1,089.0	2,230.9
All Ages	1,852.8	1,845.2	3,697.4	2,663.9	2,628.2	5,292.1

Percent Increase 1990/1970	Male	Female
Ages 0–19	27.5	27.1
All Ages	43.8	42.4

Percentage of Total Population	Male		Female	
	1970	1990	1970	1990
Ages 0–19	24.2	21.6	23.2	20.6
All Ages	50.1	50.3	49.9	49.7

Source: United Nations, *Global Estimates and Projections of Population By Sex and Age, The 1988 Revision*, New York, 1989 (Table is derived from data on pp. 4-33)

do the developed countries. The percent increase in 1990 over 1970 is much higher globally for women of all ages than for girls. Conversely, the decline in the proportion of girls in the total population of the world is greater than of women of all ages. (Compared to 1970, girls, as a percentage of total population in 1990, experienced a decline of 2.6 percentage points, in contrast to women of all ages who experienced a decline of 0.2 percentage points.)

There is no rational or documented explanation for several issues which arise from the above comparison. For instance, (i) Why should developed countries perform more or less similarly to developing countries insofar as the numerical presence of the female population is concerned?; (ii) Why should Africa and Latin America show more favorable sex ratios than developed countries with respect to girls in both 1970 and 1990?; (iii) Does the unique fact of the declining male ratio (of all ages) in Latin America between 1970–1990 reflect its considerably higher mortality for men over 20 years of age, massive male migration, or both, or does it represent a radically improved health and survival capability of Latin American women?; and (iv) What accounts for the significant decline in the number of males (of all ages) per 1,000 females in Africa from their positive ratios in the 0–19 age group in both 1970 and 1990?

Table 7 (next page) examines the sub-groups among 0–19 population to see whether gender disparity is specific to any one or more age groups. Male/female ratios are presented for both years, 1970 and 1990. For easy reference, sex ratios for all ages are also indicated. When comparing 1990 to 1970, the trend in favor of boys appears with respect to each age group and in all regions of the world, except in the age group 5–9 in the developing countries where no variation is noted. In the total population, Latin American men experience a unique decline in 1990 over 1970. Therefore, whereas women of all ages are able to improve their position a little compared to men in at least one region, girls are uniformly disadvantaged, although the extent of disadvantage varies between regions. What is disconcerting is the much higher proportion of males to females in all sub-groups of 0–19-year-olds in developed countries, over the proportion in Africa. Greater male advantage is also visible in developed countries, in comparison to Latin America, for both years and for all sub-groups aged 0–19.

Looking at the 0–19 and all ages male/female ratios, it is puzzling to note the drastic decline in male presence in the total population (all ages) in both developed countries and in Africa. The contrast with Asia and Latin America is also puzzling. The improved female presence in the total population can be attributed to their improved health and survival in developed countries, but the same explanation cannot be valid for Africa. It is difficult to suggest what combination of genetic, environmental, socioeconomic, or political factors

Table 7
Male/Female Ratios 1970, 1990
(Males per 1,000 Females)

Places	0–4	5–9	10–14	15–19	0–19	All Ages
World						
1970	1,044	1,047	1,048	1,042	1,045	1,004
1990	1,045	1,048	1,050	1,052	1,049	1,014
More Developed						
1970	1,046	1,044	1,043	1,037	1,042	930
1990	1,049	1,050	1,049	1,053	1,050	942
Less Developed						
1970	1,043	1,048	1,049	1,043	1,046	1,035
1990	1,045	1,048	1,050	1,052	1,048	1,036
Africa						
1970	1,013	1,009	1,009	1,001	1,009	981
1990	1,016	1,012	1,012	1,013	1,013	989
Asia						
1970	1,051	1,059	1,060	1,053	1,056	1,045
1990	1,056	1,061	1,065	1,065	1,062	1,048
Latin America						
1970	1,030	1,024	1,021	1,017	1,024	1,004
1990	1,031	1,025	1,022	1,018	1,025	998

Source: United Nations, *Global Estimates and Projections of Population By Sex and Age, The 1988 Revision*, New York, 1989 (Table is derived from data on pp. 4–33)
Note: 1970 figures are estimates, and 1990 figures are medium variant

(including wars, internal violence, migration, under-reporting, or over-reporting of male and female deaths) influences sex ratios within the limited context of this chapter, given the inadequacy of relevant trend data. But whatever the contributing factors, they require further examination, and not merely in developing countries. In fact, it is in the developed countries that serious and searching answers have to be found as to why gender differentials among 0–19 year olds there are not distinct from those in the developing countries. At the least, it should allow some room for skepticism in linking demographic performance to "development." In fact, based on the above evidence, it is tempting to discard the *level of development* as a positive indicator of the demographic status of girls.

To further test the unfavorable demographic status of girls, Table 8 (next page) examines the demographic status of males compared to: (i) females of all ages; (ii) those aged 0–19; and (iii) those above the age of 20. The male/female ratios are indicated for 1970 and 1990 for all regions. In addition, four countries are included in the tabular analysis as generally presumed models of least (India), more (Japan, United States), and most (Sweden) favorable overall status of women. From the table, it is easy to discern that in both 1970 and 1990, *universally,* there are fewer males per 1,000 women (age 20-plus) than per 1,000 girls (age 0–19). Moreover, as per Table 9 (page 51), the gap in male presence between women (age 20-plus) and girls (age 0–19) is widest in the more developed regions and narrowest in the less developed regions in 1990. (In 1970, it is narrowest in Asia.) In other words, in 1990, in the more developed regions, there are nearly 150 more males for every 1,000 girls than per 1,000 women (20-plus). In contrast, in the less developed regions, the number of males amounts to a little over 20 more males per 1,000 girls than per 1,000 women (20+). Among the four selected countries, likewise, India shows the smallest gap, while the United States shows the largest gap in both years. Applying the traditional (woman's) perspective, the higher gap would be perceived as a favorable development to the female, but not to girls aged 0–19.

Variation between 1970 and 1990 in the difference between males as a percentage of girls, minus males as percentage of women 20-plus, is also interesting. As seen in Table 8, the difference is most marked in the more developed regions. A positive variation in the difference suggests that women are faring better numerically than girls in such regions as Asia and Latin America, and among the four selected countries, except India. The negative

Table 8
Demographic Status of Males and Females 1970, 1990
(Males per 1,000 Females)

	All Ages	0–19	20-plus
World, 1990	1,014	1,049	989
	(1,004)	(1,045)	(969)
More Developed Regions, 1990	942	1,050	902
	(930)	(1,043)	(874)
Less Developed Regions, 1990	1,036	1,048	1,025
	(1,035)	(1,046)	(1,023)
Africa, 1990	989	1,013	958
	(981)	(1,009)	(947)
Asia, 1990	1,048	1,062	1,038
	(1,004)	(1,056)	(1,034)
Latin America, 1990	998	1,025	975
	(1,004)	(1,024)	(981)
India, 1990	1,070	1,073	1,067
	(1,071)	(1,083)	(1,060)
United States, 1990	952	1,048	917
	(959)	(1,037)	(914)
Japan, 1990	967	1,051	938
	(964)	(1,038)	(930)
Sweden, 1990	973	1,047	952
	(997)	(1,053)	(977)

Source: United Nations, *Global Estimates and Projections of Population By Sex and Age, The 1988 Revision,* New York, 1989 (Table is derived from data on pp. 4–33)
Note: 1970 figures are bracketed

variation in India, although a bleak commentary on the female's overall status in India, could suggest some kind of approximation in the sex ratio status of girls and 20-plus women. Conversely, in regions and countries where a positive variation is observed, it represents an increasing gap between the sex ratio status of girls compared to women 20-plus.

Table 10 (next page) examines the variation in male/female ratios from 1970–1990. As seen from the table, males have improved in their ratio to females in 1990 over 1970 in the 0–19 age group, in Japan and the United States, while their ratios have declined in India and Sweden. The absolute decline is greater in India (0.94) than in Sweden (0.61).

Table 9
Difference Between Male/Female Ratios for
0–19 and 20-plus Population in 1970 and 1990,
and Variation in 1990 over 1970
(Males per 1,000 Females)

Region	Difference (M/FR for 0–19 minus M/FR for 20-plus)		Variation (1990/1970)
	1990	1970	
World	5.99	7.66	-1.67
More Developed Regions	14.78	16.85	-2.07
Less Developed Regions	2.13	2.26	-0.13
Africa	5.51	6.17	-0.66
Asia	2.34	2.12	+0.22
Latin America	4.94	4.23	+0.71
India	0.66	2.25	-1.59
United States	13.17	12.34	+0.83
Japan	11.30	10.85	+0.45
Sweden	9.56	7.69	+1.87

Source: United Nations, *Global Estimates and Projections of Population By Sex and Age, The 1988 Revision*, New York, 1989 (Table is derived from data on pp. 4–33)

In the 20-plus age group, a declining male presence in relation to the female is observed only in Sweden, while in the other three countries the male presence has improved from 1970 to 1990. In fact, the rise in favor of males is highest in Japan, followed by India and the United States. For All Ages, male presence compared to females experienced a decline in three of the four countries, with Sweden showing a considerably higher decline than the United States and India. In Japan, on the other hand, the male's demographic position improved. Japan, in fact, experienced an improved male presence in all three categories, while Sweden experienced a declining male presence in all categories. In the United States, male presence improved most in the 0–19 age group, while experiencing a decline among all age groups. India showed an improved comparative presence of females in the 0–19 age group as well as among all age groups. Thus, as is clear from Table 10, the "developed" characterization of individual countries did not have a consistent impact on their male/female distribution.

Looking at the world variations in male/female ratios between 1970–1990, it is clear that the male ratios for all three age groups have improved in all

Table 10
Variation in Male/Female Ratios in 1990 over 1970
in Selected Countries and World Regions

	All Ages	0–19	20-plus
India	-0.16	-0.94	+0.65
United States	-0.63	+1.10	+0.27
Japan	+0.33	+1.33	+0.88
Sweden	-2.40	-0.61	-2.48
World	+0.94	+0.35	+2.02
More Developed Regions	+1.21	+0.73	+2.80
Less Developed Regions	+0.60	+0.26	+0.16
Africa	+0.80	+0.46	+1.12
Asia	+0.32	+0.60	+0.38
Latin America	-0.57	+0.10	-0.61

Source: United Nations, *Global Estimates and Projections of Population By Sex and Age, The 1988 Revision*, New York, 1989 (Table is derived from data on pp. 4–33)

regions, barring Latin America. (Table 10) Even in Latin America, where the male presence has declined compared to the female in 1990, as compared to 1970, the decline is not visible with respect to girls aged 0–19. It is thus evident that, over the period 1970–1990, girls have experienced a more unfavorable demographic status than females of all ages, universally.

Comparing girls with women aged 20-plus yields some interesting findings. For the 20-plus category, male gain in 1990 over 1970 again, surprisingly, shows most in developed countries and least in developing countries, excluding Latin America, with its negative variation. Also, the positive variation in male proportional presence is far more significant for the 20-plus group than for ages 0–19, or all ages in the world, but to a lesser extent in Africa. It may be surmised from the above that women 20-plus years of age may not be experiencing the extent of survival advantage over men that had come to be associated with the level of life and health capability of developed countries.

III
Another line of inquiry concerns the age at which either demographic parity is achieved between the genders, or the female exceeds the male component in the population. Table 11 (next page) presents the age groups at which twenty-one countries achieved an excess of female over male population. As the table shows, there is no apparent link between the development status of countries and how quickly they achieve female demographic predominance.

Table 12 (page 55) presents the "projected female excess" data pyramidally. The mean age at which the crossover occurs is 40.8. Slightly over two-thirds of the twenty-one countries experience the crossover between 23–59 years of age, with 19 percent achieving excess below 22 years and 14 percent above 59 years. The contention by such scholars as Bernard (1981), that females "equal the number of males in the early 20s," is only validated by less than 20 percent of the sample.

What is further reinforced by Table 12 is the somewhat illogical and unexplainable clustering of countries at entirely different levels of development, in their age of female crossover. Netherlands, Sweden, and Paraguay form as strange a grouping as Egypt, Japan, Sudan, and United Kingdom, or Korea and France. Also, Nigeria and six other developing countries in the sample achieve female majority well before France, Israel, and the United States. Significantly, the developed countries with higher income levels and more positive female health and literacy status are still well behind Gabon, Ghana, Nigeria, Mexico, Mongolia, and the Philippines when it comes to achieving a favorable demographic ratio for the female.

Table 13 (page 56) seeks to assess whether there is any link between development's other variables and the widely ranging stage of demographic

---

Table 11
Age Group at Which Female Excess was
Achieved by Selected Countries

Country	Age at Excess
1. Egypt	45–49
2. France	30–34
3. Gabon	15–19
4. Ghana	20–24
5. India	70–74
6. Israel	35–39
7. Japan	45–49
8. Republic of Korea	30–34
9. Kuwait	75–79
10. Malaysia	25–29
11. Mexico	25–29
12. Mongolia	20–24
13. Netherlands	55–59
14. Nigeria	10–14
15. Paraguay	55–59
16. Philippines	25–29
17. Saudi Arabia	65–69
18. Sudan	40–44
19. Sweden	55–59
20. United Kingdom	40–44
21. United States	35–39

Source: United Nations, *Global Estimates and Projections of Population By Sex and Age, The 1988 Revision*, New York, 1989 (Table is derived from data on pp. 4–33)

excess of women. Among the variables analyzed for their possible association with the age at which females exceeded males in the country's population are: (i) size of total female population; (ii) per capita GNP; (iii) female literacy; (iv) total fertility rate; (v) infant mortality rate per 1,000 live births; (vi) maternal mortality rate per 100,000 live births; (vii) sex ratio (female/male) for total population; (viii) sex ratio (female/male) for age 0–14 population; (ix) difference in average age at first marriage (male-female); and (x) percent of urban population in the country. The independent variables chosen were in keeping with those that typically influence the health and survival capability, as well as the status of women; data availability were the other considerations. Child mortality, for instance, had to be discarded in favor of infant mortality, mainly because gender-specific data for the former are not available. Urbanization and GNP per capita were included as standard indicators of modernization and development, and as factors most likely to make health care and other basic services more accessible to women.

Table 12
Pyramidal Distribution of Selected Countries by Age Group
at Which Female Excess Over Male was Achieved

Country	Age at Excess
Kuwait	75–79
India	70–74
Saudi Arabia	65–69
Sweden, Paraguay, Netherlands	55–59
Japan, Egypt	45–49
Sudan, United Kingdom	40–44
Israel, United States	35–39
Republic of Korea, France	30–34
Philippines, Mexico, Malaysia	25–29
Mongolia, Ghana	20–24
Gabon	15–19
Nigeria	10–14

Source: *World Fertility Survey, Cross-National Summaries*, Number 27, October 1983, and First Country Reports

The rank-difference method of correlation was applied to identify possible linkages between the countries' rankings by age of female crossover and their ranks in each of the other variables. For each variable, the twenty-one countries were ranked according to their achievement, with the number "one" representing the most achievement. The rank difference coefficient

Table 13
Rank Correlation Coefficients for 21 Selected Countries
(Dependent Variable: Ranking by age at which female excess over male occurs in a country's population)

Independent Variables	Pearson's r
1. Size of female population	-0.079558
2. GNP per capita	-0.334142
3. Female literacy	+0.038851
4. Total fertility rate	-0.095700
5. Infant mortality rate	-0.302652
6. Maternal mortality rate	-0.356382
7. Difference in life expectancy at birth (F-M)	-0.030225
8. Sex ratio (F/M), All Ages	+0.495112
9. Sex ratio (F/M), 0–14	+0.422931
10. Difference in average age at first marriage (M-F)	+0.181362
11. Percent urban population	-0.453478

Index

Coefficient	Nature of Association
.70 to 1.00 (plus or minus) =	High
.40 to less than .70 =	Substantial
.20 to less than .40 =	Low
Less than .20 =	Negligible

Note: Based on data derived from United Nations, Global Estimates, op. cit; UNICEF, Statistics on Children in UNICEF-assisted countries, 1989; United Nations, World Population Chart, 1988; and United Nations, Compendium of Statistics and Indicators on the Situation of Women, 1996. Index derived from Pauline V. Young, *Scientific Social Surveys and Research*, Prentice-Hall of India Private Limited, New Delhi, 1977, pp. 316-317

correlation was then worked out for the variables mentioned, and the outcome is presented in Table 13.

The table indicates Pearson's r values and signs for all the variables as a basis for gauging the positive or negative nature of their association with the dependent variable (hereafter referred to as Rankage). Applying the stricter criteria, it is easily inferred from the table that the stage at which the female component in a population supersedes the male does not show a "high" level of association with any of the chosen indices of development. However, a "substantial" positive association is visible with the female/male sex ratios among total population and among 0–14 year olds, and a "substantial" negative association with the percentage of urban population. "Low" negative correlation is observed between the female excess stage and GNP per capita, infant mortality rate, and maternal mortality rate. The remaining five variables (size of female population, difference in female-male life expectancy, difference in male-female age at marriage, fertility rate, and female literacy) show "negligible" positive or negative relationship. (See table for index of what constitutes degrees of association)

Relative to each other, however, the level of association with Rankage is significantly higher for some variables than for others. Sex ratios (all ages and ages 0–14), for instance, are more than fourteen to sixteen times as likely as female literacy to be linked to Rankage; urbanization is more than five to six times as likely to be associated with Rankage than the size of female population or the total fertility rate. Rankage is likely to be ten or more times as sensitive to maternal and infant mortality, and GNP per capita, than to female literacy and difference in life expectancy at birth.

One would expect the crossover age to be more influenced by sex ratios at different ages and the availability of medical attention integral to urbanization, rather than to such other tenuously linked factors as the absolute size of the female population. However, it was surprising to find an inverse relationship of Rankage with urbanization. The fact that a higher level of urbanization is not linked to the crossover of females occurring earlier suggests that urbanization affects males more favorably than females, enabling the former to maintain or even enhance their numerical advantage over women. What was also surprising was the low level of predictability of the crossover age being associated with the total fertility rate, and the even lower probability of Rankage being linked to female literacy. Literacy and fertility outcomes seemed to contradict the usual perceptions of these two variables as being of undeniable importance to enhancing the status of women. When unexpected, inverse relationships have emerged, it would be fitting to suggest that where women have some access to development's benefits men have greater access, and therefore the crossover occurs later than earlier. The main conclusion is that the point of transition in favor of the female in a population is not influenced by most of the variables conventionally associated with the improved status and prospects of women.

Looking at the Pearson's r values in Table 13, the following specific observations can be offered:

On the positive side:

1. There is a nearly 50 percent probability that as the female/male sex ratio improves, the female crossover in a population occurs earlier. Likewise, there is a 42 percent probability that as the female/male ratio improves among 0–14 year olds, the crossover will occur at a younger age for the population as a whole; and

2. There is an 18 percent probability that when the difference between male and female average marriage age increases, the crossover will occur later.

On the negative side:

1. There is a 45 percent probability that when urbanization is less, the crossover will occur early; and a 33 percent probability that when GNP per capita declines, the crossover will occur early also;

2. As maternal mortality and infant mortality rates rise, there is a 30 to 35 percent likelihood of the crossover occurring earlier;

3. There is a less than 10 percent probability that when total fertility is higher, crossover will occur earlier;

4. There is less than an 8 percent probability that the greater the size of the female population, the earlier the crossover occurs; and,

5. There is only a 3 percent predictability that as the life expectancy difference between females and males decreases, the crossover will occur earlier.

Since individually the variables did not show high levels of association with Rankage, multiple regression was applied to see if certain factors collectively had a more meaningful bearing on Rankage. (Marriage age was deleted from the multiple-regression analysis because this ranking was missing for some countries.) The analysis of the variance report showed that two variables—female literacy and infant-mortality rate—taken together, resulted in a probability level of 0.0. This suggests that these two together can be used to predict the stage at which the female crossover can occur in a population. While it is logical that these two factors should be linked to the age of female excess over male, it is curious that the analysis isolated these two variables as being most capable of predicting Rankage. As their exact relationship has not been determined and is beyond the scope of this chapter, it seems to be a legitimate and promising area for further research.

IV

In conclusion, some emerging issues need to be restated. Among social scientists and demographers, the fact that there are more women than men has been used for years to connote a higher developed status for the female, irrespective of when the female crossover occurs and whether it encompasses girls as distinct from women. Another tendency has been to associate the developed countries with a higher health and demographic status for women and, by inference, girls. This argument was based on the traditional parameters of mortality, disease incidence, and life expectancy, which have worked favorably for women in the developed rather than the developing world. However, the same advantage is not apparent when gender ratios are applied across various age groups and for all ages to measure achievement with respect to the female's demographic status, particularly both as girl and as woman. Moreover, after examining the data pertaining to a group of countries, representing various levels of female and total socioeconomic development, it is clear that neither the gender ratio nor the age of female crossover are necessarily linked to the development status of countries, or to a variety of development's indicators. In the sample studied, there are a number of developing countries where the crossover occurs early, and many developed countries in which it occurs later. It would, therefore, be incorrect to assume that where women's status is high, the transition occurs early. Conversely, if the transition occurs early, it does not mean that women's status is high. The correlational analysis also confirms that there is insufficient predictability between any of the selected independent variables and the age of female crossover in a population. It needs to be added, however, that the sample and frequencies used are small, and any wider inferences must be approached with caution. Nevertheless, as preliminary findings, they are intriguing enough to encourage further systematic studies of gender ratios in developed and developing countries, and the link of female demography with other indicators of women's development.

In view of the above, it is imperative that demographers as well as development and health planners, pay greater attention to assessing the gender dynamics of population growth and development, and to identify strategies which will help women and girls better cope with existing demographic inequities, compared to men and boys and to each other. There is a pressing need to question existing demographic beliefs and myths surrounding the status of girls and women and to launch further research into the concept of the biological and environmental viability of the female. Simultaneously, the discussion of the female gender's vulnerability to discrimination must extend from the earlier focus on South Asia and other developing countries to a genuinely global inquiry and strategic concern.

Endnote

1.   Male conceptions are estimated at 130:100 by researchers in the United States. Rates of miscarriage, stillbirths, and neonatal mortality are also higher for males, as are infection and disease in infancy. (Lott, 1994:29)

V

HEALTH AND SURVIVAL CAPABILITY
OF GIRLS

Health is a prime parameter of the well-being and overall status of a population. Mortality, disease, and life expectancy are its vital indicators. Gender differences in these three areas provide an excellent and unbiased measure of the relative value placed upon males and females in a society.

Health is directly related to genetics and environment. Birth parents are the only unknown and uncontrollable elements in the birthing phenomenon. The rest of life can be regulated, controlled, and influenced by human behavior. Socioeconomic factors, such as education, religion, law, and custom; the individual and collective resources available to a society; and the level of science and technology—all condition human and health behavior and determine access to affordability, acceptability, and utilization of health technology. Poor health and nutritional conditions, environmental hygiene, access to health care, and cultural factors influence the number of years a person can expect to live and the kinds of diseases to which she or he is exposed.

Sex differences in disease incidence and mortality are recognized as "socially or biologically caused." (Waldron, 1976 in Ware, 1981:41) Physical health, moreover, is "a function of both natural endowment and human intervention; both nature and human society treat women one way and men another." (Newland, 1979:5). Conducive or non-conducive human behavior, aided by the use or misuse of health technology, can work in favor of or against either sex from the moment of conception. As pointed out in previous chapters, it is at this point that discrimination against the female child first appears.

Where the more advanced procedures and facilities for sexual selection are unknown or unavailable, even callous neglect and, in extreme cases, infanticide, still endanger the female child. As noted earlier, infanticide is intrinsic to cultures which favor sons. Although legally banned, it is suspected to persist in a variety of countries, including Bangladesh, India, Nepal, and Pakistan. Tighter birth regulations in China and the "one child norm" were believed to account for a decline in the female-male ratio from 94.3 in 1979 to 93.5 in 1985. (Sen, 1989) Sex ratios at birth are worse. Every year, 3.6 million more boys are born than girls, the *China Daily* reported from Beijing in March, 1993. Other recent reports have suggested the sex ratio at birth has reached 114 boys for every 100 girls nationwide, and 130 boys per 100 girls in some poor rural areas. Female life expectancy in China also declined from 66.0 in 1978 to 64.1 in 1984, while male life expectancy grew marginally (Banister, 1987) In such countries as Jordan, Korea, and Syria, where the 1983 World Fertility Survey revealed strong son preference, gender selective practices are likely. (See Box 5, next page, on "The Lost Girls")

Discrimination in nutrition and overall care results in a higher death and disease rate among women. In developed countries, where medical and socioeconomic conditions make health care widely available, women's original biological advantage is reinforced. Female life expectancy in developed countries has improved over recent decades, and the gap between female and male life tenure has increased from five years in 1950 to seven years in 1985. (Sivard, 1985: 24) In developing countries, sex differences in life expectancy are narrower. In 1985, the average was 62 years for women as compared to 60 years for men. In three South Asian countries—India, Nepal and Pakistan— the difference was in men's favor. Both in Africa and Asia, higher female mortality in early childhood and childbearing ages "appears to be associated with the relatively low cultural position accorded girls and women in a number of countries." (Sivard:25)

In 1985, "the average girl in the Third World could hope for an added 18 years of life compared with her mother's generation, yet female life expectancy remains unacceptably low in many developing countries. In contrast to the average of 77 years in developed countries, fourteen of the poorer countries, representing a female population of sixty-six million, have not yet attained a life expectancy of 50 years; with one exception, these countries are in sub-Saharan Africa or South Asia." Between 1950–1985, the country difference in life expectancy between the highest and the lowest level country was reduced from 47 to 36 years, yet female babies in poorer countries "still have a shorter life ahead than those in richer countries did 35 years ago." (Sivard:24)

Ideally, infant- and child-mortality rates are sensitive and reliable indices of the health and survival status of the child population. Yet the fact that gender-specific global data on infant and child mortality are not widely available or entirely reliable is a telling comment in itself on sexism in health and

---

Box 5
The Lost Girls

That many Asian families prefer boys is no surprise; that they are having their wishes fulfilled, is. A study in the latest issue of Population and Development Review suggests that in two Asian countries, the ratio of boy babies to girl babies rose noticeably in the 1980s. This happened not only in China, whose draconian population policy has been blamed for the shortage of girls, but also in South Korea.

In China, the ratio of boys to girls has risen from 107.2 per 100 girls in 1982 to 111.3 per 100 girls in 1989, compared to the norm of 106 per 100 girls. Most of the lost girls would have been second or third children in families that already had at least one girl. A count of births in Chinese hospitals found that, for first babies, the ratio of boys to girls was a predictable 105.6, but where a mother already had one girl it was 149.4, and where she had two, it rose to an amazing 224.9.

What has happened to the missing girls? The study, by six Chinese demographers, suggests that many births of unwanted girls are never recorded. As economic growth makes Chinese society more mobile, and the state finds it increasingly difficult to keep tabs on people, it becomes easier to avoid registering a birth. A tightening of the birth-control policy in the late 1980s has probably made parents keener to ensure that they have a son.

The example of South Korea suggests that a one-child policy is not needed to change the natural sex balance. There, prosperity has cut births from 4 per woman in the early 1970s to 1.7 today, and the ratio of boys to girls has risen even faster than in China, from 106.9 per 100 girls in 1982 to 113.6 per 100 girls in 1988. The common wish among more prosperous people to have fewer babies presumably provided the motive to get rid of females, and better access to technology provided the means.

Source: Abridged from *The Economist*, September 18, 1993:38

demography. Whereas gender-specific infant-mortality data are collected and analyzed frequently, both at the national levels and globally, gender-specific mortality data for children aged above 1 year are much less frequent and unreliable. Even so, some surveys and studies are available with some indicative value. For instance, data from twenty-eight countries available through the 1983 World Fertility Survey (see Table 14, next page) indicated higher female than male deaths among 1–2-year olds in thirteen countries, and among 2–5-year olds in eighteen countries. (UNFPA, 1988:18) Because the data for the survey were derived from the mothers' reports of their children's births and deaths, intrinsic biases for males could affect the accuracy of reporting. As more than one scholar has observed, data reliability is often shaped by the prevailing attitudes toward girls. Illnesses and deaths of girls are less easily remembered or recorded than of boys. In an Algerian study, for instance, the deaths remembered yielded an infant mortality rate of 199 per 1,000 births for males and 108 for females. Follow-up counts showed true rates to be 142 and 141, respectively. "After all, it was only a girl!" seems to be the typical response to loss of young female life. (Ware, 1981:47)

Data based on vital registration systems, which are the primary source of health statistics, are likewise open to criticism as they carry their own errors and biases. Both the availability and reliability of gender- and age-specific data are matters of serious concern to health planners and analysts. Discrepancies appear even at the global level. A comparison of two sets of data on child mortality available from the United Nations and World Fertility Survey indicated, on average, a 12 percent higher mortality for girls than boys, in the latter source, as against 5 percent in the former. In the case of one country, male mortality was recorded as being higher than female in one source, and lower than female in the other. (Waldron in WHO, 1987:194–213)

A rare study analyzing child mortality trends from 1945 to 1983 (Waldron:194–213) reveals that female infant mortality is slightly higher, or approximately equal in only a few of the developing countries located in North Africa, South, and West Asia. In contrast, for children aged 1–4, female mortality has been higher than male in many developing countries in Africa, Asia, and Latin America. In the age group 5–14, girls have generally experienced higher mortality than boys in countries where life expectancy is low (below 60). For the age group 10–14, Eastern and Southern Asia, along with North Africa, exclusively indicate excess female mortality. The conclusion of this trend analysis is that factors influencing sex differences in mortality vary according to age, mortality level, and region, but gender

Table 14
Sex Differences in Child Mortality

| Country | Mortality Rates of Children Aged | | | | | |
| | 1–2 Years | | | 2–5 Years | | |
	F	M	F-M	F	M	F-M
Pakistan	40.4	26.1	14.3	54.4	36.9	17.5
Haiti	27.6	30.6	-3.0	61.2	47.8	13.4
Bangladesh	35.4	26.0	9.4	68.6	57.7	10.9
Thailand	7.3	10.4	-3.1	26.8	17.3	9.5
Syria	11.3	11.9	-0.6	14.6	9.3	5.3
Colombia	20.8	15.5	5.3	24.8	20.5	4.3
Costa Rica	7.8	7.9	-0.1	8.1	4.8	3.3
Nepal	55.0	49.2	5.8	60.7	57.7	3.0
Dominican Republic	24.5	25.2	-0.7	2.2	17.2	3.0
Philippines	15.2	14.2	1.0	21.9	19.1	2.8
Sri Lanka	11.2	7.6	3.6	18.7	16.3	2.4
Peru	33.4	33.4	0.0	30.8	28.8	2.0
Mexico	17.2	14.8	2.4	16.7	14.7	2.0
Panama	6.8	6.2	0.8	8.7	7.6	1.1
Turkey	34.2	21.2	13.0	19.5	18.4	1.1
Korea	9.4	10.0	-0.6	12.7	11.8	0.9
Venezuela	5.9	6.7	-0.8	8.4	7.6	0.8
Jordan	14.0	11.4	3.6	-7.1	7.0	0.1
Senegal	77.3	76.5	0.8	106.8	107.0	-0.2
Fiji	4.8	4.4	0.4	5.1	5.3	-0.2
Guyana	9.6	10.0	-0.4	8.4	8.9	-0.5
N. Sudan	28.2	32.9	-4.7	35.7	36.4	-0.7
Jamaica	8.7	9.3	-0.6	5.3	6.2	-1.1
Trinidad and Tobago	4.9	3.5	1.4	2.8	4.5	-1.7
Malaysia	4.9	6.9	-2.0	7.7	9.2	-1.5
Lesotho	24.4	35.3	-10.9	26.6	29.3	-2.7
Paraguay	12.5	13.4	-0.9	7.9	13.3	-5.4
Indonesia	28.2	32.3	-4.1	40.1	52.6	-12.5

Source: *World Fertility Survey 1983*, UNFPA, 1988 Report, 1988:18

disparities in mortality rates appear to be concentrated in countries with a high preference for sons and a subordination of female health and nutritional needs to those of the male. The presumed superiority of males, which determines gender biases in health care, nurturing, rearing, and the overall attention given to female well-being, allows the female less than an equal chance to grow from birth to childhood, adolescence, and adulthood. Elsewhere, it has been noted that the greater male vulnerability evinced through higher male mortality from conception through childhood has provided a biological rationale and stimulus for the prevalence of "benign neglect" of females, and "even for the higher status accorded to males in general." (McKee, 1984 in Demand, 1994:188)

In societies where males and females receive similar treatment, females live longer than male. Yet, in countries where gender biases are strong, women are just beginning to match or overtake male life expectancy, a trend that is repeated among children. In Bangladesh, for instance, life expectancy at each age group (0–1, 1–4, 5–9, and 10–14) is higher for male than female children. (UNICEF, Bangladesh, 1990) In an earlier health-status study carried out in Matlab, Bangladesh (D'Souza and Chen, 1979 in Ware, 1981:45-46), covering a 250,000 population between 1963–1974, it was reported that: (i) the crude death rate for females at 16.7 per 1,000 was higher than male at 16.1; (ii) at 0–1 month, the male death rate exceeded the female (78:68); (iii) between 1–11 months, however, 64 females died for every 53 males; (iv) at age 3, a 53 percent higher female death rate than male was observed. As Ware notes, "In Bangladesh, the advantages given to males in parental care, feeding patterns, food distribution within the family and treatment of illness (especially where financial expenditure is involved) appear to be the causes of higher female mortality." (46)

Ideally, development should affect all people equally. In reality, social and other conditions are not the same for both sexes. "One sex may be continually at a disadvantage in obtaining food, medical services, leisure or other goods because the culture consistently gives one sex priority over the other." (Ware, 1981:39) In India, age-specific death rates reveal that up to the age of 35, more females than males die at every age level. A 1986 survey in Jordan revealed infant mortality to be nearly 20 percentage points lower for males in Amman—son preference, leading to the neglect of daughters, was found to be responsible for the mortality differential.

Evidence from recent studies in Bangladesh, Egypt, India, Nigeria, and Pakistan reiterates the sex bias in health care. A Bangladesh study confirms differential health care for female children. Here, although the incidence of diarrhea was comparable between male and female children, 66 percent more male children were brought to a treatment facility. (Ravindran, 1986:10) In Egypt, "neonatal-mortality rates are significantly higher for boys and infants, and child-mortality rates are higher for girls. This pattern indicates a clear differential in treatment of children based on sex, as do nutritional evidence, medical care practices, and the fact that birth intervals are shorter following the birth of a girl." (CAPMAS and UNICEF, 1988:61)

A study in a South Indian village revealed that the money spent on treatment of nineteen first-born girls was approximately 35 percent of that spent on eighteen first-born boys. A comparison of sex and birth order with medical expenditure found a virtual absence of medical treatment for late-born females. In Lagos, Nigeria, the sex of a child was found to be one of the factors affecting use of the primary health care clinic for children, boys had a better chance of being brought to the clinics than a girl, "perhaps due to the preference for boys among the various cultural groups." Similarly, in an urban slum in Lahore, Pakistan, while the prevalence rates of various illnesses were the same for boys and girls, parents were more concerned about the health of their sons and spent more money on consultation of private practitioners and treatment for them; 58 percent of sick boys were taken to a private practitioner, compared to 37 percent of sick girls. More than twice the number of girls who were ill (27 percent) compared to boys (12 percent) were not taken for any medical treatment. However, no differences were found in the immunization rates between boys and girls. It is probable that immunizations were free of cost. To illustrate this point—in Korea, in the Kanghura Community Health Project, when measles immunizations were provided free of cost, the proportions of boys and girls being immunized were almost equal; but when a small fee was charged, the proportion of girls fell to little above one-quarter. (Ravindran:1986:10–11) There is an undeniable gender-discriminatory diagnostic and treatment behavior from the child's closest caregivers.

High death rates are the result of high fertility, poverty, nutritional insufficiency, and lack of adequate personal and environmental health amenities, such as health care and referral, safe water, sanitation, and health education. All of these factors have an impact on children but often more acutely on female children. When resources are a constraint, and access costly in terms of money, time, transport, or other opportunity costs,[1] gender bias takes over and works preeminently to the advantage of the male. "It is evident that males get better medical attention than their female counterparts, which is partially explained by differential perceptions of sickness and mortality among boys and girls." (Elahi, in Momsen and Kinnaird, 1993:89) Boys are "considered more at risk of falling sick or dying. Intrinsically, boys are valued more and because of the above perception, extreme care is taken of boys, beginning with infancy.[2] Overall, a girl receives appropriate medical attention if she is the only child or only daughter among many sons. Otherwise, at the initial state of illness, she is ignored and her illness is rationalized as either being trivial or a characteristic of her general level of health. Thus the overall mortality and health status of the girl is closely related to the total social and economic value of male children. . .Sex discrimination in favor of the male operates at an early stage and is manifested in the norms of family formation, birth delivery, illness, and health practices. This pattern continues throughout the lives of both sexes and negatively affects women, and girls." (91–92)

According to Newland (1979:47), "Women and girls feel the pinch of food scarcity earlier, and more frequently and severely, than do their husbands or brothers. In Bangladesh, in the years of food shortage, the Matlab study found that among the 1–11-month-old infants, children, and adolescents, when parents play an important role in determining nutrition and health care distribution, "excess female mortality was consistently higher than the normal differential."

Sex disadvantages, however, are not restricted to the context of scarcity. Even in normal times, when there is no famine or food shortage, females in Bangladesh were observed to obtain 83 percent of the total calories and proteins fed to males; women in reproductive years received 78 percent, and those past reproductive years 65 percent. Widowed older women received even less. (Ware:1981:45) Data from Pakistan also suggest that sex differentials in mortality and differential treatment against girls, in the form of food distribution in a family, fewer chances of getting health care during illness, and also fewer chances of parental attention, are found in urban and rural areas and across socioeconomic groupings. (Sathar, 1990:7) The unfavorable numerical presence of the girl in developed countries, too, suggests that sex ratio disparities are not inconsistent with affluence and "development."

NEGLECT AND ADOLESCENCE

Adolescence marks a stage of acute neglect for the female child. Evidence from several countries, including Bangladesh, Egypt, India, Nepal, and Pakistan, suggests that the girl, as the more deprived, depleted, and neglected child, grows up to be a malnourished and smaller adolescent, given to frequent episodes of illness which further sap her vitality. In developing countries, the girl's early induction into unpaid domestic and farm labor, often beginning at age 6 or below, and her caregiver/surrogate-mother status, prevent her from experiencing childhood, or exercising her right to being nurtured, or simply being a child—carefree and unprecocious.

Deprived of adequate nutrition and burdened with child care and other household responsibilities which entail heavy and constant physical labor, the adolescent girl "falls through the cracks" of household and public support services. There are virtually no programs aimed exclusively at this home-bound, full-time worker. Cognizance of her needs and presence is nil. Caught between childhood and adulthood, the female adolescent represents the twilight child—invisible to both parents and planners.

Difficult as the plight of the adolescent girl is in developing countries, she is far from being fully vested with all of childhood's entitlements, even in developed countries. The physiology of adolescence is only beginning to be acknowledged. Neglect of the young female's psyche, body, and growth cycle has been common to both medical and social sciences. The popular view of adolescence, according to a recent American report (Hechinger, 1992:1), is that it represents "merely an unfortunate 'phase,' something like a temporary illness from which, with time and perseverance, the patient will eventually recover."

Other than for reproduction data, female health trends are barely recorded in health statistics, in developing countries, nor are there interventions designed to understand and address the young female's *non-reproductive health needs*. Cultural and traditional health and social practices, on the other hand, exert unnatural pressure and constraints on the adolescent. Poignant anecdotal data from countries in Africa, Asia, and Latin America establish how, with the onset of puberty and menarche, the girl is forced to withdraw from life and fun and learns to live with the pain, the burden, and the confusing isolation of having grown up. Her male counterpart, on the other hand, is celebrated for his maturation into manhood and rewarded with unaccountable license and mobility.

Both culture and religion venerate fertility and define a woman's value solely in terms of her reproductive capability. The young girl is thus perceived primarily as a potential child bearer. But her reproductive value has done little to enhance her social status or individual worth. In most cultures, her fertility becomes a threat and a basis for mistreatment. Because of the reproductive risk it poses, her biological maturation causes social ostracization and imprisonment. Purdah, the custom of secluding girls, is widely practiced in Islamic and other traditional settings. The Persian word for curtain, *purdah,* is an institutionalized system of seclusion and veiling. "The purdah system keeps women excluded and isolated from the wider world. . .Purdah is imposed at puberty and from then on, the private and public spheres are clearly defined. The respect due to a family depends on the behavior of its women. To deviate from the prescriptions of purdah is to dishonor and shame the entire clan. In conventional homes, separate rooms for women form the zenana. . .These 'separate worlds' dictate the division of labor in the family and innate differences are presumed between the protector (man) and protected (women), from which an assumption of fundamental sexual inequality is generated." (Papanek, 1982, in Dankelman and Davidson, 1988:98–99)

In some cultures, even the girl's body is tampered with through excision and other means to make her "sealed and safe." Often, these invasive measures are integrated into the girl's acculturation. For example, in Sierra Leone, the manifest objective of traditional societies, especially Poro (male society) and Bondo/Sande (female society), and their affiliates, is to train young boys and girls to become full and active members of the adult community. Initiation of girls into Sande usually takes place at puberty, but some are initiated much earlier."(UNICEF, Sierra Leone, 1989:16–17) Part of this initiation is the practice of clitoridectomy, or female circumcision. (This practice is explored more fully in Chapter IX, Violence Against Girls.) Severe health and psychological outcomes are now being associated with such practices.

GIRL MOTHERS

The burden of adolescent reproduction is a significant contributor to the continued health vulnerability of the girl child. Giving birth at a young age, after an early marriage, places these adolescents at risk for their survival. The other sizable risk arises from informal sexual activity, a product of changing social mores and a necessary outcome of rapid urbanization. In recent years, the adolescent's reproductive burden has become an area of concern because of the social, economic, and health consequences of early and prolonged childbearing. The problem is manifest in both the developed and developing regions. In the former, as marriage age is high, large numbers of sexually active adolescents run the risk of becoming pregnant, particularly those among socioeconomic groups without ready access to contraception. Because almost half of the adolescent mothers are unmarried, they resort to abortion in many countries, again increasing the risk to their lives.

Recent estimates of marriage age in the developing world indicate that 50 percent of African women, 40 percent of Asian women, and 30 percent of Latin American women are married by age 18. (UNFPA, 1988:13) The pressure to marry girls off early comes from parental concern over pregnancy or loss of virginity. The girl's chastity and virginity command a high price in many cultures. Illustrative of that value-system is a statement by women from two Indian villages where the average age at marriage for girls was found to be just 14.3 years: "Society will condemn us if our daughters are not married off by age 15." Mothers in Burkina Faso echo similar concerns: "The girl has to be married as soon as possible or else she'll give birth to a tempiri—an illegitimate baby." As one of the Burkina Faso mothers recalled, "she herself had seen her washing (menstruation) only once before she left her father's house for her husband's." (UNFPA, 1988) Fear of the "wandering womb" is also prevalent elsewhere. In modern Greece, young brides are praised for having "come straight from their mother's arms," or "never going beyond the front door." (Demand, 1994:10)

In developed countries, where marriage age is much higher and increasing, it is not necessarily indicative of a companion trend towards postponed sexual activity. Marriage age is thus only an index of the formal reproductive risk to girls. The other significant risk arises from informal sexual liaison and activity. Living together is a product of changing social mores in the developed and the developing world, and a necessary outcome of rapid urbanization that compels married couples to stay apart. Where multiple marriages and liaisons are considered permissible by sociocultural norms, informal cohabitation has been a common practice, now increasingly reinforced by environmental compulsions and seductions. The cumulative impact is a heightened reproductive activity among adolescent girls. The average level of fertility among girls globally is not precisely known. For 1985, teenage fertility in developed countries was estimated to range from 4 births per 1,000 women aged 15–19 in Japan to 78 births per 1,000 in Bulgaria. In the developing regions, the fertility level among 15–19-year-old girls is reported to be highest in Africa (37 live births per 1,000 in Mauritius to 216 in the Ivory Coast), followed by Latin America/Caribbean, where the range is from 49 per 1,000 in Martinique to 138 per 1,000 in Honduras. Although lowest for Asia as a whole, fertility among 15–19-year-old girls is reported to range from 7 per 1,000 in the Republic of Korea to 239 per 1,000 in Bangladesh. Childbearing below the age of 15 is fairly common in such countries as Bangladesh, Jamaica, Mauritania, Nigeria, Sudan, and Yemen. (U.N., 1989:5)

Studies of pre-marital adolescent fertility have shown that in ten countries in Latin America, and in Israel and Gambia, between 5 and 20 percent of unmarried females were 14 years of age or younger at the time of first intercourse. Those 16 years of age accounted for 15 to 30 percent. Inter-regionally, pre-marital conceptions resulting in live births tend to be reported at much higher levels in Africa below the Sahara, followed by the Caribbean and Latin America, and less commonly in Asia, North Africa, and Oceania (Southern Pacific Islands). Among women aged 20–24 who reported a live pre-marital births, Kenya recorded 34.5 percent and Pakistan none, with remaining countries in the sample ranging from 0.3 to 20.7 percent. (U.N., Draft, 1990: 6) A large number of out-of-wedlock childbirths also occur in developed countries. As noted in an earlier chapter, three-fourths of teenage births in Denmark and Sweden were out-of-wedlock; in England and the United States, more than 50 percent of all out-of-wedlock births in 1982 were to teenage mothers. (UNFPA, 1988:22) Because there may be some debate and discrepancies between reported and actual incidence of teen sex and promiscuity in each country and society, it is appropriate for every country to investigate and refine the magnitude of its adolescent reproductive behavior within the constraints and tolerances of its own cultural context. In order to reduce the reproductive burden of the girl child, both formal and informal fertility need to be equally addressed.

The disadvantages of early (marital or pre-marital) cohabitation are well recognized in health and fertility literature. High levels of maternal, infant and child mortality, disease incidence, large family size, greater frequency of conceptions, and maternal depletion are all proven to be rooted in early marriage and early first birth. Other consequences, as pointed out in an earlier chapter, are a much longer reproductive span (18–19 years for the average African woman, who marries at around age 17, and 16–17 years for the Asian and Latin American woman, who marries between ages 17–19). Compare this with approximately 7 years in developed regions. The damage to childhood is incalculable. Early childbearing is related to low school enrollment and attendance among young girls, with its attendant outcomes earlier and higher rates of fertility and economic and social costs arising from her loss of educability.

Births to teen mothers are a growing tragic phenomenon in women's health. It is estimated that: "40 percent of all 14-year-old girls alive today will have been pregnant at least once by the time they are 20. In Bangladesh, four out of five teenagers are mothers, three out of four teenagers in Africa are mothers. In the United States, teenage girls account for one-fifth of all births. Forty percent of teenage births are to women aged 17 or under in Africa; 39 percent in Latin America, 31 percent in Asia, and 22 percent in Europe." (UNFPA, 1988:21–22)

Even in developed countries, teen reproduction, out of wedlock especially, has grave consequences. "A girl with an illegitimate child at age 16 has her life's scenario virtually entirely written out. She will probably drop out of school; not find a steady job; not be able to earn enough to provide for herself and her child; be impelled to marry someone for the wrong reasons; have few life choices and most of them bad; and an unstable environment for rearing her child." (Bernard, 1981:176)

Maternal mortality and reduced life expectancy are the most devastating and inexcusable consequences of early marriage and teen reproductive behavior. Studies have adequately established that a principal reason for greater inequality in the life expectation for women (life span is roughly shorter by 16 years in developing regions than in developed) is the greater risk that pregnancy poses for women in the developing world. A recent U.N. report affirms that maternal-mortality rates show a greater disparity between developed and developing regions of the world than any other health indicator. Rates of less than 5 maternal deaths per 100,000 live births are observed in a few developed countries in contrast to more than 1,000 maternal deaths in some developing countries. Women in developing countries face risk of death due to pregnancy that is 80 to 600 times higher than their counterparts in developed countries. (1991:57–58) Complications of pregnancy and childbirth are estimated to account for 20 to 45 percent of the deaths of women of childbearing age (15–45 years) in developing countries compared to less than 1 percent in the United States. The chance of dying from pregnancy between the years 1975–1984 was estimated at 1 in 21 in Africa, 1 in 54 in Asia, 1 in 73 in South America, 1 in 140 in Caribbean, 1 in 6,366 in North America, and 1 in 9,850 in Northern Europe. Girls under the age of 15 are 5 to 7 times more likely to die in pregnancy and childbirth than women in the lowest-risk age group of 20–24. (Starrs, 1987:13,15) The International Planned Parenthood Federation notes that the main causes of death for 15–19-year-old females worldwide are pregnancy-related. The risk of complications during pregnancy and childbirth is greater for girls under 18 because their bodies are not fully developed because they are less likely to receive early and adequate prenatal care. (UNICEF, First Call for Children, July-September, 1994:8) A recent report (U.N. 1991:3) notes that in developed and developing countries alike, mothers aged 15–19 are twice as likely to die in childbirth as mothers in their early 20s, and those under age 15 are five times as likely.

Over one-third of the fertility burden is borne by women 20–24 years of age. Adolescent fertility rates constitute from 10 to 15 percent of total fertility rates. (U.N. 1989:32) Unfortunately, age-specific maternal-mortality data are not available to identify what proportion of the fertility-related mortality burden is borne by these or younger age groups. In the absence of pertinent data, it is difficult to compare the role and liability of motherhood in young girls. Yet, these type of data are crucial to upgrading the health status of the girl-mother, and its unavailability is a major drawback to obtaining health intelligence, monitoring, and planning activity. Where national statistics are available, the findings are portentous. The evidence from the oft-quoted study in Matlab, Bangladesh, concludes that 10–14-year-old girls had a maternal-mortality rate (MMR) five times higher than women aged 20–24. Among 15–19-year-old girls, the rate was twice as high as for the 20–24-year-old women. Even in the United States, girls under age 15 show a MMR three times as high as women aged 20–24. (Belsey and Royston, in Wallace and Giri, 1990) There are studies which suggest that by confining child-bearing to ages 20–29 years, the MMR would drop by 11 percent; cessation of childbearing after the fourth birth alone would achieve a drop of over 50,000 maternal deaths per year (or 4 percent reduction in MM). (U.N. Draft, 1990) An earlier projection estimated that by confining births to women aged 20–34, maternal mortality would decline by 20 percent in Mexico, Thailand, and Venezuela, and by approximately 25 percent in Colombia and the Philippines. (Nortman, 1974, in Maine, 1982:35)

Unwanted pregnancy culminates in two ways—through an unwanted and therefore neglected at-risk child, or through abortion. In Algeria and Morocco, for instance, a recent study by International Planned Parenthood Federation notes that 2,000 unwanted babies are abandoned every year by young unmarried mothers. The social consequences of unwanted pregnancy can be severe. (UNICEF, *First Call for Children*, July-September, 1994:8) Lack of reliable hard data prevents precise understanding or treatment of the problems leading to abortion. According to the Guttmacher Institute, between 36 and 51 million abortions were performed worldwide in 1987. From 10 to 20 million are illegally performed annually, compared to 26 to 31 million performed legally. Those figures imply "close to one induced abortion for every two to three births worldwide." Moreover, demographers have calculated that "from a third to half of all women of reproductive age undergo at least one induced abortion in their lifetime." In many countries, abortion has become the primary method of family planning. In Bangladesh and Brazil, for example, demographic studies indicate that 20 to 35 percent of all pregnancies are aborted. (Worldwatch Institute, *Worldwatch Paper* 97, July 1990:24–25)

Studies of hospital records of women, treated for complications of abortion, reveal that 38 to 68 percent in Congo, Kenya, Liberia, Mali, Nigeria, and Zaire; more than 25 percent in Malaysia; and more than 10 percent in Brazil, Chile, Guatemala, Peru, and Thailand are under 20 years of age. In Jamaica, 28 percent of all births and 40 percent of abortions are to teenagers. (Sadik 1990:23) A study of 970 school girls in Freetown, Sierra Leone, "found 63 percent had sexual intercourse, and 6 percent (65) had become pregnant. Of the 65 pregnant girls, 55 had undergone abortions." (UNICEF, Sierra Leone, 1989:56) Teenage pregnancies, whether illegitimate or legitimate, whether in rich or poor countries, are catastrophic. According to recent estimates, 30 to 44 percent of all teenage pregnancies in the United States end in abortion; in Norway, almost 88 percent of pregnancies among 18-year-old girls are aborted. Teenagers also account for half of all late, and therefore more dangerous, abortions in the United States. (UNFPA, 1988:22; UN, 1989:96)

Even when carried to term, births to adolescent mothers are far more dangerous than to the more physically mature, older mothers. Babies born to a teenage mother are more than twice as likely to die in their first year of life. In Korea and Sri Lanka, babies born to under-16-year-old mothers were three times more likely to die than those born to 20–24-year-old mothers. (UNFPA, 1988:22; Sadik, 1989:9) In Sao Paolo, Brazil, 104 out of 1,000 babies born to teen mothers died before their first birthday, compared to 53 out of 1,000 born to 25–29-year-old mothers. In Iran, a saying that "the first two are for the crows" is in direct reference to early pregnancies leading to early deaths of the first two children. (Newland, 1979:53) In India, infants born to teenage mothers (under the age of 18) have been found to carry almost twice the risk of death compared to those born to mothers above age 18. (Chatterjee in Gopalan & Kaur, 1989:307) Evidence from thirty-four developing countries also shows that neonatal mortality in the case of girl mothers (aged 15–19) is in excess of 24 percent compared to births among 25–34-year-old mothers. Furthermore, there is "a clear inverse association between age of mothers and probability of death for children under age 5." (U.N., *Adolescent Reproductive Behavior*, 1989:99)

Although it is estimated that 60 to 75 percent of the world's population live in countries where abortion is legal, problems of access, affordability, and risk make it at best a secondary option for many women. It demonstrates the need to widen the availability of contraception information and practice in order to reduce the survival risk for girls and women. The International Conference on Population (Mexico 6–14 August, 1984) clearly recognized the high incidence of unwanted pregnancies and attendant risks to female health and life expectancy from resultant abortions. It urged governments to ensure that adolescents receive adequate education, including family life and sex education, and that appropriate family-planning information and services be made available to them. A subsequent review and appraisal of the World Population Plan of Action notes that adolescents everywhere appear to be among the underserved groups, along with remote rural and poor urban residents, as far as population information and services are concerned. At the recent International Conference on Population and Development, held in Cairo in September 1994, sex education and reproductive-health services for adolescents all over the world were approved as essential components of an ambitious Action Plan aimed at stabilizing the world's population. This stabilization would ideally occur with reproductive freedom, improved health, and the assurance that women had greater control over their lives.

Fortunately, there is encouraging evidence in recent studies that sex education is not linked to earlier or increased sexual activity in youth. Six out of nineteen international studies reviewed in a multi-county research project found that sex education led either to a delay in the onset of sexual activity, or to a decrease in overall sexual activity. In ten studies, sex education was found to foster safer sex practices among youth. School programs which helped youth postpone sex and explained protected sex were found to be more effective than those promoting abstinence. School-based education programs were also found to be more effective when offered before young people had become sexually active and when skills and social norms were emphasized instead of abstract knowledge. (UNICEF, *First Call for Children*, July-September, 1994:8)

MATERNAL HEALTH OF GIRLS

Maternal health, as several scholars have noted, is an area of vigorous discrimination. The female body is such that there are risks to life associated with both excessive and untimely fertility, as well as insufficient child bearing. It has also been widely established that in societies where the female is poorly fed, neglected, heavily overworked, and denied access to minimal health care, childbearing assumes much greater risks. A woman in Africa, for instance, is "200 times as likely as an European woman to die as a result of bearing her children. More women die in India in one month than in Australia, Europe, Japan, and North America combined in one year." (UNFPA, 1988:24) About one-fourth of 15–49-year-old females in developing countries die from pregnancy- and delivery-related causes, compared to 1 percent in the United States. In one-third of the developing countries, childbearing causes rank first or second in overall death rates. (Sivard, 1985:26)

Cumulatively, in the world, over 500,000 females die every year from pregnancy or birthing, or one every minute. It is important to note that "nearly half of the maternal deaths in the world could be avoided simply by avoiding unwanted pregnancies." (UNFPA, 1988:28) In Bangladesh, two studies (Chen et al., 1974) found that 20,000 women per year died as a direct consequence of pregnancy and that one-third of all deaths of females aged 10–49 were related to maternity. "By eradicating these deaths, females would have lower death rates than males at all ages between 10 and 49." (Ware, 1981:51)

Frequent and closely spaced births and births to very young or old mothers, pose major hazards to maternal and child safety. According to one estimate, "more than one-third of births in the world occur to women below 19 or older than 34." (Newland, 1979:55) Irrespective of the socioeconomic or health levels of the countries in which they live, risks to females are accentuated if they give birth too early or too late. UNFPA (1988:27) concludes that women over age 35 are two to five times more likely to die from childbirth. According to Newland (1979:53-54), in 1974, in the United States, 10 maternal deaths per 100,000 births among women in their early 20s rose to 41 deaths among women in their late 30s, and 234 deaths among women over 45 years of age. In Thailand, in 1971, 154 deaths per 100,000 women in their 20s increased to 474 per 100,000 women in their 40s. In Matlab, Bangladesh, maternal deaths among women 19 and below were found to be 860 (between 1968–1970), and among women 40 years and above were 810, as compared to 380 deaths among 20–24-year-old women and around 480 to 620 among 25–45-year-old women.

Apart from births which occur too early or too late, frequency and poor spacing of births endanger the life of both the mother and the child. Every additional birth poses escalating danger and, as Newland and others have contended, regardless of the woman's socioeconomic level, the maternal-depletion syndrome that occurs undermines both the woman's and the child's health. According to UNFPA (1988:27), Jamaican women having their fifth through ninth child are 43 percent more likely to die than women having their second; in Portugal, the risk is found to be over 300 percent greater.

Risks to babies are also ominous. (See Figures 1, next page, and Figure 2, page 80, on "Relative Risk of Dying") Babies born in quick succession to mothers whose bodies have not yet recovered from previous births are the least likely to survive. A baby born less than two years after its sibling is 50 percent more likely to die in its first year of life and twice as likely to die between the ages of 1 and 5. Yet 50 percent of all births in such countries as Colombia, Costa Rica, Jamaica, and Jordan are found to be less than two years apart. (UNFPA:27)

Mechanisms need to be identified and strengthened to provide birth-process-related information, not only to the adult but also the adolescent female (as well as to adolescent and adult males). The current (1983) contraceptive-using population is optimistically estimated to be around 45 percent in the developing world (14 percent in Africa; 50 percent in Asia; and

56 percent in Latin America). Although a substantial improvement from the 9 percent estimated user rate in the 1960s, it is still well below the desired level. (UNFPA, 1988:9) For fertility to decline to the desired one-third of its current level, parental interest in planned families must be generated. In several traditional cultures there is also a wealth of behavioral wisdom, norms, and taboos which help to postpone the next birth—at least until the previous child has been weaned. In Mali, for instance, women are advised not to go to their husbands while their child is suckling. If she does, the child risks becoming shriveled up. In Burkina Faso, pregnancy is blamed for poisoning the breast milk which will cause the baby to fall sick and have diarrhea. Post-delivery abstinence is encouraged in several cultures from seventeen months in Lesotho and Benin to other durations in other countries. (UNFPA, 1988:27) Unfortunately, modernization, urbanization, migration, and other

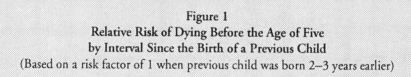

Figure 1
Relative Risk of Dying Before the Age of Five
by Interval Since the Birth of a Previous Child
(Based on a risk factor of 1 when previous child was born 2–3 years earlier)

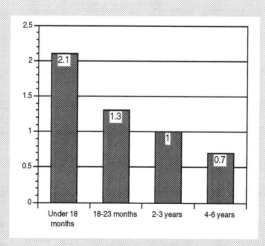

Source: John Hobcraft, "Child spacing and child mortality," *Proceedings of the Demographic and Health Surveys World Conference*, vol. 2, IRD/Macro International, 1991. Data from taken from 25 countries. In UNICEF, *The State of the World's Children 1994*, New York, p. 47.

forces are causing cultural changes. Often, sound conventional wisdom and behavioral norms are sacrificed in the process. There is a need to retrieve those conventional practices that help safeguard and restore female health and enhance the survival capability, especially for the younger female.

Of course, it is not just contraception but also safe birthing practices which need to be encouraged. Safe procedures during birth increase the health and survival capability of both the mother and the child. "Even in the late 1950s in Upper Volta, one maternal death occurred for every 100 births; and 1 mother in 20 could expect to die in childbirth. That risk was reduced to one-fourth of the level when women could give birth with the aid of partially-trained attendants, and in rudimentary maternity clinics with mud floors and minimal equipment, as against women giving birth in their own huts."

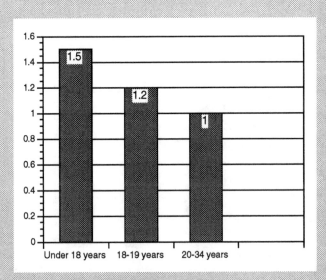

Figure 2
Relative Risk of Dying Before the Age of Five
(Based on a risk factor of 1 when the mother is 20–34 years old)

Source: John Hobcraft, "Child spacing and child mortality," *Proceedings of the Demographic and Health Surveys World Conference*, vol. 2, IRD/Macro International, 1991. Data are taken from 18 countries. In UNICEF, *The State of the World's Children 1994*, New York, p. 48.

(Ware, 1981:51) Training of traditional birth attendants in Nigeria's isolated villages caused a 50 percent drop in maternal mortality over a three-year period. (Jensen in UNDP, *Choices*, July 1992:11)

High infant mortality is a vital influence in shaping reproductive behavior in traditional and less socioeconomically well-off countries. Relative to developed countries, as Sivard contends, "fewer pregnancies result in surviving infants in the poorer countries. Infant mortality is as high as 20 percent or one birth in five in some countries." (1985:26) Approximately one-half of all child deaths occur in the first month. A woman must have eight or so births in order to have some survive, with the result that 50 to 60 percent of her reproductive years are spent in pregnancy and lactation. Every death brings the next birth a little nearer. U.N. figures from twenty-five developing countries reveal that couples experiencing the death of one child are more likely to have larger families than those whose children all survived. (UNFPA, 1988:27) High infant mortality and high fertility appear to go hand in hand, and that, in turn, leads to lower female life expectancy. Every birth and pregnancy is a drain on a woman's health reserves. According to one estimate, approximately 100,000 calories are expended per pregnancy, and about 1,800 calories per day during lactation. (Sivard, 1985:26) In the poorer countries, and in poorer families in rich countries, the capacity to compensate for that caloric consumption does not exist. It is there that women—especially girls—pay the price for that shortfall with their disease, disability, or death.

Endnotes

1. Opportunity cost refers to the opportunities forgone, and the loss incurred or implied in forgoing those opportunities, in favor of using another opportunity or set of opportunities. It reflects the trade-off between the gain from doing something at the cost of not doing something else. To apply a resource to one use means that it cannot be put to any other use. When a girl goes to school, opportunity costs are calculable based on how her time could be spent elsewhere, and the costs to her and the family that could be avoided by not sending her to school.

2. It is encouraging that current abortion laws in many countries have liberalized the basis for legal abortion to include adolescence, advanced maternal age, or infection with the AIDS virus, in addition to such conventional factors as rape. However, in most parts of the world, even though abortion is legal, it is neither readily accessible nor affordable. In India, a 1984 survey showed that only about 1,000 of a total of 15,000 physicians trained

to perform abortions lived in rural areas, although 78 percent of the country's population is rural. Not surprisingly, only 388,000 of the estimated 4 million to 6 million abortions in India were carried out in government-operated safe facilities.

In Mexico, safe abortion services are urban-based and cost from $215 to $644, compared to a monthly minimum wages of $103, thus placing safe medical abortion beyond the reach of even the middle class. In the United States, 82 percent of the counties have no known abortion providers, forcing many rural women to resort to "abortion migration."

Throughout Africa, Asia, Eastern Europe, and Latin America, the rates of induced unsafe abortion are proportional to the availability and affordability of safe abortion services. Devices for inducing abortion are drastic, ranging from the use of medicinal herbs; the ingesting of gasoline, detergents, chemicals, aspirin, or other drugs; the inserting of plant roots into the cervix; and the use of clothes hangers, knitting needles, and intensive abdominal massage to induce uterine contractions. Abortion-related deaths, disability, and illnesses are viewed as the "hidden plague" of women in the reproductive stages. From one-fifth to one-half of all maternal deaths worldwide could be prevented by providing access to safe abortion services. (*World Watch Paper* 97, 1990) Increased access to contraception information and supplies, along with improved reproductive health care, are indispensable to lowering the widespread female reliance on unsafe abortion.

VI

NUTRITIONAL INEQUITY AND GIRLS

Nutrition, health, survival, and a person's potential for development are intrinsically linked. Any deterioration in the economic climate of a country worsens the effects of malnutrition on its poor, as has been conclusively demonstrated by FAO and UNICEF. (U.N., 1989:39) Gender-based discrimination in nutrition and overall care, however, results in higher death and disease among females because they are the more neglected population group. There is ample evidence from surveys and in social custom that malnutrition occurs disproportionately among girls and women. (Sivard, 1985:25) Outright discrimination plays a part in women's greater vulnerability to malnutrition. (Newland, 1979:47)

"Relatively high levels of female mortality," as Preston notes (1976:159 in Ware, 1981:43), "are associated with poor overall nutritional levels." Females suffer more because they are undernourished and perceived as being less worthy of medical attention than males. Sex differentials in both the provision and use of health services are marked. Despite women's childbearing function, men reportedly have a higher rate of hospital-bed occupancy. (Ware:43; Sivard, 1985:27)

Women face discrimination in food allocation throughout their lives. Cultural practices and food taboos deny women nutritious foods and their equitable share of all food. Their childbearing function and the work they are compelled to do accentuate women's need for steady, sound nutrition. Absence of nutritional support endangers their health. Those who die are only a fraction of those who suffer from sickness and other disabilities caused by under-nutrition. (Ravindran, 1986; Newland, 1979:48–51)

Presumably, under-nutrition is "primarily a disease of poverty and women are more likely than men to be poor." (Newland:51) One hypothesis, based on the findings of "small-scale and infrequent studies of women's anthropometry, iron levels, and dietary intake, is that women may be at greater nutritional risk in certain societies because of cultural values or because women are especially vulnerable due to maternity or owing to the need to combine productive and reproductive roles." In Bangladesh, from 1975–1976 and 1981–1982, a study found women's nutrient intake was consistently lower than men's. In a 1984 study, it was found that half of women of Brazil did not eat enough. (U.N., 1989:41) Recent estimates demonstrate that anemia associated with poor nutrition affects as many as "two-thirds of Asian women, half of all women in Africa, one-sixth of Latin American women, and 60 percent of women worldwide." (UNFPA, 1988:19) In contrast, a study found that from 4 to 7 percent of European women and an average of 6 percent of United States women are anemic. (Sivard, 1985:25)

During and after pregnancy, under-nutrition becomes a major health hazard. According to UNFPA (18), "Between 20 percent and 45 percent of women of childbearing age in the developing world do not eat the WHO-recommended amount of 2,500 calories a day when they are pregnant." Globally, 59 percent of pregnant women compared to 26 percent of men, suffer from anemia. (U.N., Draft:55) According to another estimate, "anemia occurs between two and three times more frequently in non-pregnant women than in men and up to twenty times more frequently in pregnant women than in men." (U.N., 1989:41)

Cultural beliefs and practices influence the food rations allowed women in societies where women tend to eat last and least, and also where, as children, females receive less care than males. In conventional cultures, typically, nutritious foods are denied to women. (See Box 6, on "Gender Differentials in Nutrition") In Botswana and Tanzania, for instance, eggs are not given to women, as they are suspected to interfere with women's fertility. Fish, meat, and spicy foods are not allowed to women during menstruation and pregnancy. In many cultures, pregnant women benefit from additional diet, but women who are lactating, which is the more crucial stage, do not. A Guatemalan study showed that nursing mothers ate consistently less than they did during pregnancy. (Newland, 1979:48–9)

In several studies ranging from African countries to India, Thailand, and Guatemala, low maternal weight gain was demonstrated as being associated with "poverty and malnutrition." In India, it was discovered that "higher

Box 6
Gender Differentials in Nutrition

Several anthropological studies indicate that differential nutrition for males and females exists in a variety of cultures. In Oceania [Southern Pacific Islands], it was customary among the Torres Strait Islanders for the fathers and sons to take their meals before the mother and daughters. A like situation existed in traditional societies of the Far East. In Arabia, it is the custom for the father and older sons to eat first, and for women and children to eat what is left. In many countries in East Africa, young women and children, especially girls—those most in need of optimal health for the task of child-bearing—tend too frequently to receive the dregs of meals and to bear the brunt of traditional food taboos.

In a study of a squatter settlement in Lahore, Pakistan, a tendency for longer breastfeeding of boys and an earlier introduction of solids for girls was apparent. Mothers believed that the longer boys were breastfed, the stronger they would be. Similar ideas are found to prevail in Turkey and throughout the Arab world, where "although a girl baby is likely to continue nursing for as long as one or one-and-a-half years, the boy is nursed until he is two or two-and-a-half, and gets far more tender treatment.

In the state of Tlaxcala in Mexico, the intake of selected nutrients was examined for a sample of families. The study showed that the intake of males, relative to requirement, exceeded that of females for all nutrients examined. In the Philippines, another study looked into the intra-family allocation of food in ninety-seven households in rice-growing communities in Laguna. The study measured the food intake of members of households in a twenty-four-hour period, for three cycles of rice-farming. It was found that fathers had slightly better diets than mothers, and male children better than female children. Of all sex-age groupings among children, male pre-schoolers and female adolescents were, respectively, the best and the least adequately fed groups. This inequity in food allocation persisted even when family size, income, and food expenditure were taken into consideration. Thus, sex discrimination existed both in poor and in better-off households, implying that increasing food availability for the family would be a necessary but *not* a sufficient condition for eliminating the discrimination in food intake of female members.

(Abridged from Ravindran, WHO/UNICEF/FME 86.2, WHO Geneva, 1986:7-8)

income women consumed around 2,500 calories per day during pregnancy and put on an average of 12.5 kilograms whereas poor women consumed only 1,400 calories a day and put on just 1.5 kilograms. Research in Gambia found that women there lost an average of 1.4 kilograms in the last three months of pregnancy." (UNFPA, 1988:19)

LOWER BIRTH WEIGHT BABIES

Lower maternal weight causes lower birth weight (LBW—less than 2,500 grams) babies, and other birth and post-birth complications for the mother and the child, triggering an intergenerational cycle of disadvantage. Weak girls make weak mothers, who make weak children, who grow up to be weak adults. As a result, the individual, the nation, and the human race suffer. It is estimated that one in six babies in the world is born with LBW. The proportion of LBW babies in developing countries approximates 17 percent compared to 6 percent in developed countries. The incidence for individual regions is estimated at one in five babies in Asia, one in six in Africa, one in nine in Latin America, and one in seventeen in Europe. LBW babies are thirteen times more likely to die of infectious diseases than normal weight babies. (UNFPA, 1988:18–19) There is adequate evidence that child survival is less likely among poorer, undernourished mothers. In India, one-third of the pregnancies among poor women are ended either through abortion or stillbirth, due to malnourished mothers whose daily caloric intake amounts to less than 1,800. (Newland, 1979:48) Malnourished children account for approximately 55 percent of the thirteen million under-5 deaths in the world each year. (UNICEF, 1994:7)

MALNUTRITION AMONG GIRLS

It is currently estimated that 51 percent of 0–4 year olds and 46 percent of 5–12 year olds experience nutritional deprivation in the form of anemia. (U.N., Draft:55) Approximately 40 percent of the children worldwide experience growth failure, with the overwhelming majority to be found in Asia. Excluding China, Asia accounts for 75 percent underweight, 66 percent stunting, and 66 percent wasting of the total number of malnourished children under age 5. (Carlson and Wardlow, 1988:8) Because gender disparity among adults is most accentuated in that region, it is safe to infer that more girls than boys in Asia are confronting consequences of faltering growth. Anthropometric data from one area in India, for instance, show retarded growth among 79 percent of female infants compared to 43 percent in males; in children aged 1–2 years, the corresponding figures are 86 and 63 percent; and in preschoolers, the figures are 72 and 65 percent respectively. (Government of India, 1989) Where disparities are not observed or have not yet surfaced, the conclusion that they do not exist is unwarranted; in fact, it may call for greater refinement in nutritional surveillance.

A major difficulty in assessing the girl's nutritional profile is the fact that gender-specific information is currently missing, and where it exists it is not necessarily reflective of micro-contexts. Because much of the national information is derived from episodes recorded at public health facilities and registration systems, accessibility affects the representative quality of data. In a study of undernourished children in West Bengal, India, based on clinic data, it was found that of the 23 undernourished children between 7 and 8 months, 15 were boys and only 8 were girls. To understand the low number of under-nourished girls attending the clinic, only those children whose development was followed through home visits were studied. Three times more malnourished girls than boys (48 girls, 15 boys) were seen through the home visits, which suggests that malnourished girls were kept at home while malnourished boys were brought to the clinic. A very similar finding, also from India, is reported among children hospitalized for PEM (protein energy malnutrition), where boys outnumbered girls by between 47–53 to 1, but field studies showed that PEM was 4–5 times more common among girls. (Ravindran, 1986:10–11) Micro-studies, similarly undertaken in Bangladesh, India, and Nepal increasingly point to micro-surveillance as a means of authenticating national data.

According to UNICEF and WHO, malnutrition is the most common cause of death of young children in poor countries. Insofar as nutrition has a distinct gender dimension in the adult world, and that pattern is presumed to repeat itself among children, it follows that girls suffer more than boys from the terminal as well as chronic effects of malnutrition. In a report of the performance of the under-fives clinic in a comprehensive health care program, in Ludhiana, India, it was found that of forty-seven severely malnourished children between 15–24 months who received consistent follow-up care through home visits, more boys (42 percent) than girls (35 percent) showed definite improvement in one year, and two girls had died. The authors state that these findings were expected "since there is a tendency to give more importance to male children." (Ravindran, 1986:10–11)

It is during infancy that discrimination begins. "A catalogue of observations, disheartening in their consistency, indicates that where difficult choices have to be made about which child to feed, a boy is more likely to be fed than a girl." (Newland, 1979:47) Gender differences in feeding and weaning are fairly overt in several countries:

- In Bangladesh, it was found that under 5-year-old boys were given 16 percent more food than girls, and that girls were more likely to be malnourished in times of famine. A 30–50 percent higher mortality rate was observed for girls than boys under 5 years of age. (UNFPA, 1988:16) In another survey of 800 Bangladesh children under the age of 5, it was noted that "the prevalence of underweight and malnourished children was higher among girls than among boys; feeding practices and intra-familial food distribution were thought to be the main causes. Similar findings were reported by researchers in India, Jordan, and Pakistan. A survey in Jamaica also found that undernourished children were more likely to be female." (U.N., 1989:40)

- Studies in India found that "boys were given far more fatty and milk food than girls. Not surprisingly, girls were more than four times as likely as boys to be suffering from acute malnutrition, but more than forty times less likely to be taken to a hospital. Another Indian study found that sick boys were more likely than girls to be taken to the city hospital when they failed to recover from illness." (UNFPA:17)

- An investigation of 58 infant deaths in ten villages in a district in Gujarat, India, showed that 17 infants died during the first month of life due to conditions associated with their birth. Boys and girls were equally affected. But of the remaining 41 deaths, 27 were girls. Diarrhea, wasting, or starvation were not the most common causes. Seven of the 8 who starved to death were girls. Only 22 percent of the terminally ill girls were taken to a health facility, compared to 80 percent of the boys. "After all, it was only a girl," said a grandmother, of one of the baby girls who died when she was 35 days old without receiving any treatment. (Visaria, 1988 quoted in UNFPA, 1988:17)

- In an earlier (1971) study in India, girls with Kwashiorkor, or severe malnutrition, were found to outnumber boys by four to three. Yet, more boys than girls were hospitalized. Overall, more girls died, succumbing to a combination of hunger and neglect. In Africa, routine infections due to malnutrition caused more girls who were admitted to hospitals to die. (Newland, 1979:48)

- A 1982 study of 3–8 month-old infants in Amman, Jordan, revealed that two to four times as many male as female infants were receiving a wide variety of weaning foods, including breast milk, eggs, fruit, meats, and vegetables. Evidence from Bangladesh points to a similar disparity in the diet administered to girls.(See Box 7, on "Discriminatory Feeding in Bangladesh and Its Cultural Basis") Both stunting and wasting are higher among 6–7-month-old girls than boys. In Pakistan, 61 percent of girls, compared to 52 percent of boys under 5 years of age, were found to be malnourished. In Nepal, girls under 5 years of age are twice as likely to be undernourished as boys. Caloric intake in Ethiopia and Malawi are reported to favor the male. In Sudan, where "prolonged breast feeding is believed to diminish intelligence, which is more needed for boys than girls, boys are weaned at about 18 months and girls at about 2 years." (Sohoni, 1990:17)

Most available evidence shows conclusively that the child's gender may be the most significant determinant of its nutritional status. The politics of food distribution within the family causes lesser quantitative as well as qualitative intake by girls.

Box 7
Discriminatory Feeding in Bangladesh, and Its Cultural Basis

In two rural areas studied in Bangladesh, no apparent differences were noted between male and female children in breastfeeding and the administering of liquid foods. However, discrimination did occur once children began taking solid foods. In the study area, between the ages of 6 and 10 months, where the parents could afford it, a male child was fed one egg almost every day, but no eggs were offered to the baby girl. The discrimination was more visible at the ages of 3 or 4 years. It was observed that "male children eat with adult males while female children eat with the mother and other female household members, all of whom tend to eat what food is left after the men finish their meals. It is still held, particularly in the rural areas, that "men need more food—they do heavy work and work in the fields. . .(this is) certainly a false assumption to make of the nutritional requirements of boys and girls at a very young age."

Source: Elahi in Momsen and Kinnaird, eds., *Different Places, Different Voices; Gender and Development in Africa, Asia and Latin America*, Routledge, London, New York, 1993:80–92

INTRA-HOUSEHOLD ALLOCATION OF FOOD, AND ITS BIAS

Senauer suggests that intra-household allocation of food in developing countries and its effect on age and gender has been receiving increased attention by researchers. (Abdullah and Wheeler, 1985; Carloni, 1981; Chaudury, 1983; Haaga and Mason, 1987; Lipton, 1983; Piwoz and Vitari, 1984; USDA, 1983; in Tinker ed., 1990:156) These and other studies establish that the intra-household allocation of food exacerbates the incidence of malnutrition among women and children. In many cultures, household food distribution typically discriminates against females, both women and girls. Also observed is an age-related distribution pattern that favors the household adults. Both an age and gender bias have been found in some cases, with the male household head being the most favored individual and the young female children receiving the lowest proportion of their nutritional needs. (Senauer:156) Poverty accentuates gender inequities in nutrition. In more than one Indian study, it has been noted that under adverse circumstances, the nutritional status of females is the first compromised. (Ghosh, 1987; Sen, 1985)

Vital differences in how the sexes are treated are "most likely to occur after weaning, when the baby has to compete with the rest of the family for food, and when frequent decisions have to be made as to how much time should be spent in trying to treat diarrheal diseases. In both of these cases, girls often receive less favored treatment than boys." (Ware, 1981:47)

Gender differences, however, are not exclusive to poorer households. Evidence from Arab and Asian countries suggests that nutritional biases cut across socioeconomic divides. Without resource constraints, cultural factors and gender-role conditioning still self-determine who gets how much of what. Feeding customs and practices provide a rationale for denying certain nutritious foods to girls and women. In several African, Arab, and Asian countries, girls are barred from eating high-protein foods at menarche, probably controlling and subduing their sexuality. Food taboos also affect the woman's intake during childbearing years and, in some cultures, during widowhood. Furthermore, as Sivard notes, "in most societies it is customary for the men to eat first, boys next, girls and women last. If protein is scarce, it goes primarily to the men." (1985:25)

Practiced over a length of time, discriminatory dietary patterns short circuit long-term trends. Data from India show that girls do not achieve their full height and weight potential on account of dietary inadequacies. Thus, the expectation of improved growth in the succeeding generation is not fulfilled with respect to the girl child. Yet, it should be expected of all progressing and developed societies.

Nutritional inadequacy demands to be treated or it becomes the basis of a vicious cycle of disease and further depletion, and a mortality risk. Timely treatment and referral can mean the difference between a life saved or lost. Because hospitalization is expensive and there are opportunity costs in using health facilities, parental motivation must be high enough to overcome gender bias. In-depth studies of hospital and health-center records are rare, but where they have been attempted, they expose discrimination in the use of health services. In Matlab, Bangladesh, it has been observed that, with nearly comparable incidence levels of diarrhea, male children under 5 years of age were brought to the treatment facility much more frequently than female children. In India, Jordan, Nepal, and Pakistan, too, there is a growing perception that more boys are brought in, and more frequently, for treatment. Domestic and traditional healing methods are used on girls, and parents spend less money treating girls than boys. This lesser investment in the health care of girls is much like the discriminatory-care patterns among men and women. In India, attendance and admission figures at hospitals are found to be significantly lower for women than men. Diarrhea prevalence itself is slowly surfacing in some Asian countries as a gender-discrimination problem. Although global data may not always be available or supportive of this, micro-level observations point to higher prevalence among girls. That disparities surface at all in an area which constitutes the prime pillar of child-survival strategy should alert health and nutrition planners to the special risks and limitations that confront the infant girl.

If not overly hostile, apathetic nurturing practices constitute the chief nutritional threat to the young girl who suffers nutritional deprivation on account of both her childhood and motherhood. Up to 15 percent of fertility in the developing world, as noted in the previous chapter, occurs among 15–19 year olds. This premature reproductive burden accentuates their vulnerability to death from childbearing causes, or leaves them sick or disabled. Often, the reproductive burden is merely the last episode in a depleting nutritional saga which begins at the infant stage. If she is born a LBW baby, her probability of survival is most likely lower than a boy, as the risk of her neglect is higher. LBW or not, mothers in the more traditional cultures tend to "breastfeed the girl for a shorter duration and wean her quickly and inadequately, due to their desire to become pregnant again in hopes of having a son. A closely spaced second birth further accentuates the girl's nutritional neglect, particularly if the younger sibling should turn out to be a boy. If a girl, the second child pays a heavier price for her gender in terms of greater neglect." (Chatterjee, 1988)

The potential combined impact of nutritional deprivation on the child and adult is well researched. But it can cause proportionally graver consequences for the girl in terms of not only her life but also her progeny. This is where the life-cycle ethos comes in. A nutritionally neglected female infant faces a nutritionally deficient childhood and, with unaided adolescent growth, even greater nutritional depletion. Consequences for the growing girl can mean sub-standard growth in terms of weight and height, a lowered physical and cognitive capacity and other dysfunction, a propensity for illness, work loss, and negative impact on reproductive capability and function. (Kurtz et al., 1994; Rohde, 1983, 1990; Tanner, 1990) Thus, malnutrition and under-nutrition continue inter-generationally, with small mothers giving birth to LBW babies who grow slowly and inadequately, and the cycle of deprivation and depletion is perpetuated.

Unless specific steps are taken in cultures where the girl is undervalued compared to the boy, the probability of the girl catching-up is either ruled out or reduced. At this point, the wheel turns a full, grim circle. Lower growth potential almost certainly slows down growth during adolescence, which is an important determinant of adult body size, and a reproductive risk. A smaller stature enhances the probability of obstructed labor or ruptured uterus which account for 5–10 percent of hospital deliveries worldwide, and for as many as one-eighth of the deaths from childbirth (as in Bangladesh). Data from Ethiopia, Tanzania, and Zaire place the incidence of obstructed labor death at 13 to 18 percent. (UNFPA, 1988:19–20) Risks extend beyond pregnancy to other stages of life. As noted earlier, the nutritional deprivation cycle traps women and daughters in inter-generational and interdependent deficiency.

MALNUTRITION DURING ADOLESCENCE

Another blind spot in nutrition planning has been adolescence, with serious consequences for girls. Puberty makes society uncomfortable, as it is perceived mainly as incipient sexuality; and that is why it has not elicited a favorable or caring response from parents or society. These intrinsic attitudinal hang-ups and constraints, as noted in the previous chapter, are common to developed and developing countries. In the more open and explicit culture of the former, adolescence is overtaken by sexual overtones, while in the more traditional cultures, it suffers from sexual undertones. In either case, the perception of adolescence is bizarre and far from constructive. There is an important need to recognize adolescence as a normal foundational phase in the female's growth process. The fact that adolescence-focused medical science has not yet surfaced widely as a speciality, whereas pediatrics and gynecology have to address the needs of both children and women, is a candid statement on the professional and societal oversight of adolescence.

In most societies, it is the denial of sexuality that causes adolescence to be denied and discriminated against. The fear, as well as suspicion, evoked by sexuality are passed on to the perception of adolescence. In traditional cultures, particularly where restraints on female sexuality are rigorous, adolescence becomes almost a feared obsession. Thus, as noted earlier, the girl child is gendered, ostracized, and, in extreme instances, cauterized during or in preparation of, her adolescence. Nutritionally, she is at greatest risk of permanent damage, especially in cultures where she is barred from protein foods and kept below minimal caloric levels, as well as in cultures where she "voluntarily" starves. Even in developed countries, sadly, nutrition-related disorders are a growing hazard to adolescent health. Unlike malnutrition in poorer families and countries, such nutritional disorders as bulimia and anorexia are self-inflicted, resulting from cultural pressures, and have a serious negative impact on girls in affluent countries. The disorders exhibit themselves in dieting, starving, and unnatural ways of food elimination by girls, and are rooted in a feeling of insecurity girls have about their bodies and themselves. A 1990 State of Minnesota Women's Fund study of 36,000 adolescents in the United States, revealed that:

- Thirty-two percent of girls and 13 percent of boys worry "very much" about their appearance.
- Over 40 percent of girls at normal weight said they were overweight, compared to 12 percent of boys.
- Thirty percent of junior high and 40 percent of senior high girls have a negative body image, compared to 12 percent and 15 percent of boys.
- Ten percent of junior high and 18 percent of senior high girls were at high or very high risk for developing eating disorders, compared to 2 percent of junior and senior high boys.[1]

Other U.S. studies (Jackson, 1992; Sadker, 1994) indicate:

- Eating disorders among girls in middle and secondary schools and colleges are rampant and increasing.
- Eighty percent of fourth-grade girls have already been on their first diet.
- Girls as young as 5 are now being treated for eating disorders.
- The average female "model" weighs 23 percent less than the average woman.
- The majority of girls in grade school say they really like themselves. By high school, almost three in four girls no longer like themselves the way they are.[1]

Age at menarche is one critical indicator which is affected, and shortchanged as a result of malnutrition. Body size and weight are also affected, as is their attenuating effect on physical and mental functioning and capability. Further down the line, there is the near certainty of LBW babies, and obstetric and other fatal risks to potential mothers. Nutritionally depleted girls do not have safe maternity experiences, normal birth weight babies, or a good chance of infant and child survival. Since birth weight is a measure both of the child's nutritional status at birth, and indirectly of the health and nutritional status of the mother, the evidence is prima facie and reiterative of the neglect of adolescent girls.

Poverty and gender are closely connected, and both appear to adversely affect female adolescence. There is evidence of a differential and delay of at least one year in the age at menarche of Indian girls who come from the poorest families in comparison to those from the highest socioeconomic groups. A similar age differential is observed between rural and urban girls. Body weights of rural and urban Indian girls differ from three to four kilograms at each interval between the ages of 12 and 16. Here, the physical workload, apart from food insufficiency, low purchasing power, and nutritional habits and value systems, is a critical variable.

The heavy physical labor required of the female child, particularly during peak work seasons, carries its toll. Time-allocation studies in several countries, particularly Nepal, demonstrate that girls are engaged in household labor from the age of 6, and by age 10–15 they may be putting in as many as twelve hours per day on domestic and non-domestic work. The proportion of working girls among 10–14 year olds is also found to be four times greater in the non-land-owning agricultural households in India than among land-owning families. Income-related differences in the age-dependent weight gain observed in that country are stated to be more likely due to the necessity for women, in all but the high and upper-middle income groups, to engage in physical activity for economic reasons. Longitudinal studies of girls in some regions of India strongly suggest that the short stature of adult rural women belonging to the low socioeconomic group is almost entirely a legacy of her childhood growth retardation due to nutritional and environmental factors. (Gopalan and Kaur, 1989:132) Thus, nutritional status among poorer and harder-worked girls, aided by environmental factors, makes a life-long difference.[2] Merely freeing the female child from some of the daily burden of work can reduce its depleting effect on her. Any solution, however, must take into account the mother's work burden. In other words, any relief for the girl must not shift the burden of work to the woman; in fact, it should lead to a more even distribution of the workload between female and male members of the family.

Nutritional and health-care insufficiency is thus *generic* to girls and women. Both anecdotal and clinical evidence affirm that in food and household politics, the male child and adult have "casting" votes and the first call on the family's nutrition. That the nutritional needs of the male so easily overpower those of the female is a reflection of several factors, most of which do not originate in nutrition or in food availability *per se*. Access to food, and its quantity as well as quality, are key determinants. But the decisive factor is the food allocator, usually the mother or other older woman. The mother is accustomed to perceiving her own nutritional needs in self-effacing terms, and transfers the same self-abnegating stance to her daughter. Her gender conditioning is so conformist that she is unable to want to empower her daughter, or to enable her to experience a more equitable growth process. To alter the girl's claim on the family's food and other resources, it requires a radical reorientation and renegotiation of the patriarchal family's behavioral dynamics, leading to greater redistributive justice in resource allocation. This will entail pitting one female (the mother, and in extended families, the mother-in-law, grandmother, or other older woman) against another (the girl child). Yet, the main strength of that approach derives from the fact that it is not malice, but conditioning and ignorance, that cause a mother to behave negligently and in a discriminatory manner toward her offspring. Persistent, gentle encouragement to act otherwise will work. The economic, social, cultural, and religious factors that go into such a process will differ in each country and culture, but they will require a linked and directed tackling in each case.

Endnotes

1. Source: Linda Feltes, et al., *Creating Gender Equity*, UMWHC, Hamline University, St. Paul, MN, 1994:75-76.

2. Numerous studies have established that girls undertake heavy workloads, as well as the demands of pregnancy, from an early age. Without food intake appropriate to the requirements of physical growth, and compounded by gender discrimination in the distribution of food, the "energy expenditure required by girls' physical workloads can compromise their nutritional status and growth. Moreover, the majority of women begin bearing children during adolescence, or shortly thereafter. The reproductive cycles of pregnancy, childbirth, and lactation are nutritionally demanding, and adolescent mothers face these demands while they themselves are still growing and developing." (Tanner, 1990) Frequently, the outcome is a compromised stature or incomplete pelvic growth with consequent increased risk of maternal death from obstructed labor. (Kurz et al., 1994)

VII

EDUCATIONAL DISPARITY AND GIRLS

Education is widely accepted to be the key to human progress. It is the "first window of change," especially for women. It enables them to take on more independent and varied roles, and education encounters less resistance from the traditional minded than do most other catalysts. Unlike employment outside the home, or political participation, education for women is almost universally valued—perhaps because education is seen both as a productive investment and as a consumer good." (Newland, 1979:5)

In recent decades, women's education has been applauded as the single most relevant factor in altering the socioeconomic capability of a country. The World Bank and the U.N. group of agencies have gathered impressive evidence supporting the positive link between female literacy and reduced fertility rate, as well as enhanced employability. A World Bank study of several countries shows that nations which invested heavily in formal primary and female education benefited through higher economic productivity, lower infant and maternal mortality, longer life expectancy, and lower fertility rates than countries with lower levels of female education. Closing the gender gap in education leads to significant gains for the economy and for social well-being. (King, 1990)

An improved level of life for the family and society is associated with the female's literacy, in several countries. According to Leslie, Lycette, and Buvinic (1986:8 in Tinker, 1990:99), research undertaken in the late 1970s in developing countries showed a positive effect of maternal education on infant- and child-mortality rates, as well as children's nutritional status. Although higher levels of maternal education were found to be connected to higher levels of paternal education and household income, most research also showed a "positive effect of maternal education on child survival and health

97

separate from its association with other socioeconomic variables." The Indian state of Kerala, which had a female literacy rate of more than 60 percent (per 1981 census), compared to the national 25 percent female literacy rate, has the lowest infant- and overall-mortality rates, the highest life expectancy, the highest average marriage age, and the lowest birth rate. Kerala's female literacy varies from 72.2 percent in urban areas to 64.3 percent in rural areas. In the 10–14 age group, in rural Kerala, 83.1 percent of the girls attend school, compared to 10.4 percent in the state of Rajasthan. (Government of India, 1985:14) Other scholars also refer to a growing body of evidence which "indicates that primary education and the resultant economic productivity result in lower birth rates, later marriages, improved family health and a dramatic decrease in infant mortality." (Buvinic and Yudelman, 1990:54) (See Figure 3 for the "Impact of Girls' Education on Fertility and Infant Mortality, next page; and Figure 4, page 100 on "More Schooling, Fewer Births.")

Independent of its impact on others, and on the environment, education has intrinsic value for the female. It should enrich her, add to her self-awareness and self-esteem, and open options for her outside of her roles as daughter, wife, and mother. However, changes in gender perceptions and stereotypes through education come about slowly, because educational curricula are often based on, and reinforce, inherited gender roles. These gender biases adversely affect the entry and retention of girls in education, and are responsible for the mixed progress in this field. Although the global push for female education is only a few decades old, the numbers of women and girls taking advantage of educational opportunities are impressive. In one Indonesian village, for example, two-thirds of the women in their 30s never went to school, compared with one out of twenty teenage girls; in Tunisia, 3 percent of the women in their late 30s were literate in 1966 compared with one-half of today's female elementary-school population. Before World War II, nine out of ten Russian women were illiterate; today, there are practically none. (Newland, 1979:27)

By 1985, there had been a record increase in the number of literate women in the world, a gain of "close to 500 million since 1960 to more than 1 billion currently. Literacy has outstripped the rise in adult population as well, so that the literacy rate for women (not including China) is now 68 percent, compared with 59 percent in 1960." (Sivard, 1985:19) However, the wide gap in literacy rates between men and women has not diminished significantly with the years. In 1985, 78 percent of adult men were able to read and write compared with 68 percent of adult women. (19) According to a U.N. report (Division for the Advancement of Women, in WIN *News*, 17-3, Summer 1991:78), the global illiteracy rate for adults of both sexes decreased from 39.3 to 27.7 percent between 1960 and 1985. In spite of the female illiteracy rate decrease from 45 to 36 percent, and the fact that developed countries are close to eradicating illiteracy, in 1985 49 percent of the adult women in developing countries were still illiterate. The estimated 561 million illiterate women constituted nearly two-thirds of the 889 million illiterates in the world. Thus the number of female illiterates is increasing, not only in absolute terms but also in relation to

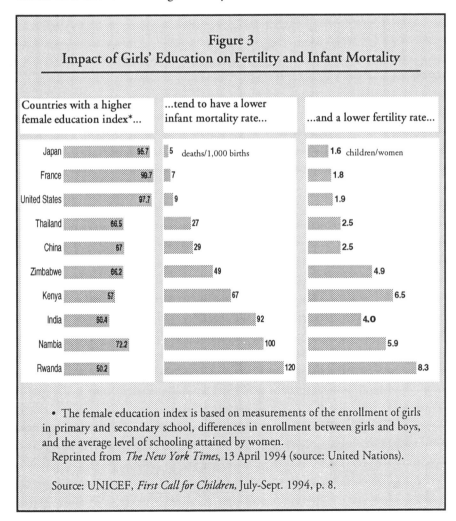

Figure 3
Impact of Girls' Education on Fertility and Infant Mortality

Countries with a higher female education index*...	...tend to have a lower infant mortality rate...	...and a lower fertility rate...
Japan 95.7	5 deaths/1,000 births	1.6 children/women
France 99.7	7	1.8
United States 97.7	9	1.9
Thailand 86.5	27	2.5
China 67	29	2.5
Zimbabwe 66.2	49	4.9
Kenya 57	67	6.5
India 56.4	92	4.0
Nambia 72.2	100	5.9
Rwanda 50.2	120	8.3

* The female education index is based on measurements of the enrollment of girls in primary and secondary school, differences in enrollment between girls and boys, and the average level of schooling attained by women.
Reprinted from *The New York Times*, 13 April 1994 (source: United Nations).

Source: UNICEF, *First Call for Children*, July-Sept. 1994, p. 8.

males. Recent updated estimates suggest a persistent female literacy handicap. Of the 960 million illiterate adults in the world, 640 million, or two-thirds, are women who either never had the opportunity to go to school or dropped out of school early. (UNICEF, 1990:23) Female illiteracy is linked overwhelmingly to poverty. More than 60 percent of illiterate women lived in countries where the average per capita income in 1980 was less than $300. In Africa and South Asia, four out of five women over 25 years of age have never had schooling. In India, which accounts for over a third of the world's illiterate female population, the gender literacy gap in percentage points widened from 17 in 1951 to 22 in 1981 in favor of men. (Government of India, 1988:72) The 1991 Indian Census showed a further increase in the gender gap to nearly 25 percentage points. (Government of India, *India*, 1993:8)

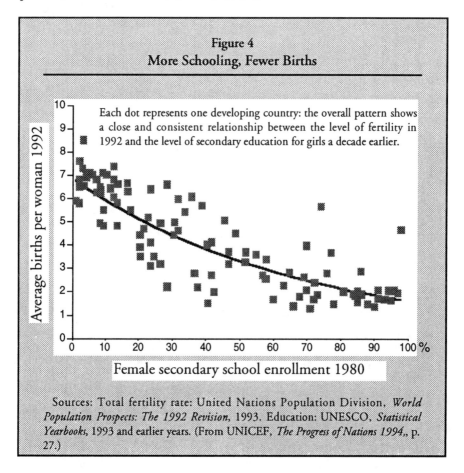

Figure 4
More Schooling, Fewer Births

Each dot represents one developing country: the overall pattern shows a close and consistent relationship between the level of fertility in 1992 and the level of secondary education for girls a decade earlier.

Average births per woman 1992

Female secondary school enrollment 1980

Sources: Total fertility rate: United Nations Population Division, *World Population Prospects: The 1992 Revision*, 1993. Education: UNESCO, *Statistical Yearbooks*, 1993 and earlier years. (From UNICEF, *The Progress of Nations 1994.*, p. 27.)

LITERACY AMONG GIRLS

It is estimated that in developing countries, at any point in time, up to three-fourths of the children not attending school are girls. Proportionally, there are not nearly as many uneducated women. But this situation appears to be improving. According to UNESCO, approximately 300 million more girls were expected to enroll in the world's schools and universities in 1985 than in 1950. Over that period, girls' enrollment was estimated to have quadrupled, and the rate of increase in enrollment was greater than the rate at which the school-age population grew. (Sivard, 1985:18)

While there has been considerable improvement in the education of girls, the gender gap has not altered significantly; in many countries, it has worsened. According to UNESCO's most recent estimates, the gap between going to school and school-age population has widened. Despite laws and constitutional mandates in most countries guaranteeing universal primary education, more than 100 million children in the world have no access to primary schooling, 60 million of whom are girls. In developing countries, approximately 60 percent of girls aged 5–19 are not in school. Absenteeism and dropout rates in the developing world are higher for girls than boys. Along with pregnancy, the disconnectedness of urban ghetto life, poverty, and domestic obligations are causing an upsurge of dropout rates among girls in the developed countries, as well. In the United States, every day, 1,512 teenage girls—mostly poor—quit high school, according to a Ford Foundation study, virtually guaranteeing a life of poverty for themselves and their children. (*San Francisco Chronicle*, December 11, 1994, p. A-18)

Although female enrollment in first-level education has matched the worldwide population growth since 1970, the ratio of girls to boys at the elementary-school level has hardly improved, at 81.6 girls to every 100 boys. (Division for the Advancement of Women in WIN *News* 17-3, Summer, 1991:78) Enrollment ratios in 1980 at the first level of schooling were estimated at approximately 78 girls per 100 boys in Africa and Asia. In Latin America, the ratios are equal. At the secondary level, there were only 54 girls to 100 boys in Africa and 63 to 100 boys in Asia. (See Figure 5, next page; Figure 6, page 103; and Figure 7, page 104, for female-to-male ratios in education)

A 13 to 18 percent difference between the primary-level enrollment of girls and boys is fairly typical of many developing countries. In the lowest-income countries, primary-level enrollment was observed to be 20 percentage points higher on average for boys than for girls. In several countries, such as Afghanistan, Benin, Guinea, Nepal, Pakistan, and Yemen, girls accounted for only one-third or less of the total enrollment. In these countries, the gender gap has widened since 1970. (King, 1990:5) A recent U.N. study of seventeen countries (seven from Latin America, five from Africa, four from Asia, and one from Europe), which examined changes in gender ratios in school enrollment between 1970 and 1985, revealed that female enrollment has declined in relation to male enrollment in a majority of countries at various levels of schooling. Decreased female enrollment at one or more levels was observed in a variety of countries, including Argentina, Bangladesh, Brazil, Chile, Colombia, Indonesia, Jamaica, Nigeria, Philippines, Sudan, and Yugoslavia. Phases of deterioration in female enrollment appeared to "have been closely linked with periods of increasing unemployment, which have often followed the onset of periods of recession. (U.N., 1989:31–34)

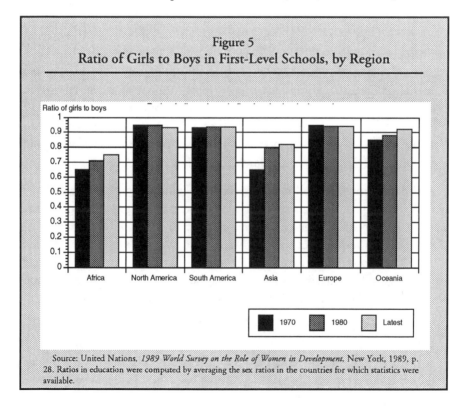

Figure 5
Ratio of Girls to Boys in First-Level Schools, by Region

Source: United Nations, *1989 World Survey on the Role of Women in Development*, New York, 1989, p. 28. Ratios in education were computed by averaging the sex ratios in the countries for which statistics were available.

Curiously, in the above study, little association was observed between the reduction in public expenditure on education and changes in female access to education. This lack of impact of reduced educational expenditures was explained in terms of the nature of allocations, characterized as "regressive," and tending to favor the "white-collar," higher-income groups over the poor. Current patterns of public spending in the majority of developing countries are such that they favor the higher, or the third level of education. (U.N., 1989:35) More than 80 percent of international aid for education also goes to secondary and higher education. (Chung in UNICEF, 1994:19) Thus, the small portion of the population, usually the richer segment, that has access to higher education, receives a large share of the expenditure on education. In a sample of countries studied by the World Bank, it was estimated that the poorer 40 percent of the population obtains 2 to 17 percent of all subsidies for higher education. In Africa, it was estimated that only 39 percent of the students in higher education have parents who come from a poor rural background, although farmers account for 76 percent of the population.

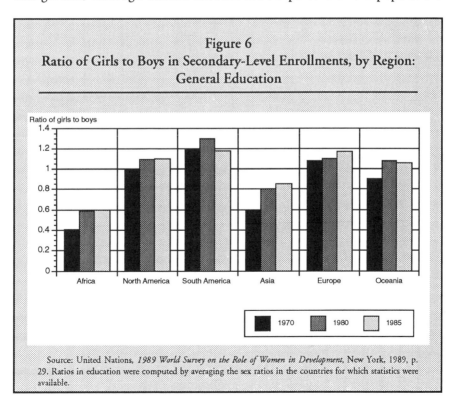

Figure 6
Ratio of Girls to Boys in Secondary-Level Enrollments, by Region: General Education

Source: United Nations, *1989 World Survey on the Role of Women in Development*, New York, 1989, p. 29. Ratios in education were computed by averaging the sex ratios in the countries for which statistics were available.

Because females usually represent a small proportion of the students in third-level schools, compared with the share they account for in first- and second-level schools, they receive a small portion of the public expenditure on education. Inequitable distribution is also attributed to the governmental tendency of spending more on urban than on rural schools. Thus, poor families, who are more likely to keep their daughters at home, benefit less from the public expenditure on education and are therefore less likely to be affected by reductions in such expenditure. (U.N., 1989:35) Other studies (Jimenez, 1986; World Development Report 1988; Staff Working Paper No. 746 by World Bank, 1985) also focus on primary education as the key to enhanced female literacy.

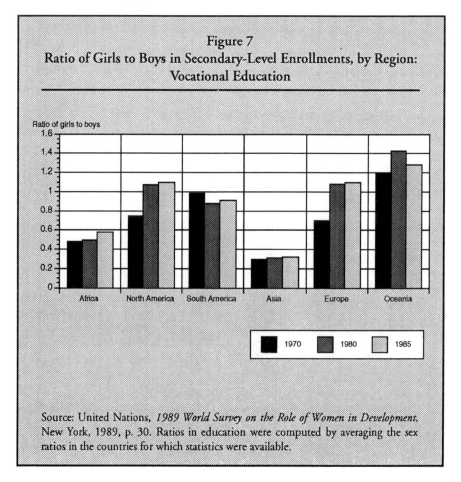

Figure 7
Ratio of Girls to Boys in Secondary-Level Enrollments, by Region: Vocational Education

Source: United Nations, *1989 World Survey on the Role of Women in Development*, New York, 1989, p. 30. Ratios in education were computed by averaging the sex ratios in the countries for which statistics were available.

Notwithstanding the above, the enrollment of girls at the highest level of education has experienced the most significant positive movement, because this had been the area where young women lagged the most behind men. Between 1950 and 1985, at the third level, girls improved from 32 to 43 percent of total enrollment (of both sexes); the corresponding increase at the primary level was from 44 to 45 percent, and at the secondary level from 42 to 45 percent. (Sivard, 1985:19) Between 1970 and 1984, enrollment of girls at the third level nearly doubled in developed countries and almost quadrupled in developing countries. (Division for the Advancement of Women, in WIN News, 17-3, Summer, 1991:78) The progress in individual countries—developed and developing—has been impressive. Japan, for instance, recorded a twenty-six-fold increase in female enrollment at the college level between 1950 and 1975, with girls accounting for one-third of the total student enrollment in college. In eastern Europe and North America, by the 1970s, girls formed one-half of the total student population in college. In western Europe and Latin America, they formed one-third, and in Asia and Africa, one-fourth or less. In such countries as Kuwait and the Philippines, there were more women than men at the college level, owing to emigration of men to other countries. In India, the number of women studying in colleges increased from 43,000 in 1951 to 656,000 in 1971, doubling their proportion of the college-enrolled population. (Newland, 1979:35-36) Currently, in the higher educational levels, Indian girls constitute 24 to 50 percent of the students enrolled, depending upon the type of courses. (Government of India, 1988:74) Enrollment levels in most countries are much higher.

Increasingly, women are enrolling in colleges and universities. In developed regions, as well as in some countries of southern Africa and western Asia, the numbers of women and men in higher education have become nearly equal. In thirty-three countries, women actually outnumber men in higher education. (U.N., 1991:46)

The content of what women choose to study, however, has not changed radically. In the majority of the world's countries, women continue to study "soft" disciplines. In Japan, for instance, more than one-half of all students in literature, arts, home economics, and teacher training were women, but only 10 percent of the students in law, politics, economics, engineering, and agriculture were women. Similar disparities were noted in female/male distribution in enrollment in the medical, legal, engineering, agricultural, and business disciplines in the United States. (Newland:36–37) Evidently, this pattern of men/women's study choice is common worldwide; it reflects as well as perpetuates occupational segregation. In both developed and developing countries, "the proportion of men students specializing in law, engineering and medicine in 1980 was twice the proportion of women students in these fields." (Sivard, 1985:21) In India, for example, although the number of girls in science courses at the higher educational level has risen to 41 per 100 boys in 1984–1985, in engineering and technology courses, only 6 girls are enrolled for every 100 boys. (Government of India, 1988:74)

A recent study by the American Association of University Women, based on a nationwide poll to assess self-esteem, education experiences, interest in math and science and career aspirations of girls and boys aged 9–15, reported that plenty of girls like math and science but as they grow older fewer and fewer think they are good in these disciplines. By the time they get to high school, 52 percent of boys think they would enjoy working in science, as compared with only 29 percent of girls. Moreover, although it was clear from the survey that most girls expect to combine a job outside the home with a job inside the home, it is also evident that very few of the girls polled believe that their outside careers should be in the technological scientific sectors—a serious disadvantage for the United States economy in a technological world. (Dworkin in *New Directions for Women*, September/October 1991:4) One major disturbing conclusion of the study was that girls do not receive the same *quality* or even *quantity* of education as boys. (See Box 8, on "American Girls and Schooling")

Occupational segregation and "soft" subject choices affect women not only as learners but also as teachers. Whereas teaching is traditionally considered a female profession, women tend to be concentrated in the lower echelons of the teaching fraternity. Data from ninety-six countries show that women form a majority of the teaching staff at the primary-school level, but their proportion reduces as the educational level rises. (Sivard, 1985:21) In the United States, in 1976, nine-tenths of the elementary school teachers were women, but only one-fourth of full-time college and university faculty were female; women also held fewer than one-fifth of the tenured positions, and fewer than one-tenth of the full professorships. In France, Germany, and the United Kingdom, women formed just 9, 5, and 3 percent, respectively, of university professors. (Newland, 1979:38) Women teachers are also over-represented in the soft disciplines, such as languages, culture, and history, and are severely under-represented in math and technical subjects. In European universities, these subjects are taught almost entirely by men. Only 2 percent of the women holding chairs in German universities are in math, physics,

---

Box 8
American Girls and Schooling

• In the early grades, girls are ahead of, or equal to, boys on almost every standardized measure of achievement and psychological well-being. By the time they graduate from high school or college, they have fallen back. (Sadker, 1994)

• Teachers interact with males more frequently, ask them better questions, and give them more precise and helpful feedback. (Sadker, 1994) White males get the most teacher attention, followed by males of color, white females, and females of color. (Sadker, 1994)

• When boys are praised by teachers, it is most often for the intellectual quality of their ideas. Girls are twice as likely as boys to be praised for following the rules of form (e.g. staying in the margins). (Sadker, 1994)

• Gifted boys have been found to be the most popular students in grades four through eight, while gifted girls are the least popular: 38 percent of gifted boys, compared to 10 percent of gifted girls, were well-liked and popular. In rating themselves, gifted girls saw themselves as the loneliest, and had the lowest opinion of their own academic ability, rating themselves lower than did both non-gifted boys and girls. (Luftig and Nicols, 1991)

• Despite medical studies indicating that a roughly equal proportion of girls and boys suffer from learning disabilities, more than twice as many boys are identified by school personnel as in need of special education services for learning-disabled students. (AAUW, 1992)

• Girls who are highly competent in math and sciences are much less likely to pursue scientific or technological careers than are their male classmates. (AAUW, 1992)

• The contributions and experiences of girls and women are still minimized or ignored in many of the textbooks in American schools. (AAUW, 1992)

• In a typical school yard, the boys' area is ten times larger than the girls area. (Sadker, 1994)

Source: Linda Feltes et al., *Creating Gender Equity.* UMWHC, Hamline University, St. Paul MN:76-79

chemistry, and engineering. (Sivard:21) Such differences are evidently a product of chronic and long-standing gender stereotypes which inhibit women from aspiring for parity with men. They serve as poor role models for future generations of female students, as well as teachers.

As in the case of health and nutrition, the female imbalance is greater in the developing than in the developed world. Behind global statistics and averages, "there are continuing major differences in national and regional patterns. Developing countries, in general, reveal greater sex inequalities in education than do the developed. At successively higher educational levels, the inequality becomes more pronounced. At the university level in developing countries men outnumber women almost two to one." (Sivard:19)

Unfettered, UNESCO and the world's leaders have committed themselves with renewed effort (March, 1990, Thailand, World Conference on Education for All) to "universalizing access and promoting equity." As the "most urgent priority," the world community accepted the need to "ensure access to and improve the quality of, education for girls and women, and to remove every obstacle that hampers their active participation. All gender stereotyping in education should be eliminated." (WCEFA/Declaration/Prov.9, March, 1991)

Although the aggregation of objectives in terms of girls and women is laudable, it is not indicative of the preeminence which girls deserve in expanded global educational efforts. Also, the rhetoric about eliminating gender stereotypes seems simplistic. Gender stereotypes in education are a reflection of stereotypes in the real world; changing text books can treat the symptoms but does not cure the causes or outcomes. Girls who cannot go to school cannot learn of "gender" roles nor of the need to revise them; and until gender roles in the real world begin to change, the girl child will continue to be barred from schooling.

Because school enrollment and the retention of girls in education is at the core of improved female status and empowerment, it is crucial to address the issue of stereotypes in the real world as a precondition of enhancing access. The level of parental awareness and their improved capability to afford the absence of the girl at home are central to her education, since it is they and not the governments that decide whether education is *universal* and *equal* for *both genders*.

There is sufficient and impressive evidence that, given the will, educability is a manageable problem, as is gender parity. Even in South Asia, where the world's overwhelming majority of unschooled girls live, Sri Lanka has achieved and maintained educational parity for girls and boys. In many other countries, at various levels of GNP (Indonesia, Kenya, Thailand, and Zimbabwe, and countries in the Caribbean and Latin America), educational inertia with respect to girls has been overcome. Augmenting the educability of younger age groups has proven to be much easier than that of older women. In Tunisia, 65 percent of girls aged 15–19 have some education, compared with 10 percent of 45–49 year-old women. In Kenya, 95 percent compared to 35 percent, respectively, have attended school.

Scant or sluggish enrollment, when it is gender specific, points to more than a shortage of educational facilities. It is reflective of underlying environmental constraints and inhibitions. In Uganda, according to UNICEF, (*Children and Women in Uganda: A Situational Analysis*, 1989:63–64), "the decreasing proportion of girls attending school at successively higher levels indicates that a choice is being made to use available funds to educate boys rather than girls." The girl's gender is the overriding constraint, along with the fact that she can offer no collateral to parents or to the socio-economy for investing in her education. In cultures where girls are "born to marry," parents see little economic value in educating a girl whose presence in the natal home is transitory. Educating a boy provides personal payoffs by way of long-term care and insurance benefits for retirement. Even when educated and employable, the fact that female skills and jobs command less pay is recognized by parents and shapes their decision not to invest in the girl's education. (See Box 9, next page, on "Unemployability of Girls Reinforces Their Illiteracy") Thus, the cycle of denial and deprivation is self-perpetuating. Since she is perceived as unemployable, the girl is kept uneducated, and as she is uneducable, she remains unemployable, reinforcing her scant economic value to the family. Even where she is likely to achieve a demonstrated earning capability, parents perceive no share in the actual or potential gain and are unwilling to invest in her. There are, in addition, opportunity costs which accentuate parental reluctance to spare the girl child for school.

A disturbing facet of discriminatory treatment of girls in education is that they tend to internalize parental perceptions and rationalize higher spending on their brothers by their parents. This has been documented by UNICEF in Bihar, India and also by researchers in Malaysia. (Heyzer, 1986)

ROLE OF PRE-EXISTING INEQUALITY

A U.N. study refers to the role of pre-existing inequality in determining the female's access to schooling. (1989:36) A household's decision to send a child to school is a "trade-off between the cost of keeping a child in school (an opportunity cost in that the child will not be used for other tasks and will not learn skills useful to the family enterprise; a direct cost in terms of school fees, equipment, books and transport) and the expected benefits of having an educated child (the child's future personal benefit and income; support for the parents)." Moreover, observation of the labor market leads families to conclude that girls have little or no chance of having a career and that they will earn less money than men. "These attitudes, which stem from women having had less access to education in the past, and from the fact that their reproductive role may have hampered their entry into the formal labor force

---

Box 9
Unemployability of Girls Reinforces Their Illiteracy

There are few wage employment opportunities resulting from primary or secondary education for girls in subsistence economies. The investment in time and money, quite apart from the risk entailed in the social and cultural mobility that goes with wage work, keeps parents reluctant to invest in the female child's education. Even if jobs were available, gender disparities favor male earners.

According to Herz et al., (1991) mean earnings for women in India were found to be more than six times lower than those for men with the same level of education and productivity. Men out-earn women in similar jobs in Latin America, too, where female enrollment is high and gender parity at the secondary level has been largely realized. Although economic policy imperfections, labor market barriers, limited access to information and resources, and shortfalls in education may combine to lock women into low productivity, the message conveyed to parents is singularly clear: investment in boys' education has a better payoff. "Men earn more, making the returns to male schooling higher, so boys are sent to school more often than girls. Girls then grow up lacking the education they need to compete."

Source: Her, et al., 1991:14–16

or obliged them to make breaks in their employment, thus constitute a vicious circle." (36)

Another factor hurting a girl's chances of being sent to school is the fact that female children perform a higher proportion of the work done in the home: if the burden of family work increases, the girl will be the one kept at home. In a survey conducted in Malaysia, the proportion of girls aged 5 and 6 doing some kind of family work was estimated at 31 percent, compared to 17 percent for boys. This pattern of sharing family work between female and male children was also found in other countries. (U.N., 1989:36) Throughout most of Sub-Saharan Africa and South Asia, as a recent study observes (Herz et al., 1991:26–29), the heavy work burden on rural women may force them to keep their daughters at home to help with care of younger siblings, time-consuming tasks on the farms, and such household chores as cleaning, cooking, and collecting fuel. Research from Malawi shows that school-age girls spend more time than boys on household chores, and spend less time the first hour after school on studying or relaxing. (Davison and Kanyuka in Grant-Lewis, 1990)

In Burkina Faso, time-use studies reveal that girls 7 years of age and older spend 3.5 hours per day on household tasks, compared with only 1.5 hours for boys. In rural Java, in the poorest households, girls aged 10–15 worked an average of 94 hours a month as compared to 38 hours of household work put in by boys. (Sajogyo et al., 1980, in FAO, 1985) In Indonesia, fewer than 3 percent of male siblings in the age-group 14–18 are involved in household care, compared to 25 percent of girls. Moreover, as teenage children grow older, boys leave school and enter the labor market, but girls leave school, reduce their leisure time, and participate more in household activities. (Evenson et al., 1980) In Gambia, 10 percent of females who drop out from primary school do so to stay home and care for siblings. (World Bank, 1990) In India, younger girls work 5.5 hours, and older girls 7.7 hours a day in adult household and agricultural tasks while younger boys spent only 1.8 hours and older boys 3.6 hours on such tasks. (World Bank, 1991) This use of girls for labor thus accentuates the opportunity cost of sending them to school.

Evidently "these different factors of pre-existing inequality have often been found to be more important determinants in households with a lower educational level and a lower standard of living: according to various surveys, poorer households are more likely to limit their daughter's access to education, a form of discrimination apparently inversely related to the family's wealth or social class." (U.N., 1989:36)

In the more protected and traditional cultures, schools are perceived as running counter to the prevailing parental and societal conditioning of the girl child. There are realistic, as well as exaggerated, accounts of how schooling "corrupts" and "alienates" the girl from tradition. In many cases, menarche is the cutoff point for the girl child's right and access to schooling. In cultures where female seclusion is practiced, the impact of that tradition on girls' school enrollment after puberty is substantial. (Kelly and Elliott, 1982; El Sanabary, 1989; Stromquist, 1987; Herz et al., 1991) Once she is biologically mature, her mobility and exposure to the outside world, in addition to intellectual challenge, pose a risk to her virginity and to the honor of the family. By tying her feet and mind, the probability of deviance and dishonor is minimized.

In those cultures, investing in the girl's education is perceived by parents as wasteful, distracting, and disruptive. In such contexts, too, strategies that begin and end with the school system cannot be fulfilling. Calling for induction of girls in schools, independent of changing the perception of girls as risky, unprofitable investments, or addressing the environmental and personal factors that control girls' education, has not worked and is not likely to work. The causes contributing to the problem need to be addressed in their totality. Of those, the following are most frequently cited:

Socioeconomic Causes:

1. Need for the girl to work in and out of the home (opportunity cost);
2. Onset of menses which makes the girl instantly and permanently vulnerable, and a biological risk to the family's reputation (the "honor" factor);
3. Early marriage (marriages continue to occur among girls below the legal, mean, or average age);
4. Purdah or sex segregation (which compels certain religious and ethnic groups to restrict the public movements and mobility of the girl).

School-Related Causes:

1. Distance of school (problems of safety of commute; opportunity cost in having to be away from home longer);

2. Fewer women teachers (UNESCO estimates that female teachers as a percentage of male, at the primary level, range from 50 in Africa, to 65 in Asia, and 77 in Latin America. But in several countries and within countries in certain regions, women still account for 10 to 20 percent of teachers);

3. Few exclusively girls' schools (especially relevant in Islamic countries and other communities where social segregation is customary);

4. Inadequate facilities (lack of toilets particularly, which compels girls to go home during school hours);

5. Time constraints (school schedules continue to ignore peak agricultural seasons, and times of the day, when opportunity costs of sending girls to school are higher);

6. Dull, dense, and heavy school curriculum (the rote method, unimaginative learning/testing methods, non-participative learning, and learning unrelated to real-life experience and needs);

7. Language (having to learn in a language which is not native to the child);

8. Length of schooling (too long, both in terms of daily hours and educational span);

9. No immediate economic value (no skills are acquired in school which can immediately enable the girl to add to the family's earnings, or to manage the household better);

10. Poverty of means (apart from opportunity costs, there are additional expenses to be incurred for school uniforms, transportation, snacks at school, books, and supplies, which are ill-afforded).

An additional problem refers to the school curricula reinforcing and perpetuating existing gender roles, and the absence of female role models. (See Box 10, next page, on "Gender Bias in Kenyan Textbooks") This is a qualitative parameter which is not intrinsic to parental limitations in keeping the girl out of school. No one keeps the female child at home because the school is not allowing her to learn new gender roles. However, this aspect is relevant to the context of gender stereotyping in the real world, and certainly needs to be addressed in order to help make a positive change in the female and male child's perception of herself/himself, their perception of each other, and their parents' perceptions of them.

Box 10
Gender Bias in Kenyan Textbooks

In 1991, a team of researchers in Kenya published their findings on the portrayal of girls and women in twenty-four of their social studies, math, science, technical and language textbooks. Stating that textbooks shaped attitudes and were sources of information on social norms, the researchers brought particular attention to the fact that in parts of Kenya where books are scarce, the textbook was highly prized by students and parents. It was viewed as a source of authority, even by teachers, who relied on it to help expose children to a common culture, ideology, or values, "The text can become symbolic of school and modernity, the future and development." Given the weight of this prestigious symbol, the task force was horrified to discover that women and girls were conspicuously absent in most texts. The task force felt that this male/female imbalance gave an impression of male activities being much more extensive than the female's.

When references to women did appear, they were negative. Women were shown as passive and retiring compared to men, as managers of people, leaders at home and in society, alert and curious, physically strong, and energetic. The task force asked: Might these more negative images of women's psychological traits be used to justify female discrimination in society, and be a reason why development has passed them by?

Math texts: The task force called mathematics the key to female entry into high paying, prestigious careers. Yet typically Kenya texts presented males as active agents in the economy—owning property, energetically working for money, and so forth. Women in math texts appeared only at home as mothers, doing unremunerated domestic chores. There was no way for girls to see women who work in the modern economy, or even handling money, despite the fact that more than 30 percent of Kenya's families are headed by women who work.

Agricultural technology texts: Surprisingly, images of adult women were sparse even in these texts, even though women contribute 80 percent of the farm economy in Kenya. At a minimum, commented Dr. Anna Obura, the author of the report, the words "the farmer and *his* wife" need to be changed to "the farmer and *her* husband."

History texts: In examining African history, the report noted that, with the exception of Queen Nzinga, women were relegated to absent or meager supportive roles. "History as written in the texts is a catalog of conquerors, kings, obas, and merchant boys." When women appear in the text and

Box 10, continued...

pictures, they are generally presented as mothers of sons waiting at home, or as possessions of rulers. In one text, the book implied that women must have been present in history, but their role was marginal.

Gendered language was also a problem. The book may read "people found food," "people gathered," "with simple tools people," and so forth. Yet in diagrams, images, and tables, the "people" shown were exclusively men.

The task force stressed the negative implication for girls when texts offer limited negative female role models. They asked: If one sex holds relative prominence in the text, doesn't that indicate that society esteems or values that sex over the other? Or, if women are depicted as marginal in history, doesn't that show that women must then be marginal to the future development of Kenya?

Corrective Strategies: On a positive note, the task force discussed how they have begun to re-orient textbook images and messages. Among suggested corrective measures are: 1) do an analysis of your own texts; 2) find examples of positive as well as negative female references; 3) hold workshops on your findings for publishers and teachers, presenting them with examples of what is needed; 4) hold workshops for parents (confronted with examples from the texts, Kenyan parents have for the first time begun to see how, even beyond the books, the current school ethos has held girls back); 5) make sure texts overtly explore gender issues, since "few people are conversant with or understand gender issues"; 6) find other ways to get positive images of women into the school curriculum.

Source: Abridged from Lyn Reese, *1993 Women in the World, Curriculum Resources*. The Task Force Report on *Changing Images: Portrayal of Girls and Women in Kenya Textbooks* is published by the African Center for Technology Studies: P.O. Box 45917, Nairobi, Kenya

VIII

EXPLOITATIVE WORK AND GIRLS

One of the most overpowering myths in contemporary development thinking and strategies is that women and children do not work. Formal labor statistics continue to report that fewer women work than men, and that women work fewer hours per week than men. However, these figures do not reflect the entirety of work done by women, nor the dual workload they carry—household chores and unpaid family work performed in the family-owned farms and cottage industries or businesses. Irrespective of the proportion of women who are included in the official definition of "labor force," "it has to be accepted that almost all women work. . .Some women work for wages, some are self-employed for profit, and some participate in the household economy receiving no cash or material compensation. But all are workers." (Ware, 1981:99–100) Whether in developed or developing countries, there are fewer women who are just housewives anymore—almost everywhere, women are bearing the dual load of work within and outside the home. Since the work women do at home has lower or no monetary value, it is not adequately reflected in family or national computations of income or wealth. Female labor, therefore, commands a lesser socioeconomic status and power than male labor.

It was not always so. In pre-modern societies, there was and currently is "no conflict between female labor and domesticity: the female farmer, the wife and the mother are one." (Wilensky, 1968:236 in Ware, 1981:213) In the rural economies of developing countries, "women spend little time on domestic work such as cooking, cleaning and child care: most of their time is spent in providing the types of goods and services which are bought for money in industrialized countries, producing and processing food and providing fuel and water." (Boserup, 1975 in Ware: 212–13)

117

It was the gender-based division of labor in modern, industrial societies, and the value given to paid labor outside the home, which caused a devaluation of women's work in and around the house. As Ware observes, industrialization caused an unnatural division in labor—paid labor was called work and unpaid labor was not. For example, when both the mistress and maid work, only the maid is counted as "worker." If the master marries the maid, she ceases to be a "worker" in national statistics. Similarly, child care is recognized as a productive activity only when it occurs outside the home and is paid.

In most modern or post-industrial societies, because women perform the domestic and men the extra-domestic role, the latter tasks have been given greater prestige, power, and monetary value than the former. Even when women have entered the extra-domestic market in great numbers, their labor has been channeled mainly into occupations which are extensions of their care-giving, healing, and service roles. In the United States, for instance, "Fully one-fourth of employed women are concentrated in 5 occupations that are consistent with prevailing cultural definitions of "femininity": secretary, bookkeeper, elementary school teacher, waitress, and retail sales clerk. These are jobs that are neither status nor cash worthy. By contrast, men are spread over numerous well-paying and respectable occupations." (FFII, 1988:92) In Australia in 1981, 63 percent of women worked in 6 out of a total of 75 occupations. In Sweden, out of 270 occupational categories in the census, more than 40 percent of women were employed in 5 jobs: secretary, nurse's aide, sales worker, cleaner, and children's nurse. The occupations which were common for women included very few men—there were 9 women to 1 man. (Sivard, 1985:16)

A recent U.N. study on the status of women (1991) affirms that almost all jobs globally are segregated by sex, with women relegated to the lower status, more poorly paid positions. Women's pay worldwide averages 30 to 40 percent less than that of men. The study also notes that women work as much or more than men in every region of the world and as much as thirteen hours more per week, on the average, in Asia and Africa. In fact, "Nowhere in the world have women entered the labor force on equal terms with men. In most countries they are concentrated in particular sectors of the economy in service jobs or in selected areas of manufacturing such as clothing and footwear, textiles, food processing, and precision and electronic engineering. In most of the less developed countries, they also make up a significant proportion of the labor force in agriculture. Within each area of work, there is still a concentration of women in the jobs with lowest pay and least status. Thus the labor market continues to be characterized by both horizontal and vertical segregation, with women's position being constrained by traditional notions about the sexual division of labor." (Doyal, 1990:588-589)

In the rural or urban economies, a bias persists between the nature of, and value assigned to, male and female work. Male farmers and laborers corner the skills and tasks which command higher wages, leaving women to perform the menial, more arduous, low-skill and low-pay tasks. In India, for instance, "in the construction industry, men do brick-laying while women carry bricks and mortar; women carry soil while men do the digging; women transplant paddy, weed, reap, pluck vegetables, and bundle the harvest produce, while men plow and sow the seeds. In terms of access to skills, women continue to be employed in monotonous, low-skilled and low-wage sectors. . .Absence or lack of enforcement of social and labor legislation hampers women's access to basic employment benefits. Women are denied rights such as minimum hours and minimum wages, and access to maternity benefits, maternal health care, day care and legal aid. There are a number of areas in which women receive no social security benefits. These factors together contribute to the insecurity of women and reinforce their inferior status as workers." (Government of India, 1988:28)

According to Bisilliat and Fieloux (1982:21, 32), "Everywhere the work of women has the same characteristics: time consuming, repetitive, meticulous tasks, neither enhancing nor appreciated; temporary work and low pay, lower pay than that received by men for identical work—pay that does not assure the survival of a family, pay predominantly by the hour or by the piece. (In India, the proportion of women working at piece-rate has gone from 25 percent to 85 percent in sixteen years.) Finally, there is the double workday, since the woman also has to assume her functions as housewife: the drudgery of getting water and wood, preparing the meals, and taking care of children." Under the pressure of commercial farming, women's time spent on farm work in many countries has increased and now exceeds that of men. In Central Africa, they work from 28 to 33 percent longer. In the Congo, women work two hundred days per year, and men thirty. In Gambia, the women devote twenty hours per week to the work on the land; the men, nine." (Bisilliat, 1982)

Whether in developing or developed countries, in the wealthy modern-industrial or the poor subsistence economies, there are some commonalties that characterize the labor of women. Newland (1979:130–131) perceives the following as similarities:

1. In both, women perform a great variety of tasks during the working day;
2. Women in both settings work a long day—longer than their male counterparts; and
3. Women in both find their output accorded little economic value. If the man did the same task in the same way—be it water or fuel fetching, cooking, or child care—it would be counted as work.

It is thus evident that women's work suffers from statistical and accounting, as well as social, invisibility. There is a vicious cycle of the myth of female non-productivity perpetuating, and being perpetuated by, the invisibility of women's work. (See Figure 8) Since the work women do remains invisible, so does their potential or actual worth to the family, economy, and society.

GIRLS AND WORK

The working child is a source of embarrassment to planners and human-rights activists. Yet, where the adults' capacity to provide independently for their dependents diminishes, children are harnessed as ready and free labor to complement the family's subsistence capability. Sadly, gender disparities in the adult work world and women's invisibility in the "formal" or "productive" work force are echoed in the world of child workers. Among them, inevitably, the more visible are boys working outside the home in factories, mines, or workshops, and in money-rewarded activity. Girls work more, and in equal numbers, but their labor, like that of their mothers and other female elders, remains obscure and unacknowledged as work of no monetary value and, therefore, not as work. That, in turn, establishes the girl's inferior status compared to the boy: she is seen by her parents as a dependent and he as an earner and supporter, therefore deserving of investment from the family in the form of food, clothing, education, skills training, rest, and even recreation. It is the parents' perception of its lack of financial worth which contributes to the underrating of the labor of the girl child. For example, a study of the value and cost of children among six hundred rural wives and husbands in Nigeria revealed that the majority of parents believed that boys were more productive than girls of the same age. Both men and women also thought that parents should invest more in their male children, particularly on their feeding and schooling. (Ourubuloye in Oppong, 1987:87–88)

Time-use studies are one way to offer convincing evidence in support of the daily engagement of girls in household and family-owned farming or other business-related labor. Such studies have been undertaken, among others, in India (Government of India, 1989), Ivory Coast (Berio, 1988), and

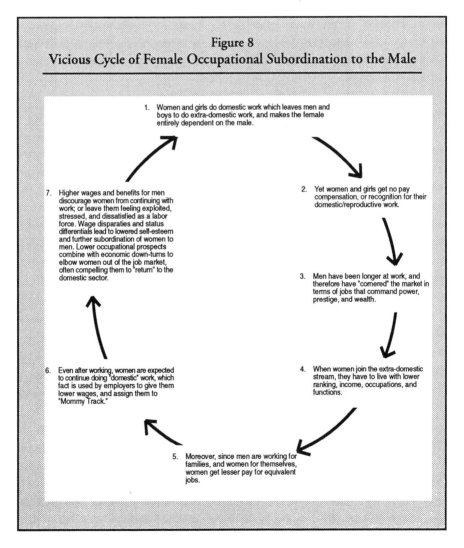

Figure 8
Vicious Cycle of Female Occupational Subordination to the Male

1. Women and girls do domestic work which leaves men and boys to do extra-domestic work, and makes the female entirely dependent on the male.

2. Yet women and girls get no pay compensation, or recognition for their domestic/reproductive work.

3. Men have been longer at work, and therefore have "cornered" the market in terms of jobs that command power, prestige, and wealth.

4. When women join the extra-domestic stream, they have to live with lower ranking, income, occupations, and functions.

5. Moreover, since men are working for families, and women for themselves, women get lesser pay for equivalent jobs.

6. Even after working, women are expected to continue doing "domestic" work, which fact is used by employers to give them lower wages, and assign them to "Mommy Track."

7. Higher wages and benefits for men discourage women from continuing with work; or leave them feeling exploited, stressed, and dissatisfied as a labor force. Wage disparaties and status differentials lead to lowered self-esteem and further subordination of women to men. Lower occupational prospects combine with economic down-turns to elbow women out of the job market, often compelling them to "return" to the domestic sector.

Nepal (Acharya and Bennet, 1979). They reveal how girls, like women, perform a variety of services for their families which free boys and men to pursue more cash-worthy activities. A typical female child, in an agrarian family, cooks, cleans, fetches fodder, fuel, and water; grazes the cattle and feeds and tends other farm animals; helps in sowing, transplanting, weeding, and harvesting; assists in family-based or family-managed cottage industry; and acts as surrogate mother to her younger siblings. In urban areas, she does most household and non-household chores. The agricultural tasks are merely replaced by chores more appropriate to the urban economy. Whether in the rural or urban sector, her labor supplements the family's and economy's output and earnings, yet her earning capability remains an unacknowledged benefit, and any call for her to be given equal "value" as her brother, remains an unheard whisper.

SEX-BASED DIVISION OF LABOR

Like adult labor, child labor is unevenly distributed, with the more time-consuming, arduous, and low-skill tasks reserved for the girl. Sex-based division of labor in rural India, for instance, is presumed to begin with the girl child as early as 6 years of age. According to a field survey of fifteen to twenty villages in Bihar, India (UNICEF, Bihar in Sohoni, 1990:39), very few tasks are gender neutral: only six out of fifty-eight activities are performed by both girls and boys. Boys' activities in agriculture are restricted to plowing (breaking clods of earth) and carrying paddy seedlings—both seasonal activities. The major share of agriculture-related work is done by girls. In silk production, boys learn the more valuable skills: collecting wild cocoons is 66 percent of the value added and weaving is 20 percent, both done by boys; spinning, which accounts for only 14 percent of the value added, is done by girls. Moreover, as in the adult world, boys do not share in the domestic activities. In households where mothers migrate or need to be away from the family for a few days, girls were found to do all household chores, including cooking and taking care of the siblings—that in addition to the economic chores they perform on a sustained basis in the eight mainstream sectors of employment: agriculture, dairy-work, khadi (spun cloth), village industries, fisheries, sericulture (production of raw silk), small animal husbandry, and handloom and handicraft industries.

A similarly uneven workload distribution is reported from other parts of the world. In Java, most young girls spend at least one-third more hours per day working at home and in the market than boys of the same age, and in some age groups, as much as 85 percent more hours. In Malaysian households, girls aged 5 and 6 who do home or market chores work as much as three-fourths more hours per week than boys of that age. In Chinese and Indian households in Malaysia, girls aged 7 to 9 work as much as 120 to 150 percent more hours than boys. (King, 1990:12) In the Ivory Coast, based on a survey, girls aged 10–14 work three-and-one-half hours and boys two hours to assist in household tasks. In Nepal, although children of both sexes work for three hours a day at ages 5–9, and more than six hours in the 10–14 age group, from age 5 onward, "girls are at a disadvantage. Females are found to work more than males in all age groups." Girls "spend the same time on animal care, but more time on agriculture, and globally more time in all activity groups than do male children in the same age group. In particular, girls spend more time replenishing the water supply, collecting fuel, and processing food than boys do." (Berio, 1988:57, 60) Fuel collection, preparation, and use are primarily the responsibility of women, assisted by girls. "Children in almost all developing societies must help their mother with these tasks. Girls especially take part in fuel preparation, cooking and tending the fire. In Tanzania, young girls begin to help their mothers as soon as they can walk; in parts of Africa, mothers take their daughters from school to help them gather fuel." (Hosken, 1979 in Dankelman and Davidson, 1988:68) As an Ethiopian refugee girl living in a Somalian camp poignantly contends, "The boys have nothing to do. For girls it is different. We have to look after the family collecting firewood as before. But we have to walk further each day to find any." ("A Girl Named Sara" in Dankelman:68)

Even in developed countries, girls experience a work or role overload. A study of Canadian girls found that 85 percent are regularly expected to do household chores and half take a major responsibility for housework for the whole family. Mothers assume most of the responsibility for housework, girls help most and boys rarely do much. (Gaskell 1992:77 in Lees, 1993:159) In the United States, where both parents work, teenage daughters do 10 hours of chores per week compared to 3 hours of chores done by boys. (Jackson, 1992:71) In Australia, sons and daughters do different amounts and different types of unpaid work. Sons do only two-thirds of the unpaid work that daughters do. For every hour of unpaid work done by a son, a daughter does 1 hour and 20 minutes. In Italy, where the average hours of remunerated work per week amount to 41.5 for men and 36.7 for women, surveys of non-remunerated work reveal a radically different picture: the average weekly hours of domestic work amount to just 5.5 hours for men, compared to 36.3 hours for women. Based on a time-use study of agricultural households, it is further reported that women (wives of farm operators) spend 5.71 hours daily in market labor and 5.23 hours in non-market labor, whereas men (farm operators) spend 8.89 and 0.95 hours respectively. That pattern of unshared non-market labor by the male is repeated among children—girls put in 4.35 and 5.01 hours daily on remunerated and unremunerated work, as compared to 7.20 and 2.11 hours respectively put in by boys. On the whole, the men of the household and the women of the household show a similar pattern. This suggests that the sexual role is stronger than age and position in the household. (Arangio-Ruiz in INSTRAW, 1990:17–28) Within the family, age and sex decide clout and both work against the girl child. Consequently, the girl is twice denied because of her age and gender, and she is twice removed from the benefits and entitlements of her childhood as well as her labor.

DISCRIMINATORY OCCUPATIONAL PATTERNS AND PRACTICES

Formal labor counts in some countries (Bangladesh, India) reveal that more girls are compelled to seek work and at younger ages, than boys, suggesting that more boys are spared from work to take advantage of schooling. (Chatterjee, 1988:73–74; King, 1990:12) Occupations of boys and girls in the labor force correspond to the patterns of their segregated roles. Girls are employed primarily as service workers while boys work in agriculture, forestry, and fisheries. (UNICEF, Bangladesh, 1990:47)

The educational and occupational choices of girls and boys are closely fashioned after the gender role models set by the adult world. Even in Sweden, which is relatively gender neutral in its development approaches, "Girls and boys choose, to a very large extent, sex-segregated education. In upper secondary schools, girls choose service health care, and cultural education and boys choose technical education. This leads to a highly sex-segregated labor force." Moreover, as a Swedish study notes, "Just as many men as women have homes and children. Nevertheless, the amount of time that men devote to caring for their children and homes is much lower than the amount of time that women devote" (Hedman in INSTRAW, 1990:159) And that pattern, in all likelihood, is replicated among boys and girls. In the United States, economic and cultural pressures are compelling girls in low-income families of color to take on the burdens of unremunerated work, often at the cost of their education. "Poor girls drop out for "family reasons" at two to three times the rate of poor boys. Oldest daughters are more likely to drop out than any other sibling in a family. . .These young women are sacrificing their teen years to accommodate crumbling economies, housing shortages, health-care inadequacies, crises in their homes and communities. Only when they get pregnant do they now get systematic and gender-specific attention—and even then, such attention is typically aimed at saving the baby." (Dworkin in *New Directions*, 1991:4)

Wage disparities are as common among girls and boys as among women and men. Evidence from India confirms that girls are paid less than boys. (Chatterjee, 1988:75) A U.S. study shows that parents are more likely to pay boys than girls for the work they do inside the home. That pattern also holds true outside the home, so that girls earn less in general. Moreover, boys are encouraged to work for "pay" and girls "out of love." (Lott, 1994:71) Also, in more traditional cultures where women's mobility and entry into the wage market is discouraged, girls are often led to fill the vacuum. The participation of 6–12-year-old females in Egypt, for example, exceeds the total percentage of female workers in the population. (UNICEF, Egypt, 198:135)

In recent years, the feminization of the export-oriented-industrial and cottage-industrial sectors has led to a different but disturbing exploitation of female labor—young female labor in particular. Educated girls coming out of high school are targeted by multinational and national employers to join industries geared to the manufacture of products intended for such global markets in textiles, garments, shoes, leather and electronic goods, pharmaceuticals, and chemicals, as well as such handicrafts as lace and embroidered goods. Girls provide a pool of educated, teachable, disciplined, dexterous, agile, and low-wage labor to fulfill the bottom-line expectations of exploitative employers. Some of their domestically acquired traditional skills, such as sewing and knitting, are easily transferable to the assembly line operations of factories. In Taiwan, for instance, the export industries— garment, leather, television, and other electronic equipment—had 56 percent female employees. The work week was forty-eight hours on the average, with only seven paid holidays. Towards the middle of 1977, 85 percent of the employees of plants in the free–trade zones were women. They worked eight-to-twelve hours a day, six days a week. Moreover, "in the free zones in Asia, not only does the unskilled female work force receive wages one-tenth as high as its counterpart in developed countries, but 34 percent of women compared to only 15.6 percent of men earn less than two hundred dollars a month." (Bisilliat et al., 1987:67) Similar situations are observed with respect to the use of girls and women in export manufacturing industries in Brazil, India, Korea, Singapore, and other parts of the developing world.

LEGAL INVISIBILITY

What the family and the census both find invisible is further ignored in law. Thus, even while working long hours in hazardous work conditions and operations, on farms or in cities, the young girl worker is unable to cash in on the law's protection. Labor laws in most instances protect and regulate occupations where there is an identifiable employer and a minimum number of employees, thus leaving out the vast majority of child workers, especially girls, because they are more represented in the informal, unrecognized sector. In the unregulated, developing countries particularly, labor avenues that employ girl children provide appalling Dickensonian work conditions with minimal compensation, long arduous hours, frequently hazardous work sites and environments, and no worker training, advancement, or social insurance provisions. (Burra, 1987) Even where the family is her employer, she has no more rights or protective provisions.

Estimates between formal and informal counts of working children continue to be widely varied due to varying perceptions. In recent years, there has been an evolution in the definition of child labor, as (i) domestic work, (ii) non-domestic work, (iii) bonded labor, and (iv) wage labor. Expanded definitions of child labor, as happens in assessing women's labor, place the numbers of working children at millions higher than the numbers officially recorded as representing the child labor force in national censuses. Reports from Bangladesh, India, Nepal, and Pakistan reveal significant gaps in recorded and actual incidence of child labor, with most of the statistical and substantive invisibility affecting the working girl child.

STREET CHILDREN AND WORK HAZARDS

A growing and troubling phenomenon are work patterns of street children, conservatively estimated at eighty million globally. (National Council of Social Development, Philippines, 1989:1) In some regions, as in Latin America, their numbers are proliferating (estimated at over fifty million), accounting for about one-third of the region's child population. Their presence is manifested in other regions as well, including developed countries.

In the United States, the number of homeless children is conservatively estimated at one million, and 50 percent of homeless women and children are reported to be in the street due to violence in the home. (*Issues Quarterly*, Vol. 1, No. 2:10) Everywhere, the denial of childhood's basic rights for both boys and girls, and a greater sexual risk for girls, is their common experience. A 1990 study of homeless, runaway, and incarcerated teenage girls in California showed 13 to be the average age for beginning sexual activity. (*San Francisco Chronicle*, December 11, 1994:A-18) Drug and sexual abuse is often experienced by girls before and after taking to street life.

A study of seventy-four street girls aged 8–18 in Metro Manila, designed to "capture their life-world," revealed that constant problems faced by them are sexual exploitation and legal harassment on grounds of vagrancy. "Their mere presence on the streets," as a Costa Rican report notes, "forces them. . .to do work that is not legally regulated. . .as women they also face patterns of sexual segregation which limit their possibilities of incorporating them into the occupations which. . .are generated for minors. Some of the options for girls fall into illegal categories which places them in a situation where the distinction between earning a living and delinquency becomes blurred." (In Sohoni, 1990:47) In California (U.S.A.), females make up the fastest growing segment of the prison and jail population. They are being committed at twice the rate of males, according to the California Delinquency Prevention Commission. Girls do not get the attention they need and their needs are frequently overshadowed by the needs of boys. (*San Francisco Chronicle*, December 11, 1994:A-18)

In addition to personal and sexual abuse, the polarizing and disorienting effect of street living is overwhelming. These are children who, without any support structures, must cope with childhood in adult terms, yet deal with adults as children. In either case, they stand *denied of their childhood,* and *exploited because of it.* Their work options and work loads globally are horrendous, ranging from street cleaning, rag picking, petty trading, and hawking, to drug and dope pushing, pornography, prostitution, begging, stealing, and kidnapping.

Although studies of street children show a greater resilience and self-confidence among them, it is maturity and savvy gained at a high personal and societal cost and at the cost of childhood's dignity.

EXPLOITATION OF GIRLS' LABOR

Whether on the street, in the home, or at the work place, the effect of child labor is constricting, and the robbing of childhood only its most demeaning and generic loss. There are other significant losses. Excessive manual and physical work lead to poor nutrition and stunted growth for the girl, much of which is irreversible. The heavy work burden, reinforced by other constraints in rural and poor urban areas, represents a strong, inhibiting factor in her participation in learning activities. While thus occupied in homes and homebound industries, girls are naturally withdrawn from schools or never sent there. Since more boys than girls go to school, their hours at school constitute a respite from work. But the girl is not so privileged.

Working in the gray zone between the black and white of census mislabeling and the reluctant arm of welfare law, the status of the working girl child violates young human dignity and is an affront to childhood's rights.

Children come *cheap* and girls come *cheaper.* In an entrepreneurial context, where the cost factor operates autonomously of ethics, girls provide labor at the lowest cost to parents or other employers. Women's wages are lower than those paid to males, and tasks exclusively or primarily earmarked for girls, as for women, command less compensation than those performed by men and boys. The same gender disparity is perpetrated within the household.

Negative socialization, one that binds the girl to her role and restrictions, comes easy and early. In anecdotal accounts, young girls from rural areas (in India, for instance) unhesitatingly affirm that they *understand* and *accept* gender discrimination. Perceiving themselves as transit passengers in their natal homes, they feel the compulsion to compensate and serve their parents and siblings, since marriage is most certainly a point from where further burden-sharing with parents is neither possible nor permitted. Their brothers, on the other hand, need to go to school and to work less at home, since the eventual onus of parental care will be on them. There is a serious and sad flaw in the acculturation process that fosters childhood, yet relegates the girl to a subsidiary, transitory role, without autonomy or entitlement, and living in the natal home principally on borrowed time.

Poor or no wages, hard work (seven to fourteen hours per day from age 6 and above), exploitative and hazardous work conditions, unskilled nature of work, no formal schooling, no provision for skills training or upgrading, no mobility or capability to choose alternate work or lifestyle, less value as worker compared with the boy, less parental pampering and recognition, and less time to dream and prepare for the future. These form gruesome scenarios wherein the young female's life and labor are contextualized, day after day, hour after hour. But even in the best scenarios afforded by developed countries, the girl is still cramped within the congested walls of her status as the subsidiary earner and gender.

IX

VIOLENCE AGAINST GIRLS

Violence against the female is symptomatic of her low status. Insofar as such violence is prevalent in both developed and developing countries, and in traditional as well as modern societies, it is safe to suggest that it has more to do with the culture of patriarchy and "gender" than with "class," "caste," "creed," "race," or the level of socioeconomic development of a people. Violence against, or the ill-treatment of, females takes several forms:

1. *Individual acts of insult, violation, and oppression,* such as eve-teasing or street harassment, sexual abuse, sexual harassment, wife beating, rape, kidnapping, and prostitution;
2. *Collective social sanctions, customs, or punishments* which are imposed on women and girls to regulate their social and sexual conduct and behavior, such as purdah, female circumcision, foot binding; and customs and laws which control and safeguard female virginity and reproductive activity, including anti-abortion, anti-contraception, and enforced widowhood measures; and
3. *Extreme types of violence* which either force a female to take her own life or lead to her murder. Examples of such violence are deaths due to *sati* (martyrdom through self-immolation of widows in India), dowry deaths (deaths of brides under suspicious circumstances because of the inability of the bride's parents to meet the exacting material demands of the bridegroom's family), and suicide of the female due to emotional and other stresses and indignities.

All of the above forms of violence are directed at the victim but rarely caused or provoked by her. Male violence is rooted in his gender and in the manner in which he is socialized. Male aggression begins early and is absorbed culturally rather than biologically. According to existing research (Montagu,

1968:88), boys with behavioral problems far outnumber girls. In one study, the ratio of boys to girls in the problem group was four to one. Undesirable behaviors reported as occurring much more frequently in boys than in girls are: "truancy, destruction of property, stealing, profanity, disobedience, defiance, cruelty, bullying and rudeness. And what is even more significant, a larger number of undesirable behavior manifestations per child were reported for boys than for girls. Boys are much less in control than girls."

Referring to an investigation of 579 nursery-school children, Montagu (1968:88) notes that among those from 2 to 4 years of age, boys were found more often to grab toys, attack others, rush into danger, refuse to comply, ignore requests, laugh, squeal, and jump around excessively. "Girls are quieter, more frequently exhibit introverted and withdrawing behavior, such as avoiding play, staying near an adult from whom they seek praise, and giving in too easily. All investigators agree that boys of all school ages are more quarrelsome and aggressive than girls." (Montagu, 1968:88)

Although aggressiveness is encouraged in the male child, the female child is urged to assimilate qualities of meekness and gentleness in her attitude as well as her behavior. Assertiveness among girls is thought of as an aberration but among boys is praised as showing independence. On the other hand, domesticity is exclusively cultivated among female children. The belief that the female is "of the home" and the male "of the outside" is carefully projected and perpetuated through child-rearing practices. The notion that men are the principal earners and anchors of the household, as well as of the economy, is fostered within the family and in schools.

A recent report on sexual violence against women in Europe observes that, "Violence against women originates in a number of assumptions about the respective roles of men and women. . .Behavior patterns and prejudices associated with sexual differences are acquired in early childhood. School offers tremendous opportunities for perpetuating or conversely transforming these stereotypes." Proceedings of a recent Inter-American Consultation of Women and Violence also point to the existing patriarchal system as being the fundamental cause of violence against women. Among the factors contributing to such violence are "domination and authoritarian relations; male power as the governing principle of social relations; economic factors; socialization norms employed in the education of children; aggressive behavior for men; passive behavior for women; and violence suffered by children in the family . . ." (WIN *News,* 1998:38-39)

Violence against the female takes place within and outside the home, and is the most potent form and outcome of sexism. It affects the female from her birth; in some cultures, from her conception. Violence against the female fetus and child occurs, as was pointed out in earlier chapters, in countries and cultures which have a distinct preference for sons. As childhood passes, the veil or purdah takes over to isolate the girl from the boy, and to begin the confinement of the female to the family. Adolescence and menarche cause further restrictions—behavioral, social, and intellectual. Girls have to stay away from any kind of social interaction to safeguard their bodies and virginity, and uphold their family's name and honor.

The isolation and imprisoning of the young girl by hiding her behind the veil is only one of the ways in which traditional societies restrict the female's freedom of movement. Drastic measures, such as foot binding in China and the practice of female infibulation or circumcision in African and Islamic countries, have been adopted. Yet another method is child marriage, which is widely practiced and provides an effective way to limit and control the emerging risk of adolescent sexuality. Rather than introducing stringent restrictions and penalties on irresponsible male sexual behavior, societies everywhere have found it easier and more acceptable to manipulate and coerce women into sexually and biologically stratified lifestyles.

Male concern for keeping the female subservient has manifested itself in a societal fixation on female chastity. This preoccupation also provides evidence of the male's envy of the female's procreative ability. Montagu (1968:53) observes that while maternity is certain beyond doubt, paternity is only an uncertain belief. Men feared betrayal by women and therefore created harsh punishments and practices to control women's sexual behavior. The use of the chastity girdle, in medieval times, and the use of infibulation in Africa, today, are some ways used to ensure female chastity. Double standards of morality were adopted, which caused female adultery to be punished by death, heavy fines, or stoning but not when committed by men. Similarly, prostitutes were punished but not as often as their male clients. Virginity in girls is prized and demanded by all cultures but not for males. In fact, obsessive concern with virginity has been responsible for stringent sexual and social behavioral norms even for widowed women. In such countries as India, widows traditionally have suffered a terribly stigmatized status and are banned from a normal lifestyle; they are denied certain types of clothing and foods, participation in cultural and religious functions, and recreational opportunities. In more extreme instances, they were (in rare cases, are) even encouraged to immolate themselves on the funeral pyres of their husbands. In other cases, they were and are forced to re-marry one of the males from within the same family in order to keep the family's assets from transferring to another person or family, and possibly also to preserve the family's lineage.

VIOLENCE AND GIRLS

The major and most devastating consequences of female gender-directed violence are borne by girls. It is they who must sometimes forfeit their lives; whose chastity is feared and tested; who are veiled, foot bound, and circumcised to keep them in check; who are married as children; who are widowed as children and forced to live bleak lives in widowhood; who face the humiliation of lack of acceptance by their husbands or their families for reasons outside their control; and who are forced to give up their childhood to act as surrogate mothers and caregivers. They are physically, sexually, or psychologically abused as children; sexually harassed in the streets, schools, and in the work place; and experience date rape and other forms of violence from young boys and men. They are denied adequate contraception knowledge and services, including abortion facilities, to prevent unwanted births from occurring; they are compelled to shape, beautify, and starve their bodies to make themselves acceptable to men; they are sexually exploited and lured into marketing their bodies in prostitution and pornographic trades; and they face the most risks of sexual abuse from family members and the community because of their age and gender.

Abuse and violence are an integral part of daily life for many girls. According to recent studies in the United States, "one out of three girls is molested before the age of 18 as compared to one out of ten boys."[1] Sadly, although girls report high levels of violence in their lives, that violence receives little attention from development. Violence in families takes the form of physical, verbal, psychological, and sexual abuse, as well as neglect. Adults who work with girls report that sexual abuse has a devastating impact on a girl's sense of self. But the trauma too often is exacerbated by the fact that victims of sexual abuse are not readily believed. "Some family members, including mothers, consciously or unconsciously collude with the perpetrator in order to keep the family intact. The pressure on girls who are victims of sexual abuse to remain silent is enormous." (Kristen Golden, "What do Girls See?," *Ms Magazine.* May/June 1994:55) A study of 450 adults in the United States who had been sexually abused in childhood revealed that nearly 60 percent had repressed their memories. The earlier the abuse and the more violent it is, the more likely it is to be repressed in memory. (Davis in *This World* in *San Francisco Chronicle*, 29 September, 1991:12) Some of the principal forms of violence against girls are reviewed in the sections that follow. Those such as early marriage and son preference have been treated in earlier chapters.

CHINESE CUSTOM OF FOOT BINDING

The custom of binding a little girl's feet began in China in the Tenth Century A.D. It originated in response to the whimsical desire of the Chinese Emperor Li Yo that the female foot should be pointed like "the points of a moon sickle." To achieve that look, cloth bindings were tied on a girl's feet when she was but 3–5 years old. The four smaller toes were bent underneath the foot and held in that bent position by a bandage or binding about 2 inches wide and 10 feet long. Due to the pressure applied, the toes were broken, eventually atrophied, and dropped off. As recently as 1934, an elderly Chinese woman recalled, "I was inflicted with the pain of foot binding when I was 7 years old. . .I was told that a girl had to suffer twice, through ear piercing and foot binding. . .it took two years to achieve the 3-inch-model foot. My toenails pressed against the flesh like thin paper. . .my feet became humped, ugly, and odiferous; how I envied the natural-footed!" (Dworkin, in FFII, 1989:16–17)

Bound feet could only have been a liability; walking must have required tremendous exertion. But the myth perpetuated was that the resultant hobbled gait so tightened the muscles in the genital region that sleeping with a woman with bound feet was like sleeping with a virgin. Western medical sources, however, point out that there was no physiological effect on the vagina from foot binding, although the direction of the pelvis was somewhat distorted as a result of bound feet. (FFII, 1989:17, 116)

Whatever its sexual effect, foot binding severely curtailed female mobility. The custom was widely followed by the wealthy classes who glorified, demanded, and could sustain the "idleness" and "immobility" of their women. Among the lower classes, the feet were bound more loosely so as to enable poorer women to walk and work. For either class of women, the custom helped to ensure "female chastity in a nation of women who literally could not 'run around.' Fidelity, and the legitimacy of children, could be reckoned on." (Dworkin:18)

The custom was widespread in China until it was outlawed in 1911. But, as Dworkin points out, it was outlawed only after millions of women, over a period of a thousand years, were brutally crippled and mutilated in the name of erotica and beauty; after millions of men, over the same period, reveled in love-making devoted to the worship of the bound foot; and after millions of mothers mutilated their daughters for the sake of a secure marriage. But this one-thousand year period is "only the tip of an awesome, fearful iceberg; an extreme and visible expression of romantic attitudes, processes, and values organically rooted in all cultures, then and now. It demonstrates that man's love for woman, his sexual adoration of her, his human definition of her, his delight and pleasure in her, require her negation: physical crippling and psychological lobotomy." (21)

FEMALE CIRCUMCISION OR GENITAL MUTILATION

Female circumcision is a euphemism for female clitoridectomy or infibulation, a widely practiced custom in such developing countries as Egypt, Ethiopia, Kenya, Somalia, Sudan, Yemen, and Muslim West Africa. The custom is their societies' way of protecting the girl's chastity. Although referred to as female circumcision, it is "hardly as harmless or superficial as male circumcision. In actuality, it equates to slicing off the glans penis or the entire penis." The extremely painful operation is performed on prepubescent girls. (Hosken, WIN *News,* 1988:116)

Female circumcision takes three forms. The traditional one entails the removal of the clitoral prepuce and the tip of the clitoris. In excision, the entire clitoris is removed. Infibulation involves removal of the clitoris, the labia minora, and part of the labia majora. The two sides of the vulva are partially sliced or scraped raw and then sewn together, so that the entrance to the vagina is closed except for a tiny posterior opening through which to allow urine and, later, menstrual blood, to drain. Fatalities result from hemorrhage, shock, and septicemia. Long-term problems include chronic urinary infections and difficulties in coitus and childbirth. The purpose of the operation is to prevent sexual pleasure so that women will find it easier to remain chaste. A popular belief holds that women by nature are so lascivious that chastity is inordinately difficult for them. (Huber, FFII:116)

World Health Organization researchers estimate that currently more than one-hundred million women in Africa have been genitally mutilated and an estimated two million young girls undergo it each year, sometimes as early as age 2. UNICEF notes that at least twenty-eight countries in Africa, Arab, and Asia practice female excision. This practice poses severe health risks, as well as emotional and psychological strains for girls as they enter adolescence and adulthood. (UNICEF, 1994:35) As populations migrate from continental Africa, clitoridectomy has been imported into Australia, England, France, Italy, and the United States. In some countries, modern health-care systems are being harnessed to carry out these operations in a safe and hygienic manner. Nevertheless, the adverse health consequences are serious and include "possible permanent health damage, hemorrhage, tetanus, infections of the urinary tract, scarring which obstructs normal childbirth, and possibly even infertility." Other associated risks are "life-long frigidity, painful intercourse, menstrual problems, fistulae, incontinence, and a number of other permanent disabilities, as well as psychological trauma." (Hosken, 1988)

Since the early 1970s, when the risks of these biologically and psychologically violative practices were publicized, an active movement grew to oppose them. Following an international seminar on traditional practices affecting the health of women and children in 1984, an Inter-African Committee on Traditional Practices was created. It is a non-governmental, nonprofit body and works through national committees in every African country. In several countries it has the support of the host government. The purpose of these groups is to execute programs combating harmful traditional practices and promoting beneficial ones. The long-range objective is to minimize and eventually eradicate genital mutilation through a concerted strategy encompassing public and parental awareness, governmental support, legal reform, vigilant enforcement, and the training of health workers to treat and rehabilitate those who have experienced mutilation. Despite these efforts, a decline in incidence is neither accurately known nor is expected to be significant.

Efforts to eradicate these harmful health practices invoke a divisive response. Those who are sensitive to the risk of western cultural imperialism strongly defend the right of developing countries to follow their own cultures and customs, without having to answer to the presumed higher moral authority of civilized western cultures. Others believe that women's causes should be supported and the mutilation of female bodies challenged universally, irrespective of cultural and national autonomy considerations. This viewpoint claims that efforts to discard these customs should be pursued while full sensitivity is shown toward traditional values and behavioral patterns. It is hard to understand why such customs as foot binding, child marriage, and widow-burning should be renounced by some cultures while other cultures are permitted the autonomy of retaining female genital mutilation if they wish. (Hosken, 1988)

Sexual tampering is not a trivial subject; certainly it is one on which there can be no ambivalence. Yet the issue, like purdah, sati, and other customary forms of violence against the female divides gender. It also pits culture against country and religion against reform. Yet, because these practices restrict and immobilize women either biologically or sociologically, they need to be tackled. If cultural autonomy did not get in the way of fighting colonialism and apartheid, a world officially committed to parity between peoples and sexes cannot afford, in this instance, to look the other way. Pressure must be mounted to confront and convince those who believe the female gender profits from culturally and biologically constraining practices. Countries can and must be allowed to believe that female infibulation, social seclusion, and other gender-directed malpractices are *their* problem to be solved by *them* in *their* way;" but their fundamental obligation to find and enforce appropriate solutions cannot remain unfulfilled. Cultural and religious autonomy must be tempered to pay homage to the supremacy of the human right of both genders to sociobiological protection and parity.[2] (See Box 11, on "General Recommendation on Female Circumcision")

DOWRY AND SATI CUSTOMS IN INDIA

Dowry and sati—essentially, murder—are two of the most serious atrocities committed against women and girls. Largely practiced in India, this form of violence is most demeaning since it is perpetrated by the girl's in-laws, with the expectation that she will have no further option than to stay married or accept death. Violence in, or as a result of, marriage is particularly debilitating in such a society as India, where less than 1/2 of 1 percent of women never marry, and a high premium is placed on the inevitability and permanence of

---

Box 11

General Recommendation on Female Circumcision

From: The Committee on Elimination of Discrimination Against Women.

Concerned about the continuation of the practice of female circumcision and other traditional practices harmful to the health of women.

Noting with satisfaction that governments, where such practices exist, national women's organizations, non-governmental organizations, and bodies of the U. N. system, such as the World Health Organization and the U. N. Children's Fund, as well as the Commission on Human Rights and its Sub-Commission on Prevention of Discrimination and Protection of Minorities, remain concerned with the issue, having recognized that such traditional practices as female circumcision have serious health and other consequences for women and children.

Taking note with interest of the study of the Special Rapporteur on Traditional Practices Affecting the Health of Women and Children, (E/CN.4/Sub.2/42) and of the study of the Special Working Group on Traditional Practices. (E/CN.4/1986/42)

Recognizing that women are taking important action themselves to identify and to combat practices that are prejudicial to the health and well-being of women and children.

Convinced that the important action that is being taken by women and by all interested groups needs to be supported and encouraged by governments.

Noting with grave concern that there are continuing cultural, traditional, and economic pressures which help to perpetuate harmful practices, such as female circumcision.

Recommends that States parties:

(a) *Take* appropriate and effective measures with a view to eradicate the practice of female circumcision. Such measures:

(b) *Include* in their national health policies appropriate strategies aimed at eradicating female circumcision in public health care. Such strategies could include the special responsibility of health personnel, including traditional birth attendants, to explain the harmful effects of female circumcision;

(c) *Invite* assistance, information and advice from the appropriate organizations of the U. N. system to support and assist efforts being deployed to eliminate harmful traditional practices;

(d) *Include* in their reports to the Committee under Articles 10 and 12 of the Convention on the Elimination of All Forms of Discrimination Against Women information about measures taken to eliminate female circumcision.

Source: U.N., Division for the Advancement of Women, Vienna, Women 2000. No. 3, 1992:9

marriage for every girl, virtually from the moment of her birth. Dowry and sati represent two exploitative and sexist responses to that peculiar cultural milieu in which the female's entity is incomplete and dishonorable, except as a married woman.

For parents eager to find a suitable match for their daughter, dowry has long been both a bait or an unofficial price for obtaining a bridegroom. Such a marital custom enhances the status of the boy and devalues that of the girl, with a similar impact on the status of their respective families. Although in theory it is a gift willingly given to enable a bride to set up her household and be somewhat self-reliant, for several centuries dowry, in practice, has evolved to mean an expected or demanded payment for marriage. "If not forthcoming, there is pressure applied to extract or even extort it. The woman becomes a hostage in the hands of the husband's people. First, her whole future is threatened by the possibility of the marriage breaking up and of her being left high and dry because the process of marriage for her is by and large irreversible. Worse still, she is in immediate danger of physical maltreatment." Being alone in a strange household, with no one on her side, she often actually suffers physical abuse. "In any case, being constantly among hostile people, she loses her mental and psychological peace. . .In this precarious situation she is exploited fully to put pressure on her parents and their reluctance (or inability) to fulfill the demands invites further wrath upon her which many a time results in extreme physical harm (even suicide or death by 'murder')." (Atre, 1988:73)

Dowry murders staged as suicides or deaths caused by "natural" causes are a widely prevalent and some suspect, a growing phenomenon in India and some of its neighboring countries. As the economic capability of families worsens due to inflationary pressures, and as their material aspirations rise, the greed for dowry is accentuated. Parents openly hawk their sons' professional qualifications and inferred earning capability over a lifetime, to extract the best dowry possible from girls. Often bride selection rests on how much dowry she is able to bring. In unusually avaricious families, dowry-seeking becomes habitual and may extend beyond one marriage. The first bride may be expelled from the house, killed, or forced to commit suicide in order to make room for another, more dowry-endowed bride. Police records in major Indian cities are filled with instances of girls who were married off at the age of 10 or 11, and who formally moved in with their husband's family only after age 18 or 19. Subsequently they were harassed, beaten, and starved to bring pressure on their parents to better cater to the dowry expectations of the husbands and their families. Such scenarios are a common experience of women from all segments of Indian society, rural or urban; poor, middle class, or wealthy; educated or uneducated. Supposedly, there is simply no alternative to a marriage that is perceived to be a "commercial" failure other than the bride's death, made to appear as some kind of accident.

Although such deaths occur annually for thousands of Indian women, the reported incidence is much less than its suspected actual incidence. Insofar as girls, because of their age, are more vulnerable to the vindictive pressures of a dowry-obsessed culture, it is evident that they are probably paying a higher price for inadequate dowry than women, often with their lives.

During the 1970s, considerable pressure was brought on the Indian government and policy-makers to deal more effectively with the dowry issue. Women activists took to the streets to protest dowry-related oppression. The media began to widely publicize instances of violence against women. Accordingly, a joint-committee of the Indian Parliament was set up to examine the Indian Dowry Prohibition Act of 1961 in order to suggest amendments to help it to cope more effectively with the dowry menace. An amended act was passed in 1984, followed by a second amended version in 1986. Under the new legislation, protection is extended to the complainant, the period of limitation for filing complaints has been removed, and the court can now act on its own knowledge or on a complaint by a recognized welfare organization. Concurrently, a new section on "dowry murder" has been introduced in the Indian Penal Code. The Indian Evidence Act has also been amended to shift the burden of proof to the husband and his family for cases where dowry is demanded and the bride dies within seven years of her marriage, except under normal circumstances. Advertisements offering consideration for marriage are now punishable.

The amended law and the activism and vigilance of women, as well as of welfare agencies, has led to social awareness of the crime, which is reflected in an increase in the number of offenses recorded. There is "no significant reversal of the trend, however, nor any visible change in attitudes even among the educated urban elite." (Government of India, 1988:139)

Unfortunately, dowry-related oppression is not confined to India. Deaths caused as a result of unrequited dowry demands are evident in other South

Asian countries. In a report from Bangladesh, Home Minister Abdul Matin told Parliament that 290 women had been killed and 545 had been kidnapped during the period January 1986 to March 1987. According to the police, many of the women died after they were tortured by husbands or in-laws demanding dowry from the brides' families. In some cases, disappointed suitors killed their intended brides by spraying them with acid. (FFII, 1989:430)

THE PRACTICE OF SATI

The custom of sati has its origins in the patriarchal society's obsession with female monogamy. It was meant to spare widows from the temptations of sexual defiance or defilement by requiring them to be immolated with their dead husbands on the funeral pyre. Widowhood was believed to be somehow unholy and inauspicious. It was considered to be an outcome of the widow's misdeeds in an earlier life, and a life-long curse. By allowing her the right to die an honorable and courageous death, the sati custom was devised as a way to help save the widow from a life of extreme simplicity and austerity entailing severe penance, denial, fasting, remorse, and shame, as well as to protect her from being ill-treated by her in-laws. There were, in addition, material reasons justifying sati. Her death prevented disputes over custody rights of the children, or her claim to a share in the husband's estate. Since re-marriage for women was almost unknown among Hindu families in India, death, destitution, or, in some instances, prostitution, were the only options open to widows. In order to encourage her to opt willingly for self-immolation, an aura of holiness or saintliness was attributed to this act so that women who committed sati were often celebrated and worshiped as goddesses.

Whatever the rationale, it is difficult to imagine or presume that a widow would willingly throw herself onto a funeral pyre. As one scholar (Daly in FFII, 1988:429–30) has observed, the issue of *willingness* is debatable. The Webster's Dictionary definition of sati as "the act or custom of a Hindu woman *willingly* [emphasis added] cremating herself or being cremated on the funeral pyre of her husband as an indication of her devotion to him" is open to serious questioning. So is the body of religious and folk mythology in India which perceives and presents sati as an act of glory *willingly* chosen by a widow. Far from being voluntary, a desperation is implied in the act which is as representative of the widow's suicidal frame of mind as her hysterical fear of having to face the consequences at the hands of her husband's relatives should she decide not to commit sati.

Although glorified and recommended, the custom of sati was not as widely practiced as the custom of foot binding in China. (FFII, 1988:116) Yet, even though sati was banned in 1829 by the British colonial administration, there were occasional known and possibly many more unknown cases of sati being committed in India. Since marriages occurred among Indian females at a very early age, and marriage to a considerably older husband was customary, it is likely that the brunt of widowhood, and of widow-related malpractices and violence, was borne by the girl or the younger woman.

A disturbing aspect of this brutal custom has been a shocking recent incident in India. An episode of sati occurred in September 1987, in Deorala, Rajasthan—an Indian state where sati commanded considerable reverence throughout history. The irony was that this time, the sati act involved a young, educated, and urbanized girl by the name of Rup Kanwar—not by any stretch of the imagination, one unable to think for herself. The effect of this modern day sati was catastrophic. It polarized Indian opinion between those who sought to celebrate and venerate the widow's and those women activists who saw it as a revival of culturally and morally sanctioned institutional violence against females. A hasty piece of legislation was put together and passed by the Indian Parliament as the Commission of Sati (Prevention) Act, 1987, in response to the national furor by Indian women. The Act equates sati with murder. It makes glorification of the sati practice an offense and "should go far in refuting the myth that sati is a manifestation of the glory of Hindu women." (Government of India, 1988:137)

Among Indian women there is still some concern that the new law, which seeks to punish whoever "attempts to commit sati and does any act towards its commission" could be interpreted as suggesting that sati could be *voluntary*. According to women and human rights activists, no attempt at committing sati can be *spontaneous* or *voluntary*, and the law needs to convey that clearly.

While law has a role in mitigating violence and injustice against girls and women, it is also imperative that supportive services be offered to widowed and estranged women to convey to the Indian society that drastic options are not only illegal but unnecessary, and that widowhood is neither a constraint nor a curse on normal life options. Similarly, to enhance the benefit of anti-dowry legislation, a cultural and societal ethos has to be generated which values girls as themselves and not as future brides or, worse, as conduits of instant material gain.

DOMESTIC AND OTHER FORMS OF VIOLENCE AGAINST GIRLS AND WOMEN

Violence within the family and society is a chronic feature not only of "primitive" but also of modern society. Such violence differs in two respects from the collective type of violence which the female gender has to face. First, it is not perpetrated out of loyalty to any lofty cultural myths or religious sanctions but represents male oppression and manipulation of the female directly in gratification of his own needs. And second, it is inflicted surreptitiously and thus is less easily detected, treated, and punished. This individualized violence is far more frightening, as it endangers the female's physical and emotional security and human dignity on a more intrusive, chronic, and widespread basis than any other kind of violence. Despite its prevalence, such violence has remained invisible in national and international statistics and in the societal accounting of crimes against women. Although it has probably been around since the beginning of human existence, it is only in the last two decades that violence against the female in the family, in the street, in the work place, and in custodial situations has become more openly and widely monitored and discussed than before.

EVE-TEASING, SEXUAL HARASSMENT, AND BATTERING

The harassing and battering of women and girls is not a new phenomenon. Men have always used their greater masculine strength in peace and war to intimidate and violate women and girls. Such aggression manifests itself through rape, battery, sexual and physical abuse and harassment which are all deployed to scare, dominate, or overpower the female. "On several occasions since 1850, feminists in Britain and the United States have initiated campaigns to end the battering of women by husbands and lovers, but have received little sympathy or support from the public. . .Sociologists systematically ignored the existence of violence against women until 1971, when journal articles and conferences devoted to the topic of domestic violence began to appear. . .Through the efforts of grass-roots activists and academics, battering has been recognized as a widespread social problem." (Ferraro and Johnson in FFII, 1989:416)

"Eve-teasing," or harassment in a public place, as violations of the female person's dignity and privacy, has been slow to surface and catch national and international recognition. Bernard and Schlaffer (FFII 1989:384-387) contend that the behavior of the "man on the street" captures, in quintessential, almost primordial form, the combination of the ordinary and the bizarre which we have learned to regard as normal. The "man on the street" is a synonym for every man. The behavior he casually accords to randomly passing women serves to identify him as a member of the ruling group to whom the streets and the society belong. It is disconcerting but common to find adult males moaning, jumping, whistling, singing, honking, winking, contorting face and body, hissing obscenities, laughing hysterically, and mumbling hoarse endearments to female strangers without apparent provocation. However odd, these single and seemingly irrational instances add up to a pattern, and the pattern spells intimidation.

In this absurd theater of the street, women are inevitably assigned a passive part. While women have recourse to a number of responses, they recognize that their responses may make no difference. "A woman can ignore what she sees or hears, she can reply, she can curse, keep walking, stop, try for a disarming smile, get angry, start a discussion. What she does has little influence. A friendly answer may stop the man, or it may encourage him to further intimacies; threats and curses may silence him, or they may prompt genuine aggression. The language itself puts us at a permanent disadvantage; it is hard to exchange serious insults without using sexual put-downs that invariably go against women. And passers-by, far from supporting a woman who defends herself, will shed their former indifference to disapprove of feminine vulgarity." (FFII:384–387)

Although it is commonly supposed that males in certain countries and cultures display this behavior more than others, in fact this form of male behavior is distributed quite evenly across the continents, races, and generations. Like other forms of sexual violence, street harassment has little to do with individual cultures or women, but is symptomatic of the wider play of masculine aggression and patriarchy's power.

The age, education and income of the man make little difference: in their street behavior, they revert to a primordially uniform condition across the lines of class and generation. Younger men tend to be more aggressive, and older men to lower their voices and whisper hastily as they pass you. Some areas are exempt altogether: small villages, where all the inhabitants know each other, and residential suburban areas. . .Harassment is a way of ensuring that women will not feel at ease, that they will remember their role as sexual beings available to men, and not consider themselves equal citizens participating in public life. (FFII: 384–387)

As Bernard and Schlaffer suggest, "Although only a minor offender, (the street harasser is) an accomplice in the more massive forms of violence against women." In cultures where the female occupies a low status, eve-teasing appears not only as a serious affront to the personal dignity but even as a threat to the physical safety, particularly of girls but also of women. In college campuses in India, for instance, it is difficult for girls to move around freely without having their dignity and sensibility constantly violated by boorish and sexist behavior, including catcalls, name-calling, obscene gestures, and occasionally even stoning. The harassment of girls by boys in United States schools, too, is emerging as a serious issue. It ranges from comments and notes, to being pinched, grabbed, and cornered, to more physical assaults and attempted rape. A recent survey reviewing two thousand responses of girls 10–18 years of age revealed 89 percent as having been the subject of sexual comments, gestures and looks; 83 percent stated they had been touched, pinched, or grabbed. (*San Francisco Chronicle*, March 24, 1993) A survey of over one thousand, six hundred students from high schools across the United States found a similar level (85 percent) of sexual harassment experienced by girls. The extent of harassment was comparable across ethnicity, ranging from 82 percent of Hispanic girls to 84 percent of African American and 87 percent of white girls. (AAUW, 1993:7)

Similar to the public place, sexual harassment at work takes many forms, including sexual overtures, verbal abuse, touching, fondling, and use of pornographic visuals in the work place. Sexist violence also includes physical and emotional harassment, and the subtle or blatant use of sex as a means of gaining control over, seducing, blackmailing, or denying to women and girls what is their due in the way of promotion, respect, and recognition. A position of authority, whether in the work place, college, or custodial institution, such as prison, police lock-up, juvenile institution, mental home, or old-age home, enables and empowers men to intimidate and exploit women. Younger girls are naturally more susceptible to such manipulation by the male.

According to Leslie Doyle (*Women's Studies International Forum* Volume 13: 6, 1990:598), the term *sexual harassment* was first coined around 1975 to describe a range of behaviors which form part of the working conditions of most women. Furthermore, it was not until the second wave of feminism in the 1970s that sexual harassment began to emerge as a public issue. Even now it is often invisible. Until very recently, women were afraid to complain and very few employers had grievance procedures to deal with the problem. Indeed, in most workplaces a degree of sexual harassment was seen as normal, as evidenced by the very large numbers of women who report having experienced it. A large-scale study carried out by the U.S. Merit Systems Protection Board in 1981 found that 42 percent of 20,314 government employees surveyed had experienced harassment. Women in higher-status positions are victims, too. In a 1982 study, 54 percent of female British managers reported that they had experienced sexual harassment. (Cooper & Davidson, 1982 in Doyle, 1990)

The scope of the harassment women experience is broad, ranging from nude calendars on the wall, through sexual jokes and propositions, to unwanted touches and caresses, and even to rape. The vast majority of incidents involve women being harassed by men, very often those in a position of authority over them. As a result, many victims have to choose between sexual harassment and lack of promotion, low pay, or even loss of their jobs. All women are potential victims of harassment at work, just as they are in the streets or in the home. However, in practice they are most likely to be harassed if they are young and have no seniority, and if they have no obvious relationship with a man. African-American women appear to be especially vulnerable. In a study of harassment against working-class women, 36 percent of the women working in a Detroit car factory reported sexual harassment, and black women were harassed more often and more severely. (Gruber & Bjorn, 1982, in Doyle, 1990)

In recent years, largely through the catalytic impact of Anita Hill's testimony against Supreme Court Justice (then nominee) Clarence Thomas, on the issue of sexual harassment, there is greater willingness and confidence among American women to protest sexually offensive behavior. Major recent court victories, along with generous victim compensation in the United States, have reinforced the unacceptability of sexually oppressive behavior in the work place.

To help women confront and overcome this type of abuse, specific services are emerging which seek to empower women and to get them to accept that they have an inalienable right to human dignity and justice, unblemished by the favors or disfavor which their gender may evoke from the cultural, socioeconomic, and judicial system, and from its male operators. They have a right to say no, to speak up against, and to expose male invasion of their bodies and privacy. They have a right to be evaluated on the basis of their skills and not their physical traits or sexual behavior, and they have a right of access to a fair legal procedure to seek compensation from their perpetrators.

DOMESTIC VIOLENCE

National and international data on the terrible phenomenon of the indignity and violence experienced by the female within or outside the home are not readily available or forthcoming. Such data as exist cannot be considered reliable since they represent merely the tip of the iceberg. In more conventional cultures there is considerable hesitation to speak openly about sexuality, or about sex-related violence. But, as a recent U.N. report has noted, "Domestic violence against women exists in all regions, classes and cultures." Domestic violence is inflicted on "a family's weakest members—women, children, the very old, and the disabled. It manifests itself in habitual physical abuse, psychological torture, deprivation of basic needs, and sexual molestation. Secrecy, insufficient evidence, and social and legal barriers continue to make it difficult to acquire accurate data on domestic violence against women—which many criminologists believe to be the most underreported crime. Most data on violence against women are compiled from small studies, giving only a glimpse of what is assumed to be a worldwide phenomenon. They cannot be used to provide precise indicators on the extent of violence against women, but they do show that violence in the home is common and that women are most frequently the victims." (U.N., 1991:19)

Among countries at radically different stages of development, the incidence of female-directed domestic violence is disturbingly similar. According to the United Nations (1991:19) and World Watch Institute (*World Watch*, March-

April 1989:14), domestic violence against the wife was cited as a contributory factor for the breakdown of marriage in seven hundred thirty-five, or 59 percent of the one thousand, five hundred divorce cases studied in Austria in 1985. Fifty-four percent of all murders in Austria were committed in the family, with women and children constituting 90 percent of the victims. In Colombia, in 1982–1983, one out of five bodily injury cases was due to conjugal violence, and 94 percent of those hospitalized were battered women. India had 999 cases of dowry deaths registered in 1985 and 1,786 in 1987. Of 153 Kuwaiti women, 80 percent said that they knew of friends or relatives who had been victims of domestic violence, and 30 percent confessed to having been assaulted. In Thailand, 25 percent of malnourished children at a nutrition-rehabilitation center were from families where mothers were regularly beaten by the husbands. More than 50 percent of married women in a slum and construction site in Bangkok stated that they were regularly beaten by their husbands. In the barrios of Quito, Ecuador, over 80 percent of women interviewed had been beaten by their partners. In Sao Paulo, Brazil, eighteen thousand cases of battering were reported to the police during 1986 and 1987. In Peru, 70 percent of all crimes reported to the police are of women beaten by their partners.

In the United States, a National Crime Survey of 1976 reported that one-fourth of all assaults against women who had ever been married were committed by their husbands or ex-husbands; in a 1975 study, 3.8 percent of the women surveyed had experienced severe violence in their marriage. (FFII, 1989:416) According to frequently quoted Federal Bureau of Investigation's statistics, one in three women in America will be assaulted or raped in her lifetime; one in four will be the victim of such an attack before the age of 18. As many as 20 percent of all hospital emergency-room cases are related to wife battering. Moreover, as contended by the National Organization of Women (Executive Director's testimony before the United States Senate Judiciary Committee): "Every 15 seconds a woman is beaten by her husband or boyfriend; every six minutes a woman is raped; and one-fifth to one-half of American women are sexually abused as children, most of them by an older male relative." (San Mateo Battered Women's Services, *Shelter News*, Spring, 1991)

In the United States, it is estimated that 95 percent of the victims of domestic violence are women. (WIN *News*, 17-3, Summer, 91:43) Although there are male victims, "the ordeal of gender-motivated crime is borne overwhelmingly by women and girls. Nearly one-third of female homicides are committed by husbands or boyfriends. . .Those crimes are part of a social pattern. . .that is founded on a deep-seated and widespread view that women's lives are worth less than men's lives." (*Shelter News*, 1991)

According to the United Nations, (1991:63) sexual assaults against women and children include defilement, indecent exposure, unlawful carnal knowledge, and rape. In Canada, women are about seven times more likely to be sexually assaulted than men. Countries are also noting increased public acknowledgment of rape. In Trinidad and Tobago, while the population increased 28 percent between 1970 and 1980, the number of men charged with rape rose 134 percent. In the United Kingdom, the number of reported rapes grew from 1,334 in 1983 to 1,842 in 1985. Despite increased reporting, crimes against women are hard to punish, given legal laxities, procedural ambiguities, and male gender biases inherent in criminal justice systems. In the United States, for instance, "Only 1 in 10 rapes are ever reported to authorities; less than 40 percent of reported rapes result in arrest; about 1 percent of rapists are convicted. . .The criminal justice system places an exceptionally high burden of proof upon rape survivors. A raped woman is often subjected to demeaning examination of her personal life and previous sexual history—even her attire is questioned. Rape survivors often report feeling humiliated, accused and alienated from the very system that is supposed to help them. . .This must stop. . .Rapists, not women survivors, must be placed on trial." (WIN *News*, 17-3, Summer, 91:43)

The issue of the female's safety in the home or the bedroom has been left mainly outside the scope of law in most countries, until very recently. Yet it is on the protection of her safety and dignity in the home that the realization of her human rights closely depends. Obviously then, there is a vital need for substantive changes in the law as it concerns the concepts underlying crimes against women. Atray (1989:133) observes that "New concepts regarding marriage, protection of women, economic security for women, punishment of defaulters, imposition of fines, delays in courts, etc., have to be introduced and certain old concepts of jurisprudence and male superiority, which in this case even extend to giving concessions to the accused, have to be discarded." In several countries, as in the United States, mandatory arrest laws have been enacted which compel the police to arrest the batterer. "Evidence indicates that mandatory arrests stop the escalating cycle of repeated violence in the home. Moreover, battered wives in some states have successfully sued police for failure to provide them the same protection as victims of any other type of assault." (WIN *News,* 1991:43)

In many cases, administrative inertia in tracking and curbing violence against women and girls reflects legislative ambiguity and dispersal. Traditionally, such violence has not elicited concerted, comprehensive legislation, or judicial processing. Yet, rather than have a widely dispersed body of law dealing with violence against the woman, which leads to unnecessary confusion, delay, and divisiveness in dealing out justice to female victims of violence, it seems reasonable, as some scholars and policymakers have suggested, to have an all-encompassing legislation: "a comprehensive law for the safety and protection of women against crimes and against exploitation which should cover all aspects of the problem confronting them from birth, through youth till death. . .There is hardly any scope for contradiction within the various branches of the law if all aspects are covered under a single canopy." (Atray, 1989:134)

Support for a comprehensive type of legislation to combat violence against women is building in several countries. In the United States, for instance, the Violence Against Women Act of 1991, seeks to reduce the intolerable level of violence against women by increasing penalties for sex crimes as well as protecting women from abusive spouses. In addition, this legislation defines gender-motivated crimes as bias crimes that deprive victims of their civil rights.

The comprehensive approach helps to single out the problem of violence and criminality against girls and women within and outside the home, for treatment at all levels of government and society, and rules out some of the inequity which traditionally pervades criminal and civil actions against perpetrators of violence against women. The underlying promise of the new legislative approach is a belief in the absolute inviolability of the female person against threats, intimidation, and physical, emotional, or sexual abuse, whether in the home, the street, the workplace, or in any other institution.

To be effective, such legislation has to be armed adequately with: i) clear and tougher sentencing guidelines, including mandatory minimum sentencing in defined situations; and ii) adequate enforcement and administrative machinery—including special women's courts, more police, prosecutorial and welfare personnel, longer prison sentences and better prevention programs, more legal aid and other assistance for victims, better-lit streets and institutional campuses, and bigger budgets.

Legislation alone, however, will not eradicate violence against the female. Protective and rehabilitative provisions in law and services, victim compensation and counseling, orientation training of justices, police and other bureaucracies placed in charge of dealing with crimes against women, more aggressive enforcement of crime prevention and preemption, as well as punishment, treatment, and rehabilitative policies, are the integral components of a more progressive and determined societal action on behalf of girls and women. Finally, massive educational campaigns to educate families, employers, children, youth, and other groups on the symptoms, nature, and magnitude of violence against, and abuse of, women and girls are central to a more effective and vigilant enforcement of law. An ethos of collective care and responsible conduct toward the female has to be created in all societies, irrespective of their superficial level of development.

Scholars, such as Ferraro and Johnson (in FFII, 1989:416), state that "Material and cultural conditions are the background in which personal interpretations of events are developed." The social and cultural expectations of women and their status within the nuclear family are widely believed to account for the reluctance of battered women to flee abusive relationships. The socialization of women "emphasizes the primary value of being a good wife and mother, at the expense of personal achievement in other spheres of life. The patriarchal ordering of society assigns a secondary status to women and provides men with ultimate authority, both within and outside the family unit. . .In sum, the position of women in American society makes it extremely difficult for them to reject the authority of men and develop independent lives free of marital violence." (417) If cultural and material factors can so significantly constrain women in one of the more affluent and supposedly liberal societies, such as is represented by the United States, the impact of those factors on the female's status and individual rights in more conventional and developing societies, and the need to launch concerted societal action to cope with those disabilities, can hardly be overstated.

RAPE

Rape is one of the feared certainties with which girls grow up in every country and culture. It affects their physical mobility and psychological liberation. Each girl, as she grows into womanhood, is taught fear.

> I have never been free of the fear of rape. From a very early age I, like most women, have thought of rape as part of my natural environment— something to be feared and prayed against like fire or lightning. . .At the age of eight. . .my grandmother took me to the back of the house where the men wouldn't hear, and told me that strange men wanted to do harm to little girls. I learned not to walk on dark streets, not to talk to strangers, or get into strange cars, to lock doors and to be modest. She never explained why a man would want to harm a little girl, and I never asked. (Griffin, in FFII, 1989:388)

As a gesture, forcible sexual intercourse typifies male aggression and domination over the female; as a crime it elicits celebrated coverage not only in the visual and print media of modern times but also in the master paintings of yesteryear. (The *Rape of the Sabine Women* is just one example.) Yet it is the least studied, analyzed, or reported in contemporary society. In most countries, criminologists and social scientists widely believe that the incidence of reported rape is several times less than its actual incidence. Considerations of female and family honor, privacy invasion, and the risk of continued trauma and social stigma are barriers to the reporting of rape in most countries. In the United States, for instance, according to the Federal Bureau of Investigation and independent criminologists, the figure of reported rapes must be "multiplied by at least a factor of ten" to approach accuracy. Calculated thus, rape emerges as the most frequently committed violent crime today—murder, aggravated assault, armed robbery, and rape are defined as violent crimes in the United States. (Griffin:388) In India, although the incidence of reported rape nearly doubled between 1976 and 1985, "the available statistics do not represent even 25 percent of the total because it is well-known that in actual practice hardly one-fourth of the cases are reported." (Atray, 1988:56)

Even when reported, rape cases remain on the back burners in the criminal justice system. In New Delhi, India, for example, of the 226 cases registered with the police over the period 1977–1979, "only 58 cases ended in conviction in the trial courts and the culprits in 130 cases were acquitted.

Leaving aside the 33 cases that were found to be false and canceled by the police the percentage of acquittals is as high as 66. It would go still higher as all the convictions in the lower court may not be upheld in the High Courts. . .The figures also bring out another unfortunate situation: that a sizable number of cases were still pending trial in 1982, a period of three to five years from the date of occurrence of the cases." (Atray:57) In the United States, rape is observed to have the highest rates of acquittal and dismissal and the lowest rate of conviction among the four major crimes of violence. For those who are convicted, the most common disposition is probation with mandatory treatment. (Lott, 1994:171)

Sluggish judicial processing in India, the United States, and elsewhere is the result of an inherently prejudiced male-dominated administrative machinery, brought up in the Freudian ethic of believing that sexual abuse of children (mostly girls subjected to incest) was wished or invited by them, and that women enjoyed being raped. (See Box 12, on "Judge Faces Recall," and Box 13, page 156, on "Fiji Probes Acquittal of Six Men in Sex Case") It is "depressing to note that to this day many judges in the United States follow these ideas. Indeed, the courts in the United States today are the most recalcitrant anti-feminist, especially in cases of rape, incest, and wife abuse." (WIN News, 16-1 1990:41) The tests applied by the judiciary, as noted with respect to India, are so ridiculous that rarely does a case of sexual assault on women succeed in a court of law. The public criticism of the Supreme Court decision in the Mathura (name of the raped girl) case acquitting two guilty policemen, who had raped a *harijan* girl in a police station on the plea that the intercourse appeared to be a peaceful affair, is only "symptomatic of the deep-rooted malaise from which the system of criminal justice suffers. . .The record of convictions is so uniformly dismal that it has dashed to the ground all hopes of building up any deterrents within the existing criminal procedure." (Atray, 1988:67)

The theory that women invite or enjoy being raped is at the root of the apathy or antipathy against the victims of rape. The perception that females enjoy being raped "extends itself by deduction into the proposition that most or much of rape is provoked by the victim. But this, too, is only myth. Though provocation, considered a mitigating factor in a court of law, may consist of only 'a gesture,' according to the Federal Commission of Violence, only 4 percent of reported rapes involved any precipitative behavior by the woman." (Griffin in *FFII,* 1989:389) Moreover, "the laws against rape exist to protect the rights of the male as possessor of the female body, and not the right of the female over her own body." (396) The legal position on rape "reflects this possessory view of women." (395) Rape, therefore, is not "an isolated act that can be rooted out from patriarchy without ending patriarchy itself." (398)

In recent years, as rape and sexual abuse as criminal problems have been given the open social recognition they deserve, there is an increasing incidence of reported sexual violence against the female. (See Box 14, page 157, on "Girls at Risk in Uganda") In India, "The number of assaults on female children is not only high but an increasing trend is very much in evidence. . .Over 300 cases with an average reporting rate of about 20 percent during the decade 1972–1981 would mean about 1,800 cases in the area

---

Box 12
Judge Faces Recall

A citizens group in Lancaster, Wisconsin, said Tuesday it will circulate petitions seeking the ouster of a circuit judge who called a 5-year-old sexual assault victim an "unusually sexually promiscuous young lady."

Diane Barton said her ouster group has decided "it was an irresponsible thing to say the child was promiscuous."

Mrs. Barton said she expected the petitions to be ready for distribution next week in the group's quest to force a recall election of Judge William Reinecke. Reinecke contended his remarks were taken out of context.

Reinecke made the remark in sentencing Ralph Snodgrass, 24, to 90 days in a work-release program for sexually assaulting the 5-year-old daughter of the woman with whom he was living.

The judge observed the girl was "an unusually sexually promiscuous young lady" and Snodgrass "did not know enough to refuse. No way do I believe Mr. Snodgrass initiated sexual contact."

The hired hand said he was sleeping and the girl climbed on top of him. The girl later was found to have been sexually assaulted.

The judge said he was simply trying to show that the girl, not really knowing what she was doing, was the aggressor.

Source: Reprinted from the *Columbus Citizen-Journal*, 20 January, 1982. Courtesy of Scripps Howard News Service, in *FFII*, 1989:395

under study and over one lakh (100,000) cases in the country." (Atray, 1988:64) In the United States, every forty-seven seconds, a child is abused or neglected, which translates to 675,000 a year. (Children's Defense Fund 1990:3) "Nearly 20 percent of all American women were sexually abused as children. In cases of incest, nine times out of ten, the victim is a girl. The first sexual abuse generally occurs at age 10—although 37 percent report abuse at an even earlier age. Approximately 70 percent of young prostitutes and 80 percent of female drug users were victims of incest. . .The average age of

---

Box 13
Fiji Probes Acquittal of Six Men in Sex Case

SUVA (Reuters): Fiji's top prosecutor said on December 7 she may appeal against a decision to acquit six men who pleaded guilty to defilement of a 15-year-old girl on the grounds that the girl looked "hefty" for her age.

Under Fijian law, defilement is sexual intercourse with a girl under the age of 16, with or without consent.

Director of Public Prosecutions Nazhat Shameem told Reuters she had asked for a report on the case, adding that if media reports of the case were correct she would lodge an appeal against the verdict.

Labasa Magistrate Moses Fernando on December 2 acquitted the six men who took turns having sex with the girl in a church in Labasa on the Fijian island of Vanua Levu on November 11.

Shameem said that if the intercourse with the 15-year-old girl was without consent, then the six men should have been charged with rape as well.

In handing down his ruling, Fernando is reported to have said the victim was "a well built girl who looked well over 16 years of age." He later told local media the girl was "hefty."

Vani Dulaki, coordinator of the Fiji Women's Rights Movement, said the acquittal was "pathetic and dangerous."

"The girl's appearance should have no bearing on the case," Dulaki told Reuters. "Just because she must be well-nourished, she's still a 15-year-old girl."

The case is the latest in a spate of questionable or lenient judgments in sex assault cases in Fiji, Dulaki said.

Source: *India Post*, Fremont, California, Dec. 16, 1994:A7

Box 14
Girls at Risk in Uganda

"My eight-year-old daughter Jane was defiled by my neighbor's son one evening as she was coming back from school," Andrew, the girl's father, said. "I reported the case to the police but nothing has happened yet. I fear to push the case further because I do not want to get into a conflict with my neighbor. So I have suggested that we settle the matter quietly."

Cases of defilement or sexual abuse of girls are reported every week in newspapers in Uganda. The problem of AIDS makes the incidence even more alarming: Current data indicate that HIV infection rates are six times higher among young girls than among boys.

According to a UNICEF-funded study, "Children and their rights: Village perceptions," conducted in seven districts of Uganda, the most prevalent form of child abuse is the practice of child marriage.

In some parts of the country, young girls are forced or kidnapped into marriages. Because many girls do not attend school, they become easy prey. Poverty also makes them vulnerable, especially in rural areas, with parents eager to obtain the money or cattle and other property traditionally given by prospective in-laws to a girl's family. But perhaps the most significant cause of sexual abuse of girls is the low status of women and children and their relative lack of rights.

Generally, because the law enforcement and justice systems are male dominated, offenders are let off lightly, even though the law on defilement calls for capital punishment. In many instances, the victims are afraid to testify in open court. The process of questioning is intimidating to girls already traumatized by the crime and often fails to elicit the necessary evidence. The police and local councils are often uncooperative, and many parents prefer to settle the matter out of court.

Uganda Women Lawyers, and other non-governmental organizations, are increasing advocacy activities to ensure that child defilement becomes everyone's concern. In addition, they are setting up a children's desk to deal with these cases and have now recommended to the Judicial Commission of Inquiries that defilement cases not be tried in open court, to reduce psychological trauma and stigmatization.

Source: Abridged from a longer article by Lillian Mulder Lubega, UNICEF, *First Call for Children*, July-September, 1994:10

recruitment into prostitution is 14 years." (Dworkin in *New Directions for Women*, September–October, 1991:3)

The age at which crimes against the female child occurs within the family and outside can be anywhere from infancy to toddler to adolescent stage, and the perpetrator is often a close relative or acquaintance. In the United States, a 1985 report (*Developing a National Agenda*, in Lott, 1994:166) estimated that incest occurs in 14 percent of families and is found in all family types and social classes. In 75 percent of the cases, fathers have abused daughters. Boys who are victims are also likely to have been sexually assaulted by men in their own families. Other estimates place children's sexual abuse at higher levels— about one in six Americans, or 25 to 35 percent of all women, and 10 to 16 percent of all men. (166) A 1993 study based on child-abuse cases that reached the offices of district attorneys found that the age of alleged victims ranged from 1 month to 17 years, with the average age being 9. Eighteen percent of victims were age 5 or younger, and the majority were between ages 9–12. Significantly, 80.3 percent of victims were girls and only 3 percent of abusers were female. The study also surmised that more than 90 percent of cases of sexual abuse of children are never brought to trial. (167)

The impact of rape and sexual abuse is long lasting for the adult female, but given the girl's tender age, innocence, and lack of physical maturation, it is far more debilitating for her. A study of more than 30,000 students in Minnesota confirmed that a disturbing number have been physically or sexually abused, and think seriously about committing suicide or have already attempted it. Girls tend to "self-destruct. And because they usually do not act out their troubles, as boys do, they often don't get the attention they need when they are hurting." (Dworkin, 1991:4) It is evident that for girls to emerge from under this spell of despairing endurance, there needs to be a radical reordering of gender relations and an end to male domination over the female within the family and in society.

DATE RAPE

Date rape is a phenomenon which affects girls and has emerged as a growing, articulated concern in some developed countries. In the United States, frequent slapping and roughing up of girls, threats or actual attacks on their lives, intimidation and terrorization of girls are being increasingly uncovered. "Recurring themes are found in many accounts by teenage girls, regardless of their cultural or economic backgrounds or sexual orientation. Almost universally, they speak of violence and jealousy as signs of love, the pressure to be in a relationship, and the unpredictable circumstances that have led them to be involved with violent men. . .As many as one in ten teenage girls may be experiencing dating-related violence. (Fitzsimmons, in "Book Review Section" of *San Francisco Chronicle*, July 28, 1991) Some U.S. studies report that 28 percent of adolescents have experienced physical violence in a dating relationship. (*Ms. Magazine* May/June 1994:56) Some college campuses report that from 47 to nearly 55 percent of college women have experienced coercive, assaultive, or abusive sexual behaviors since age 19. Yet other studies uncovered higher levels of unwanted sexual activity on dates (up to 70 percent of female respondents). Only a small proportion of respondents in various studies reported being raped to the police. There was also ambiguity or reluctance to identify sexual assault as rape, especially when the perpetrator was known to the victim. (Lott, 1994:169–170)

Sadly, many girls do not recognize date rape and violence as an infringement of their right to personal safety and dignity. Levy (1991, in Fitzsimmons) observes that since put-downs, threats, possessiveness, and physical intimidation are accepted as part of their interactions with one another, and often with adults as well, abusive behavior is difficult for many young people to identify until it escalates into overt violent behavior. Gamache (in Fitzsimmons) also notes that it is often difficult for young women to identify sexual abuse in their relationships and to decide how to respond. As illustrations of the above phenomenon, Gamache quotes the examples of a college sophomore whose boyfriend did not feel powerful until he had ordered her to perform sexual acts; an eleventh-grade girl who was scared to leave her boyfriend because he would hit her until she promised not to; and a first-year college student who was not permitted to look at or talk to anyone, or go out anywhere without her boyfriend.

Sadly, sexual violence against girls in personal relationships is not only prevalent but also considered natural or normal. A 1979 study investigating four thousand teenagers in Los Angeles (U.S.A.) found that only 44 percent of the girls and 24 percent of the boys believed that the use of force to have sexual intercourse with girls was never acceptable. More recently, in a 1988 study of seventeen hundred grade-six-through-nine students, about 65 percent of the boys and 47 percent of the girls believed forced intercourse is acceptable, if the couple has been dating for six to ten months. Twenty-four percent of the boys and 16 percent of the girls also found the behavior acceptable if the man had spent money on the woman. (Lott, 1994:176)

The most distressing feature of date-related violence is that the laws of most countries offer no protection from it. According to Levy, in the United States, only three states—California, Colorado, and Pennsylvania—include dating relationships within the definition of relationships protected by domestic-violence laws, and allow women under 18 to seek legal action under these laws. Some counseling and battered women's services are now beginning to address and treat issues of dating-related violence. In certain rape treatment centers, preventive programs aim at sensitizing school boys and girls to sexual stereotypes, peer pressure, dating roles, and acquainting them with what motivates rapists. Information on sexual violence is also offered on a targeted basis to various ethnic and other communities in the United States, including African Americans, Asian Americans, Hispanics, lesbians, gays, and prisoner groups. In the more culturally introverted communities and countries, such targeted awareness strategies can be immensely helpful in encouraging victims to recognize and expose where such violence occurs and in launching remedial strategies.

SPOUSAL AND OTHER RAPE

Along with date rape, spousal rape has long remained a widely prevalent but unidentified form of violence against women. These various forms of rape "are not new, although the sudden surge in consciousness makes it seem as though they are. What's new is our understanding that they are crimes. . . The image persists of the rapist lurking in the dark alley or waiting to leap from behind the bushes. That's why spousal rape and date rape have made such late entries into our understanding of sexual violence. . .The image of rapist-as-stranger misconstrues the nature of violence against women. Women's biggest threat has never been the stranger in the bushes, but the boyfriend, the husband, the stepfather, the acquaintance." (Banks in *The Peninsula Times Tribune*, 28 June, 1991) One could add father, brother, cousin, uncle, or other to the list.

A U.S. 1991 Justice Department study noted that "Violent crime against women is different than crime against men because it is six times as likely to be committed by their intimates. Twenty-five percent of the violent crime against women is committed by family members or men they have dated. . . More than five of six of the violent crimes by intimates that were reported by female victims were assaults, including attacks with weapons, beatings or threats." Other U.S. sources note that "every day four women are killed by batterers in the U.S.A.; every six minutes a rape is reported in this country; the FBI estimates that only one out of ten rapes is actually reported; one in four college women is a victim of rape or attempted rape while she is in college, mostly by someone known to the victim. . .Violence against women occurs within all races, ages, socioeconomic groups, religions and nations. It affects everyone." (WIN *News,* 17-3, Summer, 1991:40,42)

In recent years, recognition of the violence to which women and girls are exposed in their homes has caused federal or state legislatures in some countries to make spousal and date rape illegal, and to stress that a female's acceptance to go out with or marry someone does not give the man the right to have sex with her whenever he desires. In the United Kingdom, a landmark judgment in March, 1991, by the Court of Appeals, rejected the centuries-old English legal principle that a man cannot be guilty of raping his wife and ruled that "a rapist remains a rapist and is subject to the criminal law, irrespective of his relationship with his victim. . .the idea that a wife, because she had married, consented in advance to her husband having sexual intercourse whatever her state of health or proper objections was a fiction. This is not the creation of a new offense; it is the removal of a common-law fiction which has become anachronistic and offensive." (WIN *News,* 17-3, Summer, 1991:46)

TEEN SUICIDE

Teen suicide is linked to teen neglect and the overall social, psychological, and emotional turmoil or discrimination which they experience. Although the phenomenon is not widely studied, where it has been there is greater risk shown among teenage girls than boys. A recent national survey of more than 11,000 ninth-through-twelfth grade students carried out by the U.S. CDC found that 27 percent had thought seriously about killing themselves in the preceding year, and one in 12 had attempted it; 2 percent of respondents noted that in their attempts they had sustained injuries serious enough to warrant medical attention. The extent of intended suicide uncovered through the study was much higher than the annual actual suicide rate for this age group, estimated at 11 per 100,000. The study also found that thoughts of suicide were "significantly more likely" among girls than boys. Thirty percent of female students had seriously contemplated suicide, and 10 percent had attempted it. The corresponding figures for male students were 21 percent and 6 percent respectively. There were also significant differences in the contemplated and attempted suicide rates among ethnic groups, with the highest rates occurring among Hispanics, followed by whites and blacks. The total suicide rate for 15–19 year olds in the United States also quadrupled between 1950 and 1989, from 2.7 to 11.3 per 100,000. (*San Francisco Chronicle*, 16 Sept., 1991:A-3) Another U.S. study notes that 400,000 adolescents, over 300,000 of them girls, make unsuccessful attempts to kill themselves each year. Of the 300,000 girls, 3,000 are successful. (Organization of Deputy Sheriffs of San Mateo County, 1990:75)

International data on suicide and attempted suicide rates by boys and girls are not widely available, but could follow the pattern of higher incidence among girls. Particularly in the more sexist and feudal cultures where girls are devalued, the alienation and repression of girls would accentuate suicidal tendencies. That reported statistics do not show overwhelming numbers offers no consolation because they are not likely to be representative of actual or suspected incidence. There is ample justification for intensifying investigation and public awareness of teen suicide. To prevent, preempt, reliably record, and treat suicide attempts, especially among girls, is crucial.

PORNOGRAPHY AND PROSTITUTION

"Apart from rape, the most common forms of violence against Filipino women," notes a preliminary review of the situation of children and women in the Philippines (WIN *News*, 17-3, Summer, 1991:41), are "pornography, prostitution, sibling abuse, domestic-help abuse, and child-parent abuse. The incidence rates of these forms of violence remained unmeasured and largely unreported as certain sociocultural norms, attitudes, and prejudices tend to keep victims, as well as their families, reluctant about reporting such incidents. . .The most glaring form of sexual exploitation is prostitution." Unhappy childhood, broken homes, poverty, lack of opportunities for learning and earning, and early abusive and traumatic experience push an increasing number of women and girls, not only Filipino but those in other countries as well, into prostitution. In the United States, girls are inducted into prostitution as early as age 14.

In the Asia and Pacific region, prostitution is increasing considerably. According to the Thailand-based End Child Prostitution in Asian Tourism (ECPAT), there are 300,000 child prostitutes in India, 100,000 each in Thailand, Taiwan, and Philippines, 40,000 in Vietnam, 30,000 in Sri Lanka, and many thousands in China. An estimated 150,000 Nepali girls under age 16 are kidnapped and sold to brothels in India. Around 40,000 Bengali children are prostituted in Pakistan. (UNICEF, *The Progress of Nations*, 1994:39) Factors contributing to prostitution are economic changes, rural-urban migration, high unemployment and under-employment among young people, plus the growth of the tourist industry. "Another major factor. . .is the prevalence of the ideology reinforcing male supremacy and the subordination of women. . .According to a recent report, the traffic in women and children brings even greater profits than drug trafficking or illicit arms dealing. . .In northern Thailand, it is said that trading in girls is the easiest form of illegal trading." (WIN *News*, 17-3, Summer 1991:44) Traditional practices, such as *Devadasi*—the religious consecration of virgin girls as temple workers and "religious" prostitutes in India—also perpetuate sexual slavery of girls, turning it into a sacrament.

Adolescent reproductive health always has been endangered by exploitative sexual practices particularly trafficking which is assuming threatening proportions. Twenty percent of the estimated 100,000 prostitutes in Bombay, India are presumed to be minors. A survey of 80 child prostitutes in the city revealed over 55 percent as having venereal disease, with 30 percent having signs of syphilis. (Chatterjee, 1988, pp. 94–95) Indian studies show a relationship between child marriage and prostitution. (CINI, 1988, p. 12) Data from Thailand indicate that there are 80,000 girl prostitutes under age 16. (UNICEF, Bangkok, *Situation Analysis*, 1989) Girls complete primary schooling but have poor job-related skills. Prostitution pays much better than any job they can get. There is new concern about AIDS and sexual diseases. Almost 38 percent of the girls in a rehabilitative home in Thailand were found to be suffering from venereal disease. WHO reports that one in twenty adolescents contracts STDs (sexually transmitted diseases) each year. In the United States every year, 2.5 million teenagers are infected. In Russia, students and school children made up 10 percent of the syphilis patients in 1992. In Brazil, where an estimated 24 million children live or work in the streets, approximately 2 percent are believed to be infected with HIV. Homelessness and economic hardship has led millions of children—some much younger than age 15—to become victims of sexual exploitation with its attendant growing risks related to their health and survival. (UNICEF, *First Call for Children*, July-September, 1994:8)

The recent involvement of international tourism racketeers and drug cartels in the prostitution trade has given it added economic value. Owing to risks of catching AIDS from older women, sex trading is reported to be increasingly favoring and focusing on the younger girl and child. At least thirty-two countries from Africa, Asia, and Latin America report sexual abuse of children by foreign visitors. The young female's recruitment into prostitution and pornography is rampant in developed nations, including Belgium, Bulgaria, Canada, Czechoslovakia, Germany, Hungary, Italy, Japan, Netherlands, Romania, the United States, and the former Soviet Republic. The induction of girls into the sex trade and slavery has become commonplace. *(Time* Magazine, June 21, 1993:46) This is a sad and indefensible trend which needs to be aggressively and openly tackled. Enforcement of punishment for crimes against girls and women has always been weak and halfhearted. Within the context of this volume, while no justice can be done to that subject, it is imperative to record that physical and sexual trading and abuse are a growing problem increasingly recognized as a major blindspot in addressing the exploitation and abuse of girls. Countries which express anxiety about teen prostitution and associated sexual health risks are Bangladesh, Belize, Djibouti, India, Jamaica, Nepal, Peru, and Rwanda. However, even where sexual abuse and exploitation of girls are not openly noted, it cannot be assumed that these do not exist.

Somewhat encouraging is the lead taken by a few countries to launch progressive corrective measures. In Thailand, aided by the U.S.-based Global Fund for Women, a local Daughters Education Project seeks to prevent young girls from being lured or forced into the powerful sex industry there. The project focuses on 9–14-year-old girls at risk of being sold to brothel agents by their desperately poor parents. It provides them with financial support so that the girls can attend high school or gives them training in sewing, agriculture, or computer skills.

In Colombia, where street girls (and boys) are fair game for exploitation and violence, a half-way house has been opened in the center of Bogata by the Renacer Foundation to rescue girls from a life of addiction to drugs and sexual exploitations. The number of female teens and preteens engaged in the sex business is estimated at about 10,000, according to a most recent comprehensive survey carried out in Bogota. Most suffer from problems of drugs, venereal disease, and violence. The general prevailing pattern among girl prostitutes is abuse and rejection by their parents, who often have their own drug, alcohol, and violence problems. According to the Foundation, "Typically, the mother works as a maid or washes clothes, the family all live in one room, and the father or stepfather sexually abuses the daughters. Some are raped at age 8 or 9, and run away or are thrown out by the mother because they are competition for the father's affection."

The child in prostitution can expect to live "to little more than 25. To survive to 30 is a great achievement." The Renacer approach is to participate in the lives and problems of the girls with untiring patience and affection. Girl (and boy) prostitutes are first persuaded to escape the "freedom" of the streets and then to enter the center where medical, counseling, literacy, and craft-training are provided to cause a change in the youth's lifestyle and aspirations. The hardest part is getting the infected ones to deal with AIDS, and to find adequate community homes to shelter and house the change-seeking street children. (*San Francisco Chronicle*, March 29, 1994:A-15, and January 16, 1995:A-8–12) However effective such programs may be, they are barely able to scratch the surface of the immense child prostitution and pornography problem.

Whereas sexual violence directed against the female is a global practice, it is evident that the girl, because of her age and gender, is more prone than the boy or the woman to experiencing violence and abuse. Since it is her lesser status within the family and society that accounts for her greater abuse, it is vital that a new order of family functioning be devised enabling equality between the sexes. The myths and values which support a dominator and dominated inter-personal and global world need to be discarded in favor of equitable domestic and societal relationships. "There is in our world today a strong movement toward what I call a partnership rather than dominator family, as is the recognition of millions of people that a family based on control rather than trust is a dysfunctional family. There is also a strong movement for equal partnership in all spheres of life between women and men. . . The urgent task at hand is to accelerate this process. An effective and do-able tactic, is a Global Campaign Against Violence and Abuse in the Family." (Eisler quoted in WIN *News*, 17-3, Summer, 1991:79)

Endnotes

1. Some experts believe, however, that boys are as much at risk as girls, but the molestation of girls is more often reported. Estimates of sexually abused children of both sexes, in the United States, range from 100,000 to 1,000,000. Only one-third of all child molestations are committed by strangers; another third by acquaintances, and the remaining third by "primary relatives." (Organization of Deputy Sheriffs of San Mateo County, 1990:31).

2. In this context, it is encouraging to note the recent announcement by the World Health Organization of its intention to put an end to female circumcision, with appropriate support from governments and women in affected countries. A resolution, approved unanimously in May 1993 by its 185-nation annual assembly, asked WHO Director-General Hiroshi Nakajima to prepare a report that would call for tougher action on female circumcision.

X

AFFIRMATIVE ACTION AND GIRLS

"Equality should be a criterion of the rights and care of every child; nourishment, physical and emotional, and the way in which children are inducted into their societies should not depend on their gender." Thus contends the United Nations in a recent document. (1989:381) Miles away, in the country of Yemen, a UNICEF document makes a plea for using girls as the flag bearers of integrating women in development: "Unless there is a dramatic shift in the status of women in Yemen, the pace of social development will be restricted. By placing special emphasis on the 'girl child,' it may be possible to stimulate a change and accelerate the involvement of women and girls in the mainstream of national development." (1989:51)

The 1990s mark the closing decade of this century. They also constitute the U.N.'s Fourth Development Decade (DDIV). The residual perception arising from the previous three development decades is that socioeconomic disparities between countries and people did not diminish, and in fact may have been accentuated. Between 1960 and 1970, the world's GNP increased by one trillion dollars, 80 percent of which went to industrialized countries and 6 percent to the poorest nations. The individual average annual income in the poorer countries was below two hundred dollars. Between 1950 and 1980, the world's output tripled in real terms. Yet the income gap between developed and developing countries widened. In 1981, the richest fifth of the world's population controlled 75 percent of the world's product while the poorest fifth controlled only 2 percent. (Sivard, 1985) Recent data for 1989–1990 show a similar distributive pattern, with the United States accounting for 35.3 percent of the world's GNP; western Europe for 22.5 percent; Japan for 11.8 percent; and all other nations combined for 30.4 percent. According to Lester Brown, Director of the World Watch Institute, "the average person today in the world is four-and-a-half times richer than were his or her grandparents at the turn of the century. Nevertheless, the global wealth is unevenly spread among the earth's five billion people, one billion of whom live in unprecedented luxury, and another billion in destitution." As Brown states, "Even American children have more pocket money—$230 a year—than the half billion poorest people alive." (*San Francisco Chronicle*, 13 March, 1991:A-3)

Wealth and poverty are unequally shared not only by countries but also by the people within countries. Whatever the increase in the world's GNP, it is now widely accepted that such increase is being achieved at the expense of (i) the poorer countries; (ii) the global environment; (iii) poor people; and (iv) women. Everywhere in the world, women experience the consequences of being prevented from enjoying development's processes, opportunities, and entitlements. The feminization of poverty is now perceived as a global phenomenon. The number of rural women living in poverty in developing countries around the world has increased 50 percent in the past two decades, and they far outnumber the men in such straits, according to a U.N. analysis. Of the 930 million people living in poverty in the developing world, 554 million are women, of whom 363 million live in Asia, 130 million in Africa, 43 million in Latin America and the Caribbean, and 18 million in the Near East and North Africa. The increase in female poverty has come despite economic gains made by many developing countries during the past two decades. (*San Francisco Chronicle*, July 23, 1991:A-3) Recent UNICEF estimates suggest that approximately 600 million children under 16 years of age live in poverty in the developing world. Even in the United States, nearly 20 percent of the children are estimated to be poor, compared to an approximate 14 percent poverty rate among adults.

For women and children, particularly girls, the gender-disparate costs of development failure have been high—pushing investment in their welfare in a further downward spiral. The woman's status throughout most of the developing world continues to be circumscribed by a combination of her lack of education, monetary assets, employable skills, and the overwhelming dual burden of her reproductive and productive functions. Assessments of Forward Looking Strategies for the Advancement of Women in the Year 2000, and the U.N. Decade for Women generally affirm that *de jure* equality for women was readily advocated and accepted but *de facto* equity remains an ideal.

The focus thus must shift to the girl as the probable key to a more equitable womanhood and adulthood. The equation is not simplistic, but simple enough to have bypassed planners, and even feminists in previous decades. The argument is familiar to those who have advocated on behalf of children since the First Development Decade. In the 1960s, it was effectively established that planning for tomorrow's adults must begin with caring for the children of today; and that the costs of neglecting the younger section of the population are inter-generational and often irreparable. The girl child offers the same logic and link to the status of the adult woman, and additionally to the children she herself will bear.

But the girl-woman equation is only one reason to link future efforts to the girl child. What is more urgent is her autonomous right to childhood, and her claim to all the protective and developmental provisions which that right entails. Standing as she does with nearly twenty completed centuries of socialization behind her as the "lesser" child, this unequal half of childhood seeks a respite from the burdens of her gender, in pursuit of her legitimate positioning in the coming decades' development strategies.

The advancement of girls must be perceived and pursued as an indispensable component of human development, and as a measure of human pragmatism and justice. By protecting, nurturing, and developing the girl child, the global community will benefit through her enhanced productivity and through the reduced burden of her dependency. By ensuring her sociodemographic parity and equalizing her potential and opportunities, the goal of development for all will be better realized.

Greater hope and endeavors for human development in the 1990s provide a congenial context for integrating concerns for the girl child. There is a fortunate change in the global climate favoring a move toward a more equitable childhood. Several developing countries have uncovered disturbing differences in quality-of-life indicators between girls and boys. Where similar problems and trends have been detected, regional initiatives have been launched to generate greater understanding and tackling of key issues. (See Box 15, next page, on "Regional Initiatives on Behalf of Girls") At the global level, several programs are beginning to recognize the special needs of girls. (See Box 16, page 171, on "International Directives Concerning Girls") A major and unique thrust to parity for girlhood is embodied in the newly adopted Convention on the Rights of the Child with its strong nondiscriminatory gender clause. (See Appendix II, page 231) The more than one hundred fifty signatory nations to this Convention, which is perceived as the Magna Carta of Children's Rights, will be morally, legally, and superlatively committed to equalizing childhood. They will serve also as valuable paradigms to those who have yet to identify intrinsic gender biases in the entitlements of children. In the sections that follow, certain strategic inputs are outlined to help create an ethos of care and equality for girls.

A BETTER HEALTH DEAL FOR GIRLS

The diagnosis of what plagues girls' health and survival is impressionistic, given the present lack of gender-specific data, but its treatment cannot be so. The first step toward enhancing the girl child's health is to recognize the problem of her greater vulnerability. Health, more so than education, has

---

Box 15
Regional Initiatives on Behalf of Girls

The *South Asian Association for Regional Cooperation* (SAARC) consists of seven member countries—Bangladesh, Bhutan, India, the Maldives, Nepal, Pakistan, and Sri Lanka. Responding to increasing concern over the lagging status of girls in the region, the SAARC countries proclaimed 1990 as the Year of the Girl Child. The countries committed to developing detailed statistics to outline the problems and status of girls, and to formulating policies and programs to end their discrimination. The countries also designated 1991–2000 as the Decade of the Girl Child. Individual initiatives have already begun at the country level to improve the survival and development potential of girls. UNICEF and other U.N. agencies are extending their support to these initiatives.

In the *Arab League* group of nations, the problems and status of the girl child were addressed at a special meeting convened in May, 1990. Leading thinkers from Egypt, Jordan, Saudi Arabia, Sudan, United Arab Emirates, and YAR participated in the meeting. In the other two regions—*Africa* and *Latin America*—promising concrete initiatives aimed at girls are beginning to gain momentum.

In developed countries, the tendency to perceive the issue of "girls" as a problem specific to developing countries needs to be questioned. In the United States, a resolution (H.J. Res. 302, U.S. House of Representatives, 103rd Congress, First Session) was passed November 22, 1993, to designate 1994 through 1999 as the "Years of the Girl Child."

been gender-blind. For a sector to commit itself to achieving Health for All but to allow the benefits of health to percolate among genders differently is ironic. At the mid-point of DDIV, and with more than three decades of preventive and promotive health behind it, there is no justification for this sector to have allowed the global female/male ratio to drop from 996 per 1,000 in 1970 to 987 in 1990. The global girl/boy ratio also dropped between 1970–1990, but unlike the ratio with women/men, the decline was universally experienced.

The fact that gender disparity in the adult population is mainly attributed or confined to Asia, where half of the world's population lives, offers little relief. On the other hand, the global nature of the inferior socio-demographic status of girls, as demonstrated in earlier chapters, should be a source of

---

Box 16
International Directives Concerning Girls

Specific provisions and clauses concerning girls appear in various international policies. The UNICEF/WHO Goals and Strategies for Children in the 1990s made gender-disparity reduction and empowerment of women principles. The recently adopted World Declaration on Education for All specifically provides (Article III, paragraph 3) for girls' education as an urgent priority. The Convention on the Elimination of All Forms of Discrimination Against Women specifically refers in Article 10 to equal access of girls, with boys, to an equal standard of education in every subject at every level. Its Article 16 refers to monitoring minimum marriage age of girls. The Convention on the Rights of the Child makes reference in Article 2 to the principle of non-discrimination when applying its provision to all children regardless of race, color, sex, language, religion, political, or other opinion, etc. Article 24 refers to the state's obligation to work towards the abolition of traditional practices, such as female circumcision and the preferential treatment of male children. Among its other significant provisions are Article 29 (d), which refers to equality of sexes; and Articles 34, 35, and 36, which address problems of child abuse, trafficking and prostitution. The Human Rights Declaration that emerged from the Human Rights Conference in Vienna, in July, 1993, for the first time acknowledged the human rights of women and of the girl child to be an inalienable, integral, and indivisible part of universal human rights.

further concern. A *conscience* change is required as the key step towards seeking and enforcing a solution. To do that, health must move from its strictly medical science- and service-restricted role to incorporate the roles of *activist, change evoker, social engineer,* and *cultural discipliner.* In order to enforce a gender-just perspective, health advocates must compel society to discard what is harmful and to adopt what is beneficial to gender-inclusive human health and well-being. Health practitioners must make that vital transition from an isolated to an integrated and truly holistic approach, one that questions and draws on the strengths of society and the economy, and uses both to expand human capability for survival and life. "Living in Society," as has been aptly noted (Sen, 1989:28) "cannot be partitioned into two unlinked categories of economic living and cultural living, and the problem of differential morbidity and mortality cannot be adequately studied without associating the two with each other."

The preeminent objective and endeavor of the second half of DDIV, as of subsequent Development Decades, must be to achieve equality for women, starting with the girl child, in health's critical parameters—namely: (i) infant, child, and maternal mortality (ICMM); (ii) life expectancy (LE); (iii) adolescent growth and reproductive care (AGRC); and (iv) rearing and nurturing of children. Strategic actions that investigate, analyze, define, refine, annotate, and amplify these parameters, with a view to improving their impact on, and gains for, the female child and adult, deserve the global health fraternity's priority attention. Implications for operational changes and roles of development assistance agencies are as follows:

Operational Implications:

1. Countries and global/regional bodies must commit to gender parity in all health interventions.
2. On a priority basis, concrete time-bound targets must be adopted to equalize benefits in the critical areas mentioned above—ICMM, LE, and AGRC.
3. All health-related reporting, surveillance, and monitoring must involve gender-specific profiling of the health status of a population. Further, gender-by-age analysis should be uniformly applied to all demographic and health-intelligence activities.
4. All planning, programming, and allocation in the health sector must seek to address gender-specific health needs, balancing disparities

where they exist and undertaking affirmative interventions to bridge the gaps in coverage, use, and benefits.

5. Research and surveillance areas which will help refine and address the girl's health needs and constraints must be supported, including: adverse sex ratios in different age groups; higher female mortality, and disease-incidence patterns among girls and boys and their causes; gender differences in the use of treatment and referral services; health spending on girls and boys in the home and by public health services; female adolescent growth needs and remedies; reproductive behavior of adolescent boys and girls and means to educate them on mutual health roles, duties and rights; adverse health and social practices, modern and traditional, which affect the health and survival of the girl child, including child abuse, infibulation, circumcision, prostitution, AIDS, and other sexual hazards; the social and mental health impact of seclusion; early marriage and early motherhood; and sexist acculturation.

6. The futility of blanket policies and approaches for maternal and child health and family planning must be recognized, and changed in favor of context-and-episode-related specific interventions. Intensity and components of corrective strategies must follow the acuteness and the nature of the problems and needs to be addressed.

7. The health sector, as a whole, must move toward closer interaction with society. Synergistic action with law, social welfare, economic and social development, as well as education, will be vital to changing fertility and child-rearing patterns. Most specifically, the combined effort of national administrations should be to combat prejudice against girls; and to drastically change people's perception of her present and potential value to the society and economy. Women's organizations must make a motivated effort to convert women and men to this gender-just perspective. Private voluntary organizations must be similarly involved to convince parents. (See Box 17, next page, on "De-Gendering Parenting") Health benefits, when linked to altered social perceptions of the intrinsic right of girls to equal survival and nurturing, will make for a lasting change in gender differentials in health.

8. An outstanding all-out effort must be made to enforce and upgrade anti-early marriage provisions. A major countervailing measure to early marriage, as well as early sexual activity and fertility and their

Box 17
De-Gendering Parenting

Interesting strategies to alter traditional parental roles and responsibilities in rearing children have recently been launched. The following represents the positive experience of a project in India:

Fathers Expand Their Role in India

Every week, Jagdish Prasad and Ram Subhash Tiwari (both fathers) meet with an educational consultant to learn about their children's capabilities and weaknesses and to discover new ways of supporting their education. Since the program began, fathers have also proven to be powerful collaborators in combating social evils and superstitious beliefs. Jagdish Prasad resisted both his neighbors and his wife, who advocated the use of witchcraft when his 6-year-old daughter Urmila fell ill. Urmila was found to be deficient in vitamin A and suffering from infections; she recovered rapidly after intensive hospital care.

Stronger relationships are another of the program's results. "Papa tells me stories," Urmila said with a shy grin, dressed in her maroon-and-gray school uniform as she prepared to visit the circus with her father and brother.

In fact, supporting the health and educational rights of girls has been particularly rewarding for many of these fathers, who come from backgrounds where child marriages are usual and female literacy is discouraged.

Mr. Prasad has successfully out-maneuvered marriage proposals for Urmila. He now wants his wife to work outside the household, not for monetary reasons alone, but so that she can be his partner in planning the family's future.

Chander Pal, father of two boys aged 8 and 10, understands that unhealthy comparisons between children can be damaging, and has taken precautions so that it does not occur within his household. Another father, Raj Ahuja, helps his 3-year-old daughter cope with the trauma of sibling rivalry.

The program, brain child of entrepreneur Vikram Nair, is growing in popularity, with many non-participants eagerly requesting counseling and guidance for their own children.

Source: Abridged from a longer article by Meenakshi M. Gautham, in UNICEF, *First Call for Children*, July-September, 1994:10

attendant negative health outcomes, will be to offer viable life options to girls. The two or three years of hormone changes in the adolescent female are accompanied by a midstream growth spurt which allows for nutritional recuperation and a growth course correction. (Rohde, 1983) This opportunity for catch-up growth has to be meaningfully exploited by identifying and refining methods for normal dietary and health-care support to the adolescent girl. Her physical size and capability for safe childbearing will also be affected positively. While these measures and recommendations call on the convergent forces of all sectors, particularly education, employment, training, cultural orientation, and others, the health sector will need to provide the knowledge necessary to protect, prepare, and develop the health capability of the female adolescent.

9. The bearing of *children* by *children* must stop, irrespective of cultural, religious, or other sanctions, and the girl child must be *restored* to *childhood*. To this end, an intensive and informed campaign must be orchestrated, led by health but echoed by all other development sectors. Strategic alliances with religious and social groups, and other public moderators (media, sports, or others) must be struck. Where friendly alliances and networks do not emerge, the will of the people must be activated to press for change.

10. Women's control over their bodies, and the need to separate the female's status from her fertility, is the ultimate value system that has to be fostered. In promoting this social change, health is one of the key agents, *provocateurs,* and monitors. Current contraception-practice rates are minimal in many parts of the world, ranging from 2 percent to 75 percent in Sub-Saharan Africa, from 7 percent to 70 percent in Latin America, and from 1 percent to 70 percent in Asia and Northern Africa. Childbearing rates average between 5 and 7 births per woman in the developing regions compared to 1.8 births per woman in the developed regions. An estimated half-a-million women die every year from pregnancy-related causes, of whom 200,000 die from illegal abortions. (U.N., 1991:56,61) Antenatal and delivery care is still inadequate. Births supervised by trained attendants account for 34 percent in Africa, 24 percent in South Asia, 64 percent in Asia and the Pacific, and 74 percent in Latin America, compared to 98 percent in the developed world. Such countries as Bangladesh, Bhutan, Somalia, and Burkina Faso report 2

to 5 percent of births as being aided by trained attendants. In those countries and other acute service-scarcity regions, it will be vital to launch unusually aggressive action.

11. Although fuel, water, and sanitation have not directly figured in this discussion, provision of these services will rapidly reduce the girl's[1] burden in her maintenance role, conserve her energy, and leave her freer to benefit from other health and socioeconomic interventions. Because water and sanitation account for 50 percent of the diseases that kill children, and girls bear the greater burden of that mortality, attaining universal access targets with respect to water and sanitation acquire incomparable significance in improving the health and survival prospects for girls. Moreover, women's demonstrated success in promoting, servicing, and sustaining these sectors must be broadened to benefit from the resource represented by the adolescent female.

12. Providing community-based and community-managed child care is another way to free the girl from doubling as surrogate mother. In this context, the experiences of several African, Asian, and Latin American projects need to be adopted so that safe, affordable, flexible, and mobile care is made available to communities. The strategy of combining a nutritional-feeding, life-education, non-formal program for adolescent girls, with the care of younger siblings, needs to be considered as a multi-beneficial, mutually reinforcing approach.

13. Aggressive laws and enforcement mechanisms, especially in developing regions, will be required to combat the growing mis-application of science and technology in reducing or eliminating female fetuses. (See Box 18, on "India Outlaws Sex Test")

14. In developed regions, there is need for greater understanding and treatment of the asymmetry between the demographic presence of girls, as compared to women.

15. Effective health service necessitates a rapid building of rapport between the service and the people. The frontline worker is not only the spokesperson and the provider of the health service, often she or he *is* the service. In the context of diminishing health budgets and the reduction of available health services and infrastructures, emphasis must be placed on the use of trained semi-skilled health workers from the community, who have a surrogate-service effect.

Documented feedback from dozens of projects reinforces the value and behavior-transforming effect of a community-based health worker, who can go door-to-door, day-after-day, to help shape people's lives. Health planners should pursue health like political campaigns, where door-to-door canvassing will cause people "to cast their ballots" in favor of health. This is the one way to democratize, popularize, and internalize health.

Box 18
India Outlaws Sex Test

New Delhi (Reuters): Indian social activists rejoiced after Lok Sabba (lower house of Parliament) passed a law to ban the misuse of medical tests that have led to thousands of abortions of female fetuses.

"I think it is an important step and a tool in the hands of social action groups," said Mira Shiva of the Voluntary Health Association of India. "We have been campaigning against this since 1982."

The Lok Sabba voted unanimously to regulate amniocentesis, a fluid test and ultrasound tests. Members said they expect the upper house to clear the law without a hitch.

The tests, meant to track pregnancy disorders, have been used to detect and abort female fetuses, with girls widely considered to be a social liability in India where parents must spend huge sums in dowries to get their daughters married.

Ultrasound tests are also widely used in China for the same purpose.

"Dowry is to a large extent the problem in what someone called demographic fundamentalism," Shiva said.

"Sex tests are a part of our social fabric of prejudice," said communist Malini Bhattacharya.

The Bill orders compulsory registering of genetic counseling centers, which will face closure if there are complaints of abuse. It stops doctors from disclosing the sex of unborn children and advertising sex tests.

Doctors and abusers could be fined and jailed for three years.

Lok Sabba's members had grappled with scientific details and the question of genuine medical needs for three years since the bill was first introduced.

Source: *India Post*, Fremont, California, August 5, 1994:A-6

Specifics for Development Assistance Agencies

1. Assistance agencies should focus on countries and communities with adverse sex ratios, and with high gender differentials in critical health parameters, such as ICMM, LE, and AGRC.

2. Funding agencies should adopt, and encourage countries to adopt, specific time-bound, country-relevant targets to eliminate gender disparity in health outcomes and benefits. The reduction of maternal mortality must receive equal ranking with child survival as a strategic priority of such agencies as UNFPA, UNICEF, and WHO. Specific time-bound targets must be adopted to make safe birth knowledge and trained attendants available to women and girls to ensure safer deliveries and reduce maternal risks.

3. Agencies should promote and support the inclusion of *age-* and *gender*-specific health monitoring, planning and performance data at the global, regional, country, and community levels.

4. Funding agencies should conduct pilot growth-promotion and reproductive-care projects for adolescent girls. These should be combined with other objectives of sibling care; of basic education; of skills training; of water, sanitation, and fuel provision; and of the cultural empowerment of girls and young mothers.

5. Multilateral and bilateral agencies, including religious/cultural charities, should help launch a major offensive against discriminatory health practices aimed at girls, and devise methods for localized exposure and redress of such deleterious practices as infanticide, feticide, circumcision, infibulation, bride burning, devadasi, purdah, dietary, and menarche rituals. High-visibility pilot demonstration projects should be set up. Where successful programs exist (such as Somalia's effort to reduce female circumcision), their experiences should be transferred and adapted elsewhere. Health care and surveillance must reach out to child and teen prostitutes, street girls, or girls in custodial situations (welfare homes, prisons, mental hospitals), as well as girls affected with AIDS or STDs.

6. Agencies must resolve to openly support contraceptive information and services to all children and adults of both genders above primary-school age.[2] Fertility must be perceived as a joint responsibility[3] and a meaningful composite wish of both parents, not as solution for a socioeconomically hard-pressed family. Parents

educated about their joint responsibility towards their offspring and about nurturing a gender-just attitude will be the true social foundation of equity in health and life.

7. The World Health Organization's evaluation of the Strategy for Health for All by the Year 2000 indicated that, in spite of the availability of modern technology, the major obstacle to implementing the strategy in developing countries is the weakness of the health infrastructure. Governmental and non-governmental, donor, and people-provided structures and resources need enhancement in order to better attain vital health objectives. In the 1980s, UNICEF'S child-survival and development program, which enforced and relied on these synergies, was a significant success in many countries. By facilitating the participation and responsibility of all sectors for the child's protection, it enabled financial and human resources, which traditionally had not been available, to be mobilized for health. It also created a vast, viable constituency for health, united in a common quest. The same constituency must now be used to reduce the gender gap in human birth, life, and death. This is the minimum foundation on which the children's Covenant of Rights will rest.

REDUCING NUTRITIONAL INEQUITY

Nutritional inequity between genders is a *societal* issue, as is its solution. Because life is an integration of social, cultural, and economic, the solutions to problems have to be addressed in an integrated manner. This implies that public and political policy must be willing to deal with the technical and behavioral parameters of nutrition. The bottom line in nutritional equity is the interdependency of food and custom, and while planners may feel their mission ends with providing an enlarged food basket per household, their mandate must extend to ensuring the food is consumed equitably. Legitimizing the girl child's claim on the family's food and other resources will require a radical re-orientation of the patriarchal family's internal dynamics and distribution system. The role of mother as food allocator will have to be morally redefined to better serve the notion of equity. The family's responsibilities to practice a bias-free family culture will need to be highlighted. Assuring the girl her equal share in foods and all other resources throughout her growth process is a message that must be vigorously conveyed to all care givers. The girl, as the greatest casualty of nutritional discrimination, must be protected.

If nutritional inadequacy is not remedied it becomes the basis for a vicious cycle of disease and further depletion. Timely treatment and referral make the difference between a life saved or lost. If the child survival and development revolution is carried out by health practitioners, its foundation must be nutrition. The principal aim of nutritional strategies should be to prevent, and remedy the effect of, nutritional *contraction* among girls. To help achieve that objective, the following approaches should be considered:

Operational Implications

1. All quests for nutritional information and monitoring must be *gender sensitive,* and the knowledge thus acquired must be harnessed for setting up *differentiated* strategies. It is also necessary that micro studies be encouraged and used to authenticate national trends and to activate appropriately responsive programs.

2. The correctional process can start anywhere—with the female infant, child, or primary-school-age girl—but it is perhaps most fitting to begin with the adolescent girl, as she provides a *bifocal* point for *retroactive* and *proactive* nutritional correction. The probability that direct feeding and nutritional support, combined with enhanced educational and earning competence, will enable the adolescent girl to catch up on lost growth, as well as empower her to be a better, safer, and more equitable mother, are two reasons for focusing on this group. The female adolescent thus must be perceived and assisted to perform as the *leading edge* of enhanced societal capability for child survival and development.

3. The counter face of the above strategy is the added focus on maternal care and education. The maternal and child health emphasis of the past has focused more on the child than the mother, and this emphasis must be made more equal. In addition, there is pressure to direct health care, nutritional support, and educational-empowerment strategies to mothers in their own right as women.

4. As growers of most of the world's food, and as its manufacturers and distributors within the household economy, women as mothers are advantageously placed to work as nutrition's *avant garde*. But to do this they must be nutritionally sound and well-versed in their

knowledge of beneficial food, health, and environmental habits. Nutritional strategies thus must involve and engage women in assessing the strengths and weaknesses in household- and community-consumption patterns, and in identifying what support systems they require and are willing to sustain. For every unhealthy nutritional taboo, there are several that have a contextual relevance and fill a felt need for people's health and nutritional protection. These need to be integrated into nutritional programs.

5. The same determined effort must preclude and dispose of customs, rituals, and beliefs that are nutritionally harmful. Some cultural food practices brazenly discriminate between genders, and rationalize or sanctify discriminatory responses to the economics of scarcity. Among the most debilitating attitudinal constraints is son fixation, which has some valid origins or explanations but its manifestations need to be addressed and rectified. The *economics* and *ethics* of *childhood* have to be stated in simple, believable terms to children and adults, with concrete interventions in the form of exclusive girl-focused feeding, care, learning, education, and skills-enhancing provisions in areas where only segregated provisions will work. In non-segregated contexts and in all routine nutritional support interventions, gender parity must be demanded and enforced.

6. The mother's and father's ability to imbibe and practice a bias-free family culture has to be enhanced. This is not a goal that can be realized overnight or over one decade; but the task must begin, and where beginnings have been made they must be carried through to the next and ultimate stage. Nutritional support directed to the household as a food subsidy is a family-centered benefit. But with supplementary awareness of the equal or specific needs of growing children, food subsidization can be made more equitable and focused. Anemia in the woman and the girl has to be addressed separately, especially in households and regions where it is believed to be acute. Exclusive feeding centers, of the kind that are put up during emergency relief efforts, are likely to be directed and have high visibility, as well as symbolic value. Where home-grown nutritional sources of food are being encouraged, making them cash capable or marketable can double the advantage to the household.

7. Both nutritional status and strategies should be viewed as a balance between intake (of food and nutrients) and expenditure (physical

work, illness, infection, or pregnancy). Nutrition studies and interventions typically target food availability and intake without addressing energy expenditure. (Kurz et al., 1994:2) That narrower approach has to be revised. In this context, particularly valid are community-based and managed child care, and water and fuel collecting and distribution systems which can be promoted either on a cooperative or a low profit private entrepreneurial basis. Proximity, affordability, and regularity of these services are factors that are known and frequently reported as being indispensable to their effective utilization. Providing water pumps, cheaper energy-saving devices, and community kitchens are other measures that can improve the nutritional and health capability of girls and women.

8. Female employment in the monetary economy, and female literacy, are two variables which influence in-house division of food and other services. They also influence women's and girls' access to health centers, markets, and other public services and facilities. Since these are micro-issues, micro-solutions need to be encouraged which can best prepare women and girls to be more productive.

9. Breastfeeding, LBW babies, and anemia are considered the critical parameters in the nutritional field. The importance and benefits of breast feeding to the infant and child are undeniable. But in the context of the nutritionally depleted girl-mother, breastfeeding must be presented in balanced terms—although breastfeeding is important for her child, it poses a risk to her own health unless she is willing and assisted in protecting her own nutritional status. Prolonged breastfeeding, beyond six months, without supplementary weaning foods, can have negative effects both on the child and the mother. Moreover, in the urban, modern sector, when women's mobility may be vital to their employment security, the benefits and disadvantages of breastfeeding must be assessed in a manner that is beneficial to both the child and mother.[4]

10. LBW babies are a maternal nutrition-dependent phenomenon, and are well-recognized as a critical challenge to child survival and development strategies. The requirement here is for proactive nutrition interventions, starting with the adolescent girl and reaching the expectant teen, young, and older mother. It is also urgent to generate and ensure equal care for the LBW child. Lack

of equal nutritional care is what currently causes subtle female infanticide.

11. Finally, combating anemia and LBW, and promoting equal breast feeding and weaning for female and male children, should become the operative clause in a gender-just nutrition strategy.

Specifics for Development Assistance Agencies

1. The principal aim for assistance agencies should be to help protest, prevent, and remedy the effect of nutritional "contraction," which is recognizably more severe for girls than for boys.

2. Remedial and preventive action must begin with the adolescent as a way of correcting the girl's growth status, and potentially improving the child and maternal health and survival scenario.

3. The nutritional status of girls and young mothers must be directly and indirectly assisted through a variety of supports, some aimed at conserving her nutritional resources (labor-reducing devices, food conservation, storage) and others at expanding them (cash or food subsidy, supplementary feeding, home gardens, cash-worthy crops, and skills). The third set of supports consists of her gaining power through improved knowledge of nutrition and child care, greater equity in family life, awareness of the strengths and limitations in traditional childrearing, nutritional and social values, and fostering the equal valuing of girls and boys.

4. The sometimes conflicting aims and gains for the mother and the child in promoting breast feeding should be carefully considered and harmonized. The same concern for harmony should guide and temper labor-reducing strategies.

CLOSING THE GENDER GAP IN EDUCATION

The problems listed in Chapter VII ("Educational Disparity and Girls") establish the range of solutions possible for closing the gender gap in education. Whereas public policy can address some, the rest involve the support of the parents and the community, and of community-based organizations and workers.

At the public policy level, proposing gender parity through 100 percent enrollment and 85 percent retention and completion of girl's primary-school education is the simplest solution. But in order to avoid frustration from overly ambitious, unaccomplished targets and to maintain realistic goals,[5] there is a need to adopt a "cafeteria" approach to educating girls as well as parents. Every delivery channel, including the primary school, needs to be considered, and *non-formal* education needs to gain *social esteem* as well as *economic utility*.

Unfortunately, unlike health, education has been slow to change. It is governed by a vertical, monolithic, uniform, static, and inflexible structure. Past and present policies are focused on building schools and school equipment. When innovations have been tried, many have had considerable impact. Even without a formal building or equipment, or trained teachers, dedicated community work and door-to-door motivation have brought literacy, numeracy, and what may be aptly described as life education to women and girls. The success of these innovative approaches demonstrates the significance of moving away from having one primary school per village to providing one or more educators for every village. The term educator does not necessarily connote a formal or conventional teacher but, instead, a person who can relate basic functional knowledge about health, nutrition, the local society and economy, and human capability and well-being. This approach replicates the proven effective presence of the community-based paraprofessional health worker.

The *context* of learning in this approach is particularly pertinent. Education in this case is *not imparted* but *learned* by the women and girls analyzing their own situation, and recognizing areas and skills where they feel handicapped. Such education succeeds in enhancing their know-how of existing laws, public services and provisions, and benefits them through both improved access to and use of existing mechanisms and psychological empowerment. (See Box 19, on "Seeking Empowerment Through Women's Groups") It also reduces the hegemonic nature and impact of conventional education.

New ways to expand the catchment area of schools for girls are increasingly required and are being tested. There is considerable instructive experience available in various countries. For instance, a combination of innovative and relevant curricula, simple teaching techniques using a cadre of paraprofessional teachers recruited from the community, and enlisting community participation has proved effective in Bangladesh. Now famous as the BRAC program, it has managed a daily attendance rate of more than 95 percent. An equal number have been able to join the fourth grade after completing three years in the BRAC project's three thousand schools. Girls account for 70 percent of the enrollment in these schools and 75 percent of the teachers are women. Sadly, enrollment does not include married girls on account of traditional restrictions on their public mobility. The BRAC schools meet flexibly for two to three hours, and respect local daily and seasonal work loads and parental preferences. They have demonstrated effectively that gender (as well as poverty) is not an insurmountable obstacle to primary education.

Nepal's *Cheli Beti* program is a non-formal education program for out-of-school girls who are economically and socially deprived. The program offers a six-month course to groups of twenty girls. The completed course is deemed equivalent to a third-grade academic level in literacy and numeric skills.

Box 19
Seeking Empowerment Through Women's Groups

In Bolivia, for many women on the outside of development's benefits, joining a women's group has made an unprecedented difference in their everyday lives. Attending meetings provides a welcome diversion from a life of drudgery and, in many cases, of physical violence. They feel a comradeship with the group and can discuss problems and work together.

In the opinion of many women interviewed, although adequate housing, water supplies, and cash for food, clothing, and medicine are essential, their greatest need is for education. "Popular education" programs help women recognize ways in which they are oppressed and help challenge the worst aspects of their exploitation—the self-confidence and management skills gained from group organization and leadership have a life-long duration.

Education is an essential component of grassroots development. In Latin America it is called "conscientization." Whatever the label, it translates as empowerment—giving people tools, not just to solve one immediate crisis, but to analyze and respond to new and emerging problems.

Source: J. Benton, "The Role of Women's Organizations and Groups in Community Development; A Case Study of Bolivia," in Momsen and Kinnaird, eds., *Different Places, Different Voices: Gender and Development in Africa, Asia and Latin America,* 1993:241-42

Following the course, many girls are able to join formal schools even when they did not have the opportunity of attending school earlier. Parents in rural areas appreciate the program and the demand for it is growing.

In Dominica, Montserrate, and Saint-Lucia, training and support services are offered for girls who are forced to withdraw from the formal school system because of pregnancy. Services include basic education, training in child care, food processing and other skills, family life education, counseling, and educational outreach for parents and partners. In all three countries, the projects combine income-generating with health-education components. (Sohoni, 1990:44)

Other experiments directly address the difficulties parents encounter when sending girls to school. Among them are:[6]

1. *Feeder or satellite schools within walking distance of homes* are being set up in several countries. In Bhutan, preliminarily these show, higher enrollment and retention of girls. These schools offer from two to three years of primary education and are linked to regular, central primary schools for girls. Schools are also being set up at specified walking distances from villages, as in Nepal and Pakistan.

2. *Expanded use of existing facilities* (school places, teaching, and space) is being successfully attempted in Bangladesh and Liberia. Although specific gender-supportive data are not available, such approaches can only help maximize the cost-benefit ratios, and with a focused attempt to deploy women teachers, such multiple use of school systems could make a dent on current female school teacher shortages.

3. *Culturally sensitive* measures, such as creating boundary walls around schools, providing closed latrines for girls, recruiting female teachers, and establishing girls' schools are being employed to placate parents. Flexible and shortened school schedules are also being successfully attempted, among others, in India and Nepal.

4. *Mosques, churches, temples, and other religious centers* can provide a credible channel for delivering education, although risk to secular notions is clearly present, as is the concern that such schools would tend to reinforce gender, class, and religious stereotypes. However, these very reasons make such schools attractive in the more conventional cultures and are certainly able to attract girls'

enrollment. Mosque schools are working convincingly enough to receive government accreditation in Bangladesh, Kenya, Mali, and Pakistan. In Mali, enrollment of girls in the schools has grown speedily.

5. To significantly *enhance the base of women teachers*, rural-based training institutes have been set up in Nepal and Pakistan, where rural girls are trained for recruitment as rural teachers. The rural female teacher is a tremendous role model in her community. In separate studies of the Integrated Child Development Services (ICDS), in India, it was found that adolescent girls in rural, urban, and tribal areas look up to teachers working in the ICDS centers and creches. Even without elaborate training institutes, a cadre of rural-recruited and rural-based teachers/facilitators can be quickly built up by countries through basic and continuing extension training programs. It has also demonstrable value as a concrete employment avenue for girls and their parents.

6. *Economic incentives* are suspect to those who believe in education for enlightenment's sake, or in self-reliance. Yet, in the context of extreme poverty, food and income subsidies are highly attractive and desirable propositions. The cost of providing such incentives has to be weighed against gains from postponed marriage and fertility of girls who, without schooling, are also without any other option than marriage. Direct subsidy to parents in the form of scholarships has been tried successfully in Bangladesh and Guatemala. In Guatemala, a U.S. four-dollar-per-month-scholarship stipend was given to parents for each daughter who attended school for 75 percent of the time and who did not get married or become pregnant. More than 90 percent of the six hundred scholarship-holding girls completed the school year. In Bangladesh, female enrollment in secondary schools in project areas, where scholarships were offered to girls, increased from 27 percent to 43 percent (over a period of five years or less), more than double the national average for girls' enrollment at that level. This also postponed their marriage and showed attendant gains from deferred fertility. Increased employability and self-transformation are other likely gains. In Nepal, the principle of providing stipends and school uniforms to poorer girls has been instituted and these provisions will cover up to 5 percent of the girls' total enrollment. (Sohoni, 1990:45)

7. *Direct subsidy* to girls in the form of supplementary food at the school or non-formal education center is a directed, multi-benefit incentive. Apart from enhancing attendance, it is a monitored, sustained, and disciplined way of supplementing the nutritional intake of girls. This approach has been effective in Tamil Nadu, India, where overall retention of girls in school, with school-feeding provision, ranged from 83 to 93 percent. The average gain in height of these girls was comparable to schoolgirls from socioeconomically stronger families without school-feeding support. (Sohoni, 1990:45)

8. *Child-care arrangements* at or adjacent to school sites are a felt need and a priority intervention service. Sibling care is a major responsibility of young girls, and has been found to be related to lower rates of school enrollment and achievement of girls. In such contexts, child care can be effective as a strategy toward universal education. Provision of child care at the girls' schooling facility is bound to improve both enrollment and retention. It may also serve as a compelling incentive for young married mothers to join the educational system.

The public policy implications of the preceding discussion can be summarized as follows:

Operational Implications

1. It is vital for countries to commit to *closing the gender gap* in education at all levels, but especially so at the *primary level*. This is the surest way of retaining the girl in the educational stream and is also a proven way to defer early marriage.

2. In support of the above, it is essential for countries to adopt concrete targets and timetables for closing the gender gap for girls in education. Recently, it is encouraging to note that a number of countries—including Bangladesh, China, Nepal, and Pakistan in Asia; Benin, Burundi, Burkina Faso, Malawi, Namibia, Rwanda, and Uganda in Sub-Saharan Africa; Algeria, Egypt, Morocco, and Yemen in the Middle East and North Africa; and Ecuador in Latin America—established the reduction of gender disparity in primary-school enrollment and completion as a mid-decade goal. Both the outcomes enable the girl to experience a more normal and extended

childhood than would otherwise be possible. Many countries conducted surveys on gender discrimination, while others, including Burkina Faso and Morocco, developed specific plans of action for girl's education. A Pan-African Conference on the Education of Girls called on governments to reduce gender disparity in education and to report progress at the 1995 World Conference on Women in Beijing. (UNICEF, *Annual Report* 1994:71-72)

3. A "cafeteria" approach which makes multiple and innovative use of the primary (and secondary) school, and which relies on a diversity and plurality of channels to facilitate learning, is desirable.

4. There is a need to replicate, in the field of education, the community-based health worker, who can serve as a paraprofessional educator or facilitator. It is equally necessary to develop life-related curricula. On the whole, education needs to be decentralized, demystified, simplified, and taken out of the confining format of an immobile primary or secondary school, and away from the stranglehold of bureaucrats and administrators. As several countries have adequately demonstrated, education can be universalized through an intensive community-based approach. That approach has worked in public health and there is no reason to believe that it will not work in education.

5. Curriculum reform is urgently required to eliminate gender stereotyping believed to be the cause underlying inter-generational gender disparity in education. In regions and countries where gender parity is achieved (such as in Latin America and Sri Lanka), this aspect is emerging as a growing concern. More remunerative skills continue to be taught to boys than to girls.

6. An aggressive purposeful campaign must be launched and sustained to elicit parental support and participation in educating girls. (See Box 20, next page, on "Your Daughter Will Never Be as Good as a Son, Unless You Give Her a Chance") By the same token, legal provisions pertaining to the minimum age at marriage must be rigorously enforced and monitored. An extraordinary effort must be made to enroll married girls in education.

7. Evidence from India and elsewhere suggests that even when education is free of cost for boys and girls up to the tenth grade, the opportunity costs are high and may require additional incentives to the family. In a stubborn context, unless there is greater awareness of

the compensations from educating girls, even incentives may not work. Mobilizing public opinion in favor of girls is of seminal value; so is the emphasis on vocational training to allow for readily employable skills and an improved female earning potential.

8. Such group incentives as cash prizes, provision of wells, televisions, and other facilities, in recognition of 100 percent enrollment and retention of girls are also viable incentives and are being considered or implemented in Nepal, Pakistan, and elsewhere. Giving publicity to successful communities also has valuable symbolic and competitive effect.

9. Privatization of schooling costs is another area receiving broader attention. This is the self-help approach in education; it entails the creation of a revolving fund from which non-governmental organizations are provided with funds to run schools on a cost-sharing basis. On a similar basis, the community can be involved in managing and maintaining the schools.

10. Finally, no affirmative action to close the gender gap for girls in education can work in isolation of reduced illiteracy among women. To reinforce the effect of enhanced educability of girls, countries

---

Box 20
Your Daughter Will Never Be as Good as a Son,
Unless You Give Her a Chance.

For centuries, the Indian woman has lived up to a pre-ordained image. She has cooked and fended, borne children and adversity with equal patience, suppressed her individuality, frittered away her native intelligence in daily chores. Because that was the role given to her. She had no education, no opportunity, and no choice in the matter. She was glorified and then treated like a second-rate citizen. In the context of the twentieth century, and an India poised for the future, do your bit to emancipate the Indian woman, and give her the opportunity to gain knowledge and the freedom to use it. Start with your daughter.

Your country needs your conscience.

Source: From a poster designed by Ulka Advertising, Bombay (Meera Pillai and Subhash Tendle)—(Winning Entry—1984, Ashok Jain Award for National Awareness Advertising)

must commit to specific targets and time frames to reduce illiteracy among women, beginning with those age, socioeconomic, and religious/ethnic groups where the gender gap in illiteracy is widest.

Specifics for Development Assistance Agencies

Gender parity at the primary level and minimum basic learning for younger women must be the central objective and the touchstone of education promotion internationally. Toward that end:

1. Funding agencies should focus their educational endeavors on *low-income* countries with a *demonstrably wider gender gap* at the *primary* level.
2. In countries with the demographically largest illiterate populations, funding agencies should concentrate on regions and pockets where the gender gap and income/facility level are most adverse.
3. Agencies should focus their funding and dissemination support on innovative experiments in alternative educational channels; creative use of schools, teacher training, and learning methods; and incentive systems. Increasingly, too, where such experiments have been tested and proven to have an impact on reducing the gender gap (Bangladesh, Guatemala, Nepal, etc.), a directed effort should be made to scale up and replicate them.
4. Agencies should not support *routine* or *conventional* teacher training, school expansion, school-equipment and textbook-production programs, except as the last relates to removing gender stereotypes. These should be left to governments and to such mainline educational funding organizations as UNESCO.
5. Gender-based targeting, performance, and monitoring criteria need to be fostered in all educational-support activities, and governments must be stimulated to plan their interventions on a similar basis.
6. The global community should address the need for *changing parental attitudes* toward the *education of girls* and *adolescent mothers*, and support massive, cooperative, public-participative alliances to achieve that. Again, the focus should be on countries where the attitudinal constraints are most acute.

MINIMIZING THE BURDEN OF WORK

When the *division* and *value* of labor *globally* require *total gender readjustment*, the problem is too *generic* to be solved in one study, or one way.

There is also the context of poverty and privation that necessitates child labor, sometimes even making it an obligation. Where the stakes are survival and not slipping below the subsistence line, children may feel an obligation to cooperate. But, such compulsions are not restricted to the culture of poverty. In privileged developed regions with increasing incidence of single parent, and both-parent-working families, domestic and non-domestic, monetary, as well as non-monetary, chores are increasingly involving children. Even when economic compulsions are not there, children are consciously encouraged by parents to fulfill their consumer aspirations by their own labor. Some of these compulsions that are engaging children in paid labor are also keeping them away from school and from future employability, with depressing implications for the economic growth and prosperity of such countries. The attenuating effect of labor participation by children in these countries, too, is likely to affect girls more than boys, since gender stereotyping continues to place the additional burden of sibling care and household tasks on girls.

The search for solutions must be rooted in the reality that child labor *exists* and will *need to continue* until development's benefits and support systems become greater than its liabilities. There is a pressing case, however, to make child labor *less exploitative* of both gender and age, and to make it more purposeful and gainful, along the following lines:

Operational Implications

1. The first step in that direction is to convert the *compulsion* or liability for children to work into an *opportunity*. This requires a shift in perspective from one that pathologizes children's labor to that which creates safe, non-exploitative work conditions, along with opportunities for skills training with improved earning potential. Recasting work patterns and aspirations between girls and boys, and between men and women, is the ultimate objective and benefit intended.

2. The second significant need is to give the girl child's work greater visibility and added value. This is a problem that affects women and girls concomitantly. Their contribution to the economy and society has to be acknowledged and given monetary value, which then can be used to quantify their economic, resource-conservation, and resource-generation function and capability. Women need their work and worth to be accepted as a real, and not a proxy, indicator of GNP. Publicizing the monetary value of their work will enhance their national worth, not only to development planners and decision

makers but also to their families, to girls and women themselves, thus adding to their self-esteem.

3. Conceptual changes are not enough. There is an urgent need to go beyond those and to provide safer, more creative, and less exploitative options for children who must work. *More conventional* education cannot enhance economic gains for poorer children, particularly girls; consequently, it has not been able to attract or interest girls or their parents. In its current incarnation, primary education provides no hope of immediate or permanent remedy for the hard-pressed girl child. The urgent need is to set up shorter and quicker learning processes and courses which will build on, add to, and refine the efficacy of skills applicable to the context of the girl. Skills taught must result in quick and concrete economic returns as the longer gestation period is ill-afforded by poor families. Even among non-poor but conventional parents, there is a protective tendency which makes them suspicious of schooling that keeps the girl away from home for more than a minimal length of time. Her "marriageability" and the biological risk of her fertility are chronic, real anxieties that call for speedy and compressed learning and skills development. Some countries in the three developing regions of Africa, Asia, and the Middle East, but especially in Asia, have begun experimenting successfully with compressed, focused training.

4. In order for girls to benefit from training, learning, and earning opportunities, providing support systems has to take priority. Until alternatives are available to households for replacing the girl's work, it would be unrealistic for them to release the girl[7] to any other arrangement, state subsidized or free. This necessitates community-managed and cooperative systems of fuel and water collection, cattle grazing, marketing, and child care.

5. Enhanced skills must generate employment if they are to become more than a basis for frustrated aspirations. This means identifying and generating not only skills but also employment opportunities at the community level, and within the parameters of available raw materials, local markets and needs, and training opportunities. Appropriate technologies that feed the benefits of employment back to the community and use trained adolescent girls to further empower their people, are especially pertinent.

6. Legal and welfare provisions, and their active enforcement, are the foundation of a safe and protected working environment. The protective reach of welfare provisions must encompass both the

unorganized and unregulated employment sectors, as well as households. Just as physical abuse and violence within the home have become legally questionable practices, work conditions and labor distribution in the home must be accountable legally. Parents and development planners have to recognize and ensure that the *sanctity* and *justifiability* of the *child's rights do not diminish* because the *violators* of those rights *are parents* or *other relatives.*

7. Since effective enforcement is a participative and not a coercive process, it is vital that parental- and community-awareness programs and campaigns be widely promoted to explain the risks in overburdening young girls, and in leaving them to cope with hazardous life-impairing activities without adult supervision.

8. Gender stereotyping is both the overriding cause, as well as the symptom, of sexism. It cuts across all sectors and therefore requires treatment by each individually, as well as synergistically. It is necessary for labor-protection programs to work towards the removal and reduction of stereotypes affecting the girl's right *not* to work as a child. When girls must work they need a safety net that reduces personal and occupational hazard, and they need fairer work distribution and compensation. This requires multi-level campaigning aimed at replacing the myth of the girl being an economic liability with the reality of her being a capable economic and human asset. The need to shape, nurture, and protect that asset by investing in her care, food, nutrition, education, skills training, leisure, and freedom must be fostered.

Gender roles tend to change quickly in response to shifting economic urgencies. Women workers are now seen riding motorcycles and bicycles in the remotest parts of Bangladesh and India; women "hand-pumpers and bicycle mechanics" are self-employed entrepreneurs in the interiors of Nigeria and Ghana; cooperative child-care arrangements, street-child education, and skills-training programs are being created and managed by women in Latin America and the Caribbean; and women are transporting goods and raw materials to neighboring markets to get better prices in scores of countries. If economic pressures and economic-awareness campaigns have begun to change economic (gender) roles, why can't social pressures and social-awareness campaigns have the same transforming effect on social values and social (gender) roles? Evidently, a new work ethic and composition which is non-exploitative, free of gender stereotype, and non-discriminatory toward girls, is the task at hand. It is also the crucible.

Corrective strategies recently envisaged or initiated in countries include: i) creation of rural vocational training institutes, with mobile teams to induct girl trainees; ii) recruiting door-to-door campaigners to enlist girls to participate in training and learning programs; iii) home-directed canvassing on behalf of the economic value and intrinsic worth of girls; iv) setting up girls' economic groups at the community and micro-planning levels to promote girl-specific, self- and wage-employment policies; v) lowering the legal age of youth employment and training programs, as well as affirmative provisions, to equalize their benefits and access for girls; vi) training in the managerial aspects of producing, storing, transporting, and selling food, craft, and other products; vii) provision of collateral-free loans and subsidies to assist girls in entrepreneurial ventures; and viii) training and employment of rural and urban adolescent girls to work the frontline in health, education, child care, or agricultural extension work.

Specifics for Development Assistance Agencies

1. Child labor has been the blind spot of assistance activity. This has to be rectified by adopting a more *candid, constructive*, and *developmental* approach to *children who work*. Child labor and gender-discriminatory labor practices have to be tackled by assuring greater visibility and legitimacy to children's labor, and making it safe, non-exploitative, and equitable by law.

2. While the child's right *not* to work has to be tempered with realism and respect for the compulsions of socioeconomically weak families, the utmost care has to be taken to ensure that the girl is not exploited or victimized *because* of her gender and age.

3. There is a need to focus action on improving the employability of girl children who are forced to work. Skills which draw on existing knowledge; hands-on training, and apprenticeship learning; and strategies which combine *learning* with *earning* will be the more convincing and profitable instruments. The thrust of these approaches should be to assist girls to become quickly functional and to enhance their cash-earning capability and productivity. The overriding objective should be to assure the *economic,* as well as *cultural* and *personal autonomy* of the *girl.*

4. In order for girls to benefit from such training, support services, including community-managed cooperative child care, fuel, water, fodder, and transportation arrangements must be set up. These *respite* services are *crucial* to break the cycle of an overburdened girl child who is unable to take advantage of existing services on account of her work burden.

5. Agencies which advocate and work on behalf of children, such as UNICEF, must assume the ethical responsibility to be spokespersons and ombudspersons for the rights of children. The *rights of countries and cultures to their integral autonomy* have to be *superseded* by the *greater and higher call of preserving and protecting the dignity and integrity of childhood*. This is a recommendation for a catch-all mandate which will bring children who are victims of human rights violations under international protection.

6. As a pre-emptive strategy, agencies need to address gender stereotypes and how they affect gender distribution of labor both in and outside the home and in the marketplace. Legislation, legal reform and enforcement, legal and cultural empowerment of girls, research in socioeconomic and cultural-religious stereotypes and how they affect the growth patterns of girls and boys, and the identification of unconventional, context-related vocational skills for girls, are some areas which could benefit from the funding agencies' presence and participation.

In essence, what has to be acknowledged and advocated is that the workplace is a reflection of the interpersonal human world, and until the basis of disparity is understood and tackled in the home, gender equity in the workplace will remain unattainable.

COMBATING GENDER VIOLENCE

Violence is a manifestation of male domination and control over women. To understand the female's control by the male one has to look at women's "economic position in relation to the means of production and their power in domestic and public realms." Moreover, it is necessary to identify "where power and control are located, how they are exercised and reproduced, and the extent of their impact on women's activities and consciousness." (Keesing in Obbo, 1990:210)

One of the main sources of female degradation and *super-imposition* by the male is the female's reproductive capability. Almost universally, men grow up having been taught, believing, and knowing that they own women and their bodies. Anecdotal and other evidence suggests that men who batter their wives express surprise when they are told in counseling and therapy sessions, or by police and other law enforcers, that they have no right to beat, force sex upon, or endanger the life of their female partner. Culture and religion foster the perception that it is natural for males to suppress females; language, media, literature, arts, and pornography reinforce and glamorize the female's subjugation, negation, and degradation.

Violence against girls is also a result of their tender age and defenselessness, exacerbated by their socioeconomic, racial, caste, class, or cultural background. Whatever their background, girls have to deal with psychological and physical aggression from male children and adults from an early age. They have to moderate their behavior, appearance, and dress to avoid provoking violence in the male, and to defuse the possibility of triggering male aggression. Among the younger age groups, the probability of sexual abuse—from close relatives and acquaintances particularly—is likely to be much greater than formal statistics can ever hope to uncover. Secrecy about the occurrence of such abuse perpetrated by persons within or outside the family is a product ultimately of the *self-renunciation* which the girl experiences through her *selfless* identification with the family.

Although there is growing comprehension of the fact that the long-standing "structures of male dominance and privilege are not sacrosanct, nor indeed given in the genetic inheritance, but are social impositions." (Young in UNESCO, 1986:12) In fact, "the nature of the dynamic of women's subordination to men is still very poorly understood." (10) For girls and women to behave differently, it is now being increasingly realized, they must begin "deductively from the analysis of their subordination." (12) It is imperative to know what causes the female's subordination and how it can be replaced with more equitable gender relations.

In recent decades, through creation of women's studies, research, and publication centers, and through consciousness-raising programs, women have begun to challenge the culture of violence and female subjugation. The sanctity of traditional patriarchal beliefs and practices, as well as gender arrangements, is being questioned, and alternative knowledge, beliefs, and culture are developing. A new knowledge about women is being rapidly built and disseminated to assist in transforming the inherited inequitable power arrangements in society. According to Dale Spender (ISIS, 1983:188), "There can be no more radical educational goal than transforming the inferiority of women into independence and autonomy. The potential that adult education affords for the achievement of this goal is great. When women come together and question and query the arrangements under which they are required to live, the basis for the construction of women-centered knowledge is being laid; the learning is obvious, the changes are predictable. This is a form of political resistance in a patriarchal society." As inherited patterns of male power and female powerlessness are questioned and deconstructed, there is hope that the pervasiveness of violence perpetrated on the young and adult female will lessen.

In the construction of a new, more equitable culture, one promising solution proposed and gaining broad support is a deliberate confusion or hybridization of gender roles encouraging, enabling and, when necessary, compelling both genders to enter each other's separate arenas. But far more significant a solution, and one with incredible "transformatory potential," (to borrow a phrase from Young, 1986:16) is ensuring that the mesh occurs at younger ages—in the manner in which boys and girls are socialized and educated. For a *new gender-fair social system* to be *constructed,* the *process of deconstruction of genders must begin in childhood.* Even as in the adult world, women re-examine and restate "institutionalized normality" through challenging the conventional view of marriage, family, work, housework, sexuality, and the political economy, they must "do more than fight. . . sophisticated adult issues. (Women) must not just reinvent (themselves), but also reach out to reinvent childhood." (Pogrebin in Gersoni-Stavn, 1974:xiii)

Sexism and aggression begin in childhood. Attitudes about sex roles and gender-related violence are formed during childhood and adolescence. There is, therefore, a need to challenge and dispel the underlying assumptions and beliefs that cause sexism and sexist violence. It is important to examine not only the effect of sex-role stereotyping on children but their sexuality, and their human and other rights under the law. According to Gersoni-Stavn, "Most anthropologists agree that in almost all cultures girl and boy babies are treated differently and that the subordination of the female happens to occur with 'remarkable persistence in a great variety of cultures.' When a human relationship occurs with great frequency across space and time, we must suppose that there are determinate reasons for it. Culture itself is a form of 'destiny'. . ." (Harris in Gersoni-Stavn, 1974:xviii)

Such destiny must be reversed or reshaped. For that to occur, both culture and nurture have to rise above sexism and misogyny. As a scholar contends, "Only individual desire and ability, not presumed or behavioral norms or outside pressures, should determine what girls and boys become and do." (Gersoni-Stavn: xxviii) To quote another scholar (Freedman in Gersoni-Stavn:9), ". . .our children, both boys and girls, all have the right to a healthy personhood." In seeking the psychological liberation of girls and women, and an environment free of gender violence, ending the sexist programming of children constitutes a valid *means* and *end.*

Other measures that will help reduce the risk of gender violence are listed below for consideration by developed and developing countries, and governmental and inter-governmental bodies:

1. The most crucial is the process of vesting the female with basic human rights and ensuring that such rights accrue to all females irrespective of their age, race, ethnicity, religion, class, caste, calling, and country. An environment free of sexism and gender violence should be a fundamental right appearing in all global and national charters of human rights and liberties. The state, in the abstract collective sense, and men (as well as women) individually, need to become guarantors of those rights. Since aggression occurs both in the public place and in the home, the state must be prepared to engage, encourage, and compel the male population to restructure their behavior and be accountable for their violation of the female population's rights. (See Box 21, next page, on "Women's and Girls' Rights as Human Rights")

2. The sanctity of the female's basic human right to protection against violence in the home, public place, workplace, and in all other societal space must be acknowledged, respected, and defended. Clearly formulated laws and stringent enforcement and monitoring mechanisms are necessary to flesh out abstract rights. Mechanisms to bring deviant governments, societies, families, and individuals to task are an integral part of enforcement guarantees. Creating relevant forums—local, national and global, and governmental and non-governmental (See Box 21, also, for "Office of Special Investigator,

Box 21
Women's and Girls' Rights as Human Rights

Unprecedented steps have recently been taken by the global community in advocating and accepting women's and girls' rights as human rights. The U.N. Human Rights Declaration, which resulted from the Human Rights Conference in Vienna, July, 1993, noted, in Article 18, that the human rights of women and of the girl-child are an inalienable, integral, and indivisible part of universal human rights. The full equal participation of women in political, civil, economic, social and cultural life, at the national, regional, and international levels, and the eradication of all forms of discrimination on grounds of sex are priority objectives of the international community. Gender-based violence and all forms of sexual harassment and exploitation, including those resulting from cultural prejudice and international trafficking, are incompatible with the dignity and worth of the human person, and must be eliminated. This can be achieved by legal measures and through national action and international cooperation in such fields as economic and social development, education, safe maternity and health care, and social support. The human rights of women should form an integral part of the U. N. human rights activities, including the promotion of all human-rights instruments relating to women. The World Conference on Human Rights urges governments, institutions, inter-governmental and non-governmental organizations to intensify their efforts for protection and promotion of human rights of women and girls.

(Source: *Voices for Compassionate Society* Vol. 2, No. 1)

Office of Special Investigator,
Violence Against Women and Girls

In April, 1994, the U. N. Human Rights Commission appointed the first U.N. Special Investigator on Violence Against Women and Girls. This Office will help ensure that the enforcement of human rights, relative to women and jobs, is monitored at the highest international level. The investigator will look into not only violence against women but also its causes and consequences, and make an annual report to the U.N. Human Rights Commission. Women's human-rights groups across the world have welcomed this Office as a long overdue step toward establishing government accountability for violations of women's human rights.

(Source: *San Francisco Chronicle*, Wednesday, April 27, 1994:A-14)

Violence Against Women and Girls")—to help expose atrocities and infringements, will be indispensable to the process.

3. Mobilizing women and girls to group themselves as activists, advocates, and watchdogs is central to the realization of their rights. Equally significant is the creation of local, national, and international institutions with a strong female presence that can activate the attitudinal and structural change necessary to create a gender-fair, gender-sensitive, local, national, and global environment. In this context, and to overcome resistance from existing agencies of patriarchy and female oppression, it may be necessary for women to *launch a global non-violent movement of non-cooperation with abusive structures and forces.*

4. Insofar as structural change entails changed attitudes toward children and their upbringing, as well as toward the female's health, education, marriage, employment, and assimilation into socioeconomic, cultural, and political power, it will need to rely on broader agencies than just the religious, political, and cultural ones. The media, in particular, must be persuaded to operate with dignity and responsibility, as well as being used to widely disseminate knowledge about female human rights.

5. Informed and objective scholarship and its dissemination are central to overcoming ideological and practical resistance to conceding human rights to the female. A process of what some scholars refer to as systematic "mining" (Mazumdar and Sharma, 1990) of history, religion, theology, and other cultural legacy is needed to take the discourse on female human rights beyond the anecdotal stage to systemic change.

6. Since the experience of violent sexism is universal, its treatment and solution must be *global.* Countries and cultures can no longer take refuge in the logic of autonomy, if such autonomy infringes on the autonomy and dignity of the female or endangers her person. National and international NGOs and U.N. groups of agencies need to give up their reluctance in judging female-discriminatory cultural behavior. They must assume an active role in the destratification and transformation of the global culture to help rid it of gender violence.

7. Finally, as men are the major perpetrators of violence inflicted on women and girls, it is they who must assume the burden of transforming gender relations, and reducing the burden of girlhood.

Endnotes

1. During the early 1980s, 70 percent of the rural population in Africa, nearly 60 percent in Latin America and the Caribbean, and 50 percent in Asia lacked access to safe water. Only 18 percent of the rural population in India, 12 percent in Zaire and 1 percent in Ethiopia enjoy safe drinking water. (U.N., 1991:74 and Bisilliat et al., 1987:77) According to United Nations (75), small-scale studies in Asia and Africa show that women and girls spend an average of 5 to 17 hours per week collecting and carrying water. Fuel collection takes up to 7.5 hours weekly in India, 2.5 hours in Nepal and Bangladesh, and about 1 hour per week in Burkina Faso, Guatemala, and Indonesia.

2. Population education and related interventions aimed at adolescent girls have been tried effectively in the Latin American and Caribbean Regions. These need to be distilled and replicated. For joint UNICEF/WHO/UNFPA strategic thinking on this, see The Reproductive Health of Adolescents, Geneva, 1989.

3. Fertility regulation has traditionally targeted women, although male participation in reduced fertility is recognized. Male methods account for approximately one-third of the estimated two hundred and fifty million people of the world currently using contraceptives. (Stokes, 1980, in Christine Oppong, 1987:166) Data for 1988 indicate that methods used only by men account for 10 percent, and those used by couples (rhythm and withdrawal) account for an additional 15 percent. (World Population Plan of Action, 1988:15)

4. Advocacy of breast feeding needs to be tempered with realism. Flex-time and employee guaranteed breast-feeding time and facilities are a luxury of the developed world. In the developing world, where 80 percent of the women may be employed in the unregulated, informal sector, a feeding break may mean on-the-spot firing and replacement. This is not feminist rhetoric. It is the stark reality of the sometimes irreconcilable moral choices that women have to face in the developing world.

5. In India, for instance, recent projections indicate that at the existing rate of progress, it will require up to one hundred years or more in at least four Indian states to bring their population up to 85 percent literacy: for women to achieve that literacy level will require an additional thirty-nine to one hundred forty-nine years! (See Recent Literacy Trends in India, Office of Registrar General, Census Commission, New Delhi, 1987) Broad-sweeping enrollment and retention targets require shrewd assessment and tempering with realism. Bangladesh, "given its booming population and limited resources, will need seven hundred fifty years to eradicate illiteracy if its efforts remain at their current level." (Forecast made by an Expert Group Meeting in Dacca, in the San Francisco Chronicle, September 6, 1991.) "Recent projections for Universal Primary Education (UPE) made by the Ministry of Education in Yemen (YAR) state that UPE for boys will not be achieved until 2005 and for girls until 2015 A.D." (UNICEF, YAR, Annual Report, October 1989:51)

6. For a detailed account of several of these, see Elizabeth M. King, 1990, and Herz, 1991.

7. Reports from India note the perception of women workers all over the country is that the only way for women to earn a living wage is to use female children, both for economic support as well as for housework.

XI

CONCLUSIONS AND RECOMMENDATIONS

ENHANCING THE ENVIRONMENT FOR THE GIRL

Meeting human obligations to childhood is a *universal* responsibility. Nations, regional, and global entities have an unquestionable obligation to provide an *equal* childhood to all, irrespective of gender. All components of human society—governmental, non-governmental, and intergovernmental, cultural, religious, social, economic, and political; developed and the developing—have to lend their committed energy, time, and resources to *restore childhood and dignity to girlhood.*

There are immediate steps that can have an extraordinary symbolic value, and others that will require sustained effort. Some of these have been outlined in this book; others are already being advocated or implemented in some countries. The 1990s or 2000s could be designated as the Decade of the Girl, at least in regions and countries where her greater vulnerability is already recognized. And where it is not, a conscientious effort could begin to assess whether, and where, girlhood is hampered from exercising its full potential and aspirations.

As constituent elements of a longer-term strategy to reduce gender disparity in childhood, the following could be considered for promotion by governments and development strategists. Among others, governments could:

1. *Adopt* specific policy statements and legal instruments committing political and societal support to reducing disparities in the short run; and eliminating the bases for discrimination in the long run;
2. In support of declared policies, *formulate* specific time-bound targets and designated actions to reach the girl both within existing

programs, and where contexts justify (i.e., where disparities are acute), through *exclusive* interventions aimed at her;

3. In further support of designated policies and programs, *create* responsible and reliable monitoring arrangements, gender-wise, particularly in maternal and child survival, and young human-resource development. Monitoring mechanisms must play a proactive, reactive, advocacy and activist role in improving the perspective and prospects for girlhood;

4. *Design and launch* effective information and communication support to create awareness of the greater vulnerability and special development needs of the girl, as well as the justification for affirmative, redressive, and proactive action;

5. *Mobilize* resources and conceptual, as well as operational support, to create a global caring, just, and violence-free *ethos* for the girl. The process must encompass the various religious, cultural, political, administrative, and socioeconomic custodians of human behavior, beginning with parents and family;

6. *Launch* specialized research and investigation into the status and profile of the girl; create a database on her; build up anthropological, religious, legislative, and socioeconomic evidence relating to her unequal status and greater vulnerability; and disseminate the findings of such research;

7. *Commit* society as a whole to work collectively toward a change in the image and potential of the girl. *Formulate* specific legal and social provisions to counteract the girl's unacceptable negative image in traditional and non-traditional media, education, religion, and culture; and

8. *Encourage* the participation of girls at all levels—social, cultural, political, and economic—with a view to enhancing their self-confidence, self-reliance, and self-worth, *autonomously* of brothers, fathers, mothers, husbands, or their own offspring.

Accepting gender parity as the prime indicator and measure of child development is the *central* premise and objective of remedial approaches. Setting gender-specific and quantifiable goals; generating gender-specific data, canvassing and alliance-building, garnering political leverage, and increasing the visibility and legitimacy of girls are the principal modalities. More than technology and budgets, a transformation of attitude is required, as well as a fundamental turnaround in parental and popular perception of the girl. The task necessitates unprecedented political and popular will and sustained support by parents. Governments will need to perceive and project parents as front-line workers on behalf of equalizing childhood. Through informed awareness and sensitization, parental reluctance to investing resources in girls will need to be overcome, and enhanced parental capability to practice a bias-free family culture ensured.

A subtle coaching about the value and place of women and girls, in comparison to men and boys, occurs in all societies. Such ideas are "conveyed in concrete form through differences in entitlements to resource shares, experienced from childhood and reinforced as adults teach their children the old norms. Differences in entitlements have been studied in terms of their ultimate consequences for health, well-being and survival; a focus on how these entitlements are communicated may suggest ways of unlearning as well as learning. Since inequality depends on social learning in the first place, it can also be unlearned." (Papanek, in Tinker, 1990:180)

Part of the social-mobilization campaign will need to be addressed to the *girls and boys themselves*. Values are acquired in childhood and adolescence. Sensitization and instructional processes will need to capitalize on the *learning and unlearning* capability of the young. A gender-neutral formal and informal nurturing of children and adolescents will make for greater gender harmony in the adult world.

In the collective- and individual-conscience transformation that is being sought, non-governmental and private voluntary organizations have an incomparably valuable role to play. In the last decade, especially, they have acquired unique experience by empowering and mainstreaming women in development. This reservoir of mature, sensitive experience will need to be effectively drawn upon by governments and inter-governmental bodies to spearhead a gender-equal and human-rights-vested childhood. People's participation and active support will be the lifeline of this societal turnaround in human behavior and value systems affecting children of both sexes.

International partners in human development have a special role and responsibility in promoting global gender harmony. Donor agencies, within the U.N. system or outside, could seek to realize and reinforce that goal by assisting in creating a more equitable, gender-neutral childhood. Among others, they could devote their energies most profitably to:

1. *Aiding* research, analysis, documentation, and dissemination of gender-disparate outcomes of childrearing and development;
2. *Devising* redressive interventions focusing on countries and communities with adverse sex ratios, and with higher gender differentials in child survival, protection, and development;
3. *Assisting* countries in formulating policies, legislation, and structural support targeted toward creating a more just and caring ethos for the girl;
4. *Promoting and adopting* age-by-gender analysis in all monitoring, planning, programming, budgeting, and performance evaluation in all sectors of development, and at all levels—global, regional, national, and community;
5. *Aiding* countries to tackle harmful traditional and other practices and attitudes detrimental to the safety and development potential of girls;
6. *Helping* pilot new approaches to enhance the educability and employability of girls, and to upscale and transfer successful strategies across countries and population groups;
7. *Enhancing* the pace of supportive services (fuel, water, child care, etc.) and structural adjustment processes to reduce the burden of premature adulthood on girls;
8. *Advocating* equal rights for girls in all international and national forums, and assisting in the creation of requisite enforcement and monitoring mechanisms;
9. *Designating and apportioning* donor budgets specifically to equalizing opportunities for girls;
10. *Extending* inquiry into the unequal status of girls to developed countries, with a view to rapidly closing existing or potential gaps in life opportunities for girls.

In conclusion, it is worth recalling that the girl as a beneficiary is *not* new to human development. Special concern for her *is*.

A strategic shift in the treatment of the gender factor in development came with the designation of 1975 by the United Nations as International Women's Year. The first International Conference on Women was convened that year. For the very first time, a formal agenda was devised for mainstreaming women in development. Twenty years later, as the world prepares to convene the Fourth U.N. Conference and NGO Forum on Women, cumulative experience suggests that gains in gender-parity have not been significant. To bridge the gap between women's contribution to, and returns from, development requires that "women receive equal (sometimes even preferential) access to services. Empowering women for development should, therefore, be both a means and an end." (UNICEF, *Strategies for Children in the 1990s*:36)

Arguably, just as children are perceived as the starting point of an international development strategy that emphasizes human development, girls should be perceived as the entry point of a global movement that seeks to achieve gender parity and women's development. Based on the preceding evidence, it should not be difficult to concede that strategies for empowering girls are the beginning of women's empowerment.

As the world moves to dismantle patriarchy, gender costs and debts in contemporary human development need to be squarely addressed by the shapers of the future. The triple human and societal asset which the girl represents (as child, potential woman, and mother) makes her neglect *costly*, and the case for attending to her needs *compelling*. Alleviation of that neglect equates to *reducing* existing differentials compared to boys, *compensating* for cumulative past disparities, and the *prevention* of future differences. These form, in essence, the main benefits and agenda of the approach recommended.

The case for the girl is currently invisible. Political will at the country level and collective will at the global level, coupled with societal support, will give the cause the *visibility and credibility* it so desperately needs and justly deserves. Visibility is of the essence; so is *legitimacy*. On behalf of childhood, several national and international mandates already exist. But in 1990, the most elaborate world instrument on human rights of children came into force. To quote UNICEF, it provides a "legal as well as moral basis" for the protection, survival, and development of children. It should be a mission of the signers of the Convention of the Rights of the Child that this *magnum opus* and its resultant strategies at national, regional, and global levels, end up benefiting *both genders* among children, equally.

The next century is less than half a decade away; it will be a fitting goal for today's children to enter the Twenty-first Century with *equal* protection and preparation.

Postscript

If the thrust and preoccupation of the preceding discourse has been with the developing world, it is because the neglect of the girl is more manifest there. Gender discrimination and sexism exist in developed countries, too, but the impact is less overt and debilitating. Nor is the outcome of gender differentiation in developed countries so germane to the female's very survival. Access to basic services of protection, care, and development is broadly available to all but the very poor or disenfranchised in the developed countries.

Women and girls in the developed world consequently suffer less, or not at all, from demographic invisibility, but are obscure in many other respects. Their collective experience is that equality between genders is easy to concede semantically, but in the real world the male/female equation continues to remain skewed in favor of the male. If millions of girls and women are becoming demographically "lost" in the developing world, then in the developed world they are "lost" in a more poignant cultural, political, and personal sense. Gender-divisive benefits in developed economies, too, are a by-product of patriarchy and the cultural role casting which values functions and roles that are intrinsically male, while devaluing such "female" functions as reproduction, caregiving, home management, and household economic sustenance.

Male control over reproductive decisions, over issues of human peace and survival, and over the allocation of funds to human rights and gender justice, adversely affect women and girls from both worlds *equally*. There are heavy costs and burdens to the female, caused by men's spending priorities, which are borne by women *globally*. The shared results are the feminization of poverty and various forms of female victimization, devaluation, and marginalization.

Many of these outcomes are being passed on to the girl, universally. Sibling care and other forms of unrecognized labor by female children, teen school drop-out and pregnancy, a lack of vocational and family-life education, the impact of high divorce rates, health and other risks of unrestrained and uninformed sexuality, and emotional fracturing, are some of the traumas that are narrowing the gap between the unconscionable reality of day-to-day life for girls in the two worlds.

The unacceptable common reality for girls, as for women, is that in either world—developed or developing—both the female and her functions derive their *value only in terms of the male.* For caregiving, homemaking, reproductive, and non-monetary productive functions to acquire a "respectable" (economic) value, all four functions will need to acquire social and monetary value, as well as be performed or assisted by men. Any development short of that ultimate role sharing can only mean a frivolous and reluctant concession to gender parity, either for today's girl or tomorrow's woman.

Bibliography

AAUW, *The AAUW Report: How Schools Shortchange Girls—Fact Sheet.* A joint publication of the AAUW Educational Foundation and National Education Association, Washington, DC, 1992

AAUW, *Hostile Hallways, The AAUW Survey on Sexual Harassment in America's Schools*, Washington, DC, June, 1993

Acharya, M. and L. Bennett, "The Rural Women of Nepal: An Aggregate Analysis and Summary of Eight Village Studies," *CEDA News*, Vol. 2, Part 9, 1979

Amadiume, Ifi, *Male Daughters, Female Husbands: Gender and Sex in the African Society*, Zed Books Ltd., London, 1989

Arangio-Ruiz, G., "Work and Activities: How to Measure Them," in *Statistics on Women*, pp. 158–70 (Compilation of Papers presented during the Second Joint INSTRAW/ECE Meeting on Statistics on Women, Geneva, 13–16 November, 1989:17–28, 1990)

Aries, P., *Centuries of Childhood: A Social History of Family Life*, Knopf, New York, 1962

Atray, J. P., *Crimes Against Women*, Vikas Publishing House Pvt. Ltd., New Delhi, 1988

Banister, J., *China's Changing Population*, Stanford University Press, Stanford, 1987

Barry, H., M. Bacon, and I. Child, "A Cross-Cultural Survey of Some Sex Differences in Socialization," *Journal of Abnormal and Social Psychology*, 55:327–32

Baum, Charlotte, Paula Hyman, and Sonya Michel. *The Jewish Woman in America.* New York, New American Library, 1975

Belsey, Mark A. and Erica Royston, "A Global Overview of the Health of Women and Children," in Wallace and Giri, eds. *Health Care of Women and Children in Developing Countries*, Third Party Publishing Company, Oakland, CA, 1990

Berio, Ann-Jacqueline," The Analysis of Time Allocation and Activity Patterns in Nutrition and Rural Development Planning," *Food and Nutrition Bulletin*, Volume 6, No. 1, 1988

Bernard, Cheryl and Edit Schlaffer, "The Man in the Street: Why He Harasses," in Richardson/Taylor eds. *Feminist Frontiers II, Rethinking Sex, Gender and Society*, McGraw Hill, Inc., New York, 1989, 1986, pp. 384–387

Bernard, Jessie, *The Female World*, The Free Press, New York, 1981

Bisilliat, J. and M. Fieloux, translated by E. Amann and P. Amann, *Women of the Third World*, Associated University Presses, Inc., Cranbury, New Jersey, 1987

Boserup, Ester, *Woman's Role in Economic Development*, Allen & Unwin, London, 1970

Boserup, Ester, "Employment of Women in Developing Countries," International Population Conference, *Liege, 1973*, Vol. 1, IUSSP, Liege, 1973

Boserup, Ester, "Economic Change and the Roles of Women," in Irene Tinker, ed., *Persistent Inequalities*, Oxford University Press, New York, 1990

Bruce, Judith, "Homes Divided," *World Development*, Vol. 17, No. 7, 1989, pp. 979–991

Burra, Neera, "Sight Unseen: Reflections on the Female Working Child," paper presented at the National Workshop on the Girl Child, New Delhi, 1987

Buvinic M. and S. Yudelman, *Woman, Poverty and Progress in the Third World*, Headline Series, No. 289, Foreign Policy Association, New York, Summer, 1989

CAPMAS and UNICEF, *The State of Egyptian Children*, Cairo, June, 1988

Carlson, Beverly A. and Tessa Wardlaw, "A Global, Regional and Country Assessment of Child Malnutrition," UNICEF Staff Working Paper No. 7, UNICEF, New York, January, 1990

Chatterjee, Meera, *Both Gender and Age Against Them: A Status Report on Indian Women from Birth to Twenty*, Mimeo, New Delhi, 1988

Chen, L. C. et al., "Maternal Mortality in Rural Bangladesh," *Studies in Family Planning*, 5 (11):334–341, 1974

Chen, L. C. et al., "Sex Differentials in Morality in Rural Bangladesh," *Population and Development Review*, 6 (2) 257–70, 1980

Chen, L. C. et al., "Sex Bias in the Family Allocation of Food and Health Care in Rural Bangladesh," *Population and Development Review*, 7(1):55–70,1981

CINI, State Level Workshop on The Girl Child, 20-22 June, West Bengal, 1988

Chodorow, N., "Being and Doing: A cross-cultural examination of the socialization of males and females," in V. Gornick & B. Moran, eds., *Woman in Sexist Society: Studies in Power and Powerlessness*, Basic Books, Inc., New York, 1971

Chodorow, N., "Family Structure and Feminine Personality," in Richardson and Taylor, eds., *Feminist Frontiers II, Rethinking Sex, Gender and Society*, McGraw-Hill, Inc., New York, 1989, 1986, pp. 43–57. (Note: As in the text, this source is referred to hereafter as *FFII*)

Chung, B. et al., *Psychological Perspectives: Family Planning in Korea*, Hollym, Seoul, 1972

Chung, Fay, "Education for All Can Still be Achieved," in UNICEF, *The Progress of Nations*, 1994, New York, p. 19

Cochrane, S., "Education and Fertility: What Do We Really Know?" World Bank Staff Occasional Paper No. 26, Washington, DC, 1979

Cochrane, S., D. O'Hara, and J. Leslie, "Parental Education and Child Health: Intracountry Evidence," *Health Policy and Education*, 2 (March): 213–250, 1982

Daly, Mary, "Indian Suttee: The Ultimate Consummation of Marriage," in *FFII*, pp. 429–30

Dankelman, Irene and Joan Davidson, *Women and Environment in the Third World*, Earthscan Publications, Ltd., London, 1988

Davis, Kingsley, "The Continuing Demographic Revolution in Industrial Societies," in Seymour Martin Lipsit, ed., *The Third Century, America as a Post Industrial Society*, Stanford, CA: Hoover Institution Press, 1979, pp. 37–64

Davis, Lisa, "I Remember Daddy Did It," in "This World," *San Francisco Chronicle*, 29 September, 1991, pp. 11–12

Davison, J. and M. Kamyuka, "An Ethnographic Study of Factors That Affect the Education of Girls in Southern Malawi," in S. Grant-Lewis et al., "Constraints to Girls' Persistence in Primary School and Women's Employment Opportunities in Education Service" *A Report of the Ministry of Education and Culture*, USAID Malawi, 1990

Demand, Nancy, *Birth, Death and Motherhood in Classical Greece*, Johns Hopkins University Press, Baltimore, 1994

Desai, Neera and M. Krishnaraj, *Women and Society in India*, Ajanta Publications (India), Delhi, 1990

Dixon, R., "Measuring Equality Between the Sexes," *Journal of Social Issues*, 32:19–31, 1976

Dixon, R., Rural Women at Work, *Strategies for Development in South Asia*, Johns Hopkins University Press, Baltimore, 1979

Doyal, L., "Waged Work and Women's Well Being," *Women's Studies International Forum*, Vol. 13, No. 6, 1990, pp. 587–601

D'Souza, S. and L. Chen, *Sex Biases of Mortality Differentials in Rural Bangladesh*, International Centre for Diarrheal Research, Bangladesh, 1979

Dworkin, Andrea, "Gynocide: Chinese Footbinding," in *FFII*, cited above, pp 15–24

Dworkin, Susan, "Can We Save the Girls?" in *New Directions for Women*, Sept./Oct., 1991, pp. 3–4

Dwyer, D. and J. Bruce, eds., *A Home Divided: Women and Income in the Third World*, Stanford University Press, Stanford, 1988

El Sanabury, N., "Determinants of Women's Education in the Middle East and North Africa: Illustrations from Seven Countries," *PHREE Background Paper Series.* World Bank, Washington, DC, 1989

Elahi, K. M., "Gender Relations in Rural Bangladesh," in J. H. Momsen & V. Kinnaird, eds. *Different Places, Different Voices: Gender and Development in Africa, Asia and Latin America,* Routledge, London & New York, 1993, pp. 80–92

Evenson, R., B. Popkin, and E. Quizon, "Nutrition, Work and Demographic Behavior in Rural Philippine Households," in H. Binswanger et al., eds., *Rural Household Studies in Asia,* Singapore University Press, Singapore, 1980

Feltes, Linda et al., *Creating Gender Equity,* Upper Midwest Women's History Center, St. Louis Park, MN, 1994

Ferraro, K. J. and John M. Johnson, "How Women Experience Battering: The Process of Victimization," Reading 45 in *FFII,* pp. 416–428

Gans, Janet E., *America's Adolescents: How Healthy are They?,* Vol. 1, Profiles of Adolescent Health Series, American Medical Association, Chicago, 1990

Gaskell, J., *Gender Matters: From School to Work,* Oxford University Press, New York, 1992

Gersoni-Stavn, Diane, *Sexism and Youth,* R. R. Bowker Company, New York, 1974

Ghosh, S., "The Female Child in India—A Struggle for Survival," *NFI Bulletin,* Vol. 8, No. 4, October, 1987

Gilligan, Carol, Nona Lyons, and Trudy Hanmer, *Making Connections: The Relational Worlds of Adolescent Girls at Emma Willard School,* Harvard University Press, Cambridge, MA, 1990

Global Estimates and Projections of Population by Sex and Age, The 1988 Revision, United Nations, New York, 1988

Gopalan, S. and Suminder Kaur, *Women and Nutrition in India,* Nutrition Foundation of India, New Delhi, 1989

Government of India, Department of Women and Child Development, *The Lesser Child: The Girl in India,* New Delhi, 1989

Government of India, *National Perspective Plan for Women 1988-2000 A.D.,* New Delhi, 1988

Government of India, *Women in India,* Country Paper, New Delhi, 1985

Griffin, Susan, "Rape: The All-American Crime," Reading 41 in, *FFII,* pp. 388–398

Gross, Susan Hill, *Wasted Resources, Diminished Lives: The Impact of Boy Preference on the Lives of Girls and Women,* Upper Midwest Women's History Center, St. Louis Park, MN, 1992

Halder, A. and N. Bhattacharya, "Fertility and Sex of Children of Indian Couples," *Etudes Demographiques,* Recherches Economiques de Louvain, No. 4. Universite Catholique de Louvain, 1970

Hechinger, Fred M., *Fateful Choices: Healthy Youth for the 21st Century* (Executive Summary), Carnegie Council on Adolescent Development, New York, April, 1992

Hedman, B., "Statistics and Indicators on the Role and Situation of Women and Men: The Swedish Approach," in INSTRAW/ECE, *Statistics on Women*, 1990, cited above

Herz, B., K. Subbarao, M. Habib, and L. Rainey, *Letting Girls Learn, Promising Approaches in Primary and Secondary Education*, World Bank Discussion Paper 133, Washington, DC., 1991

Heyzer, Noeleen, ed., *Working Women in South Asia: Development, Subordination, and Emancipation*, Open University Press, Philadelphia, PA, 1986

Hosken, F., "The Hosken Report: Genital and Sexual Mutilation of Females," WIN *News*, Lexington, MA, 1979

Huber, J., "Trends in Gender Stratification, 1970-1985," *Sociological Forum* 1:476–495

INSTRAW *News*, "Women and Development," No. 12, Summer, 1989, Santo Domingo, 1989

ISIS, *Women in Development, a Resource Guide for Organization and Action*, Geneva, 1983

Jackson, Donna, *How to Make the World a Better Place for Women in Five Minutes a Day*, Hyperion, New York, 1992

Jay, R., *Javanese Villagers: Social Relations in Rural Modiokuto*, Cambridge, MA, 1969

Jensen, Lois, "Who Cares for the Mothers?" in *CHOICES: The Human Development Magazine*, Vol. 1, No. 2, UNDP, New York, July 1992, pp. 9–12

Jiminez, E., "The Public Subsidization of Education and Health in Developing Countries: A Review of Equity and Efficiency," *Research Observer*, Vol. 1, No. 1, January, 1986

Johansson, Sheila Ryan, "Sex and Death in Victorian England," in Martha Vicinis, ed., *A Widening Sphere*, Indiana University Press: Bloomington, IN, pp 163–181

Jones, G., "Trends in Marriage and Divorce in Peninsular Malaysia," *Population Studies*, 1980

Jones, R., "Sex Predetermination and the Sex Ratio at Birth," *Social Biology*, 20:303–308, 1973

Kelly, G. and C. Elliott, eds., *Women's Education in the Third World: Comparative Perspectives*, State University of New York Press. Albany, NY, 1982

King, Elizabeth M., *Educating Girls and Women: Investing in Development, Summary Report*, World Bank, Washington, DC., 1990

Kocher, J., *Rural Development, Income Distribution and Fertility Decline*, Population Council, New York, 1973

Kocher, J., "Rural Development and Fertility Change in North East Tanzania," paper presented to Population Association of America, St. Louis, MO, 1977

Kohlberg, L., "A cognitive-developmental analysis of children's sex-role concepts and attitudes," in E. Macoby, ed., *The Development of Sex Differences*, Stanford University Press, Stanford, CA, 1966, pp. 82–173

Kurz, Kathleen M., Nancy L. Peplinsky, and Charlotte Johnson-Welch, *Investing in the Future: Six Principles for Promoting the Nutritional Status of Adolescent Girls in Developing Countries*, International Center for Research on Women, Washington, DC, 1994

Lee, H. and S. Lee, "Boy Preference and Family Planning," *Psychological Studies in Population/Family Planning*, (Seoul) 1 (1) 1–35

Lees, Sue, *Sugar and Spice: Sexuality and Adolescent Girls*, Penguin Books, London, 1993

Leslie, J., M. Lycette, and M. Buvinic, eds., *Weathering Economic Crises: The Crucial Role of Women in Health*, International Center for Research on Women, Washington, DC, 1986

Levy, Betty, "The School's Role in Sex-Role Stereotyping of Girls: A Feminist Review of the Literature," in Gersoni-Stavn, cited above, pp. 49–69

Lott, Bernice, *Women's Lives, Themes and Variations in Gender Learning, Second Edition.* Brooks/Cole Publishing Company, Pacific Grove, California, 1987, 1994

Luftig, Richard L. and Marci L. Nichols, "Parent and School Influences: An Assessment of the Social Status and Perceived Personality and School Traits of Gifted Students by Non-Gifted Peers," *Roeper Review*, Vol. 13, No. 3, (1991), pp. 148–153

Madan, T., *Family and Kinship: A Study of the Pandits of Rural Kashmir*, Asia Publishing House, Bombay, 1965

Maine, D., *Family Planning: Its Impact on the Health of Women and Children*, Center for Population and Family Health, Columbia University, New York, 1989

Mazumdar, V. and K. Sharma, "Sexual Division of Labor and the Subordination of Women," in Tinker, 1990, cited above, pp. 185–97

Mernissi, Fatima, *Beyond the Veil, Male-Female Dynamics in a Modern Muslim Society*, Wiley, New York, 1985

Miller, Barbara D., *Son Preference, Daughter Neglect and Juvenile Sex Ratios: Pakistan and Bangladesh Compared*, Working Paper #30, Michigan State University, 1983

Minnesota Women's Fund, *Reflections of Risk: Growing Up Female in Minnesota*, The Minnesota Women's Fund, 1990

Montagu, A., *The Natural Superiority of Women*, Macmillan, New York, 1953, Rev. Ed., 1968

Moore, Kristin, *Facts at a Glance*, Child Trends, Inc., Washington, DC, January, 1992

Morris, M., *Measuring the Condition of the World's Poor*, Overseas Development Council, Pergamon, New York, 1979

National Council of Social Development, Manila, Philippines, *The Street Girls of Metro Manila: Vulnerable Victims of Today's Silent Wars*, Manila, April, 1989

National Health, Vol. 8, No. 1, 1990, Karachi, Pakistan

New Directions for Women, September/October, 1991:4

Newland, Kathleen, *The Sisterhood of Man*, W. W. Norton and Company, New York, 1979

Nortman, Dorothy, "Parental Age as a Factor in Pregnancy Outcome and Child Development," *Reports on Population/Family Planning*, Population Council, New York, August, 1974

Obbo, Christine, "East African Women, Work, and the Articulation of Dominance," in Tinker, cited above

Oppong, Christine, ed., *Sex Roles, Population and Development in West Africa*, Heinemann, Portsmouth, NH., 1987

Orubuloye, Oyetunji, "Values and Costs of Daughters and Sons to Yoruba Mothers and Fathers," in Oppong, cited above

Papanek, Hanna, "To Each Less than She Needs, From Each More Than She Can Do: Allocations, Entitlements, and Value," in Tinker, 1990, cited above, pp. 162–84

Pogrebin, L. C., "Foreword," in Gersoni-Stavn, 1974, cited above

Pohlman, E. H., *The Psychology of Birth Planning*, Shenkman, Cambridge, MA, 1969

Preston, S., *Mortality Patterns in National Populations with Special Reference to Recorded Causes of Death*, Academic Press, New York, 1976

Pugliesi, Karen, "Employment Characteristics, Social Support and the Well-Being of Women," *Women and Health*, Vol. 14 (1), 1988

Ramanamma, A. and U. Bombawale, "The Mania for Sons: An Analysis of Social Values in South Asia," *Social Science and Medicine*, 14(B):107–10, 1980

Ravindran, Sundari, *Health Implications of Sex Discrimination in Childhood*, A review paper and an annotated bibliography prepared for WHO and UNICEF, Geneva, (WHO/UNICEF/FHE 86.2), 1986

Ravindran, Sundari, "Son Preference," in Helen Allison, Georgina Ashworth, and Nanneke Redclift (eds.), *Thinkbook V, Hard Cash: Man-Made Development and Its Consequences: A Feminist Perspective on Aid*, issued by CHANGE, with support from War on Want, U.K., pp 14–15, June 1986

Richardson, Laurel and Verta Taylor (eds.), *Feminist Frontiers II: Rethinking Sex, Gender and Society*. McGraw-Hill, New York, Second Edition, 1986, 1989

Rohde, Jon E., "Why the Other Half Dies; The Science and Politics of Mortality in the Third World," *Assignment Children*, Vol. No. 61/62, 1983

Rohde, Jon E., "Principles and Strategies of Programming for Adolescent Girls," *Indian Journal of Maternal and Child Health* 1(1):3–7, 1990

Sabru-Abdalla, Ismail, "Heterogeneity and Differentiation: The End for the Third World?" *Development Dialogue*, No. 2, 1978

Sadker, Myra and David Sadker, *Failing at Fairness: How America's Schools Cheat Girls*, Charles Scribner's Sons, New York, 1994

SAARC, *Report of the SAARC Workshop on the Girl Child*, New Delhi, 19–23, September, 1988

SAARC, "Year of the Girl Child, 1990," *Information Kit, The Girl Child in India*, New Delhi

SAARC, Workshop on Social Indicators, Kathmandu, December 4–6, 1989

Sadik, Nafis, *The State of World Population 1989*, UNFPA, New York

Sadik, Nafis, *Safeguarding the Future*, UNFPA, New York

Sadik, Nafis, *Investing in Women: The Focus of the 90s*, UNFPA, New York

Sadik, Nafis, "Development Challenges of the 1990s: Maternal and Child Health Care and Family Planning," Mimeo. 8 February, 1990

Sadik, Nafis, "The UNFPA Contribution: Theory to Action Programmes," in Special Issue of Development: *Journal of the Society for International Development*, SID, Rome, 1990:1, pp. 7–12

Sajogyo, P. et al., "Different Perspectives, West Java Project on Rural Household Economics and the Role of Women," in FAO, *Women in Developing Agriculture*, Rome, 1985

San Mateo County, Organization of Deputy Sheriffs, *Child Abuse, Teen Suicide and Missing Juvenile Prevention Manual*, Stuart-Bradley Productions, Inc., Walnut Creek, CA, 1991

Sathar, Z., "Uneven Odds in Life and Death," in *National Health*, Special Supplement on the Girl Child, Vol. 8, 1, January, 1990, Karachi, Pakistan

Schultz, T.P., "Return to Women's Education," PHRWD Working Paper No. 001, World Bank, Washington, DC, 1989

Sen, Amartya, *Commodities and Capabilities*, Lectures in Economics, Vol. 7, Oxford University, U.K., 1985

Sen, Amartya, "Women's Survival as a Development Problem," *Bulletin of the American Academy of Art and Sciences*, Vol. XLIII:2, November 1989

Sen, Amartya, "Gender and Cooperative Conflicts," in Tinker, 1990, cited above, pp. 123–49

Sen, Amartya, "More Than 100 Million Women Are Missing," *New York Review of Books*, December 20, 1990, pp. 16–66

Sen, G. and C. Grown, *Development, Crises, and Alternative Visions, Third World Women's Perspectives*, Monthly Review Press, New York, 1987

Senauer, Benjamin, "The Impact of the Value of Women's Time on Food and Nutrition," in Tinker, 1990, cited above, pp. 150–61

Sivard, R. L., *Women. . .A World Survey*, World Priorities, Washington, D. C., 1985

Sohoni, Neera Kuckreja, "Child Without Childhood, Report on Girl Child," submitted to UNICEF, Mimeo, 1990, UNICEF, New York. (A summary based on this report was published and issued by UNICEF in 1990. See citation below)

Srinivasan, K. and Tara Kanitkar, "Demographic Consequences of Low Status of Women in Indian Society," in Gopalan and Kaur, cited above. 1989

Starrs, A., *Preventing the Tragedy of Maternal Death*, A Report on the International Safe Motherhood Conference, Nairobi, Kenya, cosponsored by World Bank, WHO, UNFFA, February, 1987

Stivers, Camilla. *Gender Images in Public Administration*, Sage Publications, Newbury Park, CA, 1993

Stromquist, N. "School-Related Determinants of Female Primary School Participation and Achievement in Developing Countries: An Annotated Bibliography," World Bank Discussion Paper No. 83, Washington, DC, 1987

Sundaram, C., "The Literacy Transition and Female Nuptiality: Implications for the Status of Asian Women," paper to Eighth Seminar in Population, East West Population Institute, Honolulu, United Nations, 1977

Tanner, Jim, *Foetus into Man: Physical Growth from Conception to Maturity*, Harvard University Press, Cambridge, MA, 1990

Thomas, D., J. Strauss, and M.H. Henriques. "Child Survival, Height for Age and Household Characteristics in Brazil," in *Journal of Development Economics*, 1990

UNDP, *Human Development Report, 1990*, Oxford University Press, New York, 1990

UNESCO, *World Declaration on Education for All: Meeting Basic Learning Needs*, WCEFA/DECLARATION/PROV., Jomtien, Thailand, 9 March, 1990

UNESCO, *Framework of Action to Meet Basic Learning Needs*, WCEFA/FRAME/PROV., Jomtien, Thailand, 9 March, 1990

UNESCO, *A Review of Education in the World: A Statistical Analysis*, ED/BIE/CONFINTED 41 Ref. 1, Paris, Oct. 1988

UNFPA: *1988 Report*, United Nations Population Fund, New York

UNICEF MENA Regional Office, "Girls' Adolescence, The Lost Opportunity, Summaries of Presentation and Recommendations of Regional Workshop," Amman, 23-26 March, 1985

UNICEF, *Two Dialogues on Women*, Bogota, Colombia, 1988

UNICEF, *Progress Report on Achievements Made in the Implementation of UNICEF Policy on Women in Development*, E/IDEF/1989/L.1., New York, 2 February, 1989

UNICEF, "Guatemala, Street Girls Study," Report of the Workshop on the Systemization of the Investigation Experiences with Girls "Of" and "On" the Streets in Mexico, Central America, Panama and the Dominican Republic, Antigua, Guatemala, March 13-17, 1989

UNICEF, *Strategies for Children in the 1990s*, New York, May, 1989

UNICEF, *Convention on the Rights of the Child*, A DCI/UNICEF Briefing Kit, New York, May, 1989

UNICEF, *Revitalizing Primary Health Care to Protect African Children*, New York, August, 1989

UNICEF, Bangladesh, Seminar on Strategies for Children in the 1990s, 8–9 October, 1989

UNICEF: *Statistics on Children in UNICEF Assisted Countries*, UNICEF, New York, 1989

UNICEF, *Situation Analysis of Children and Women in Thailand, Bangkok, 1989*

UNICEF, *The Children and Women of Sierra Leone, Freetown, 1989*

UNICEF, *Children and Women in Nigeria: A Situation Analysis*, Lagos, 1989

UNICEF, *Children and Women in Uganda: A Situation Analysis*, Kampala, 1989

UNICEF: *The Girl Child: An Investment in the Future*, UNICEF, New York, 1990

UNICEF, *An Assessment of UNICEF's Implementation of the Women's Dimension in 10 Countries*, New York, 22 January, 1990

UNICEF, *The Girl Child in Bangladesh, A Situation Analysis*, Bangladesh, January, 1990

UNICEF, Bangladesh, Child Survival Programme, Final Evaluation Report, Dhaka, February, 1990

UNICEF, UNICEF Meeting on the Girl Child, Islamabad, 1990

UNICEF, *The State of the World's Children*, New York, 1990, 1994

UNICEF, *First Call for Children*, New York, July-September, 1994

UNICEF, *The Progress of Nations*, New York, 1994

UNICEF, *Annual Reports*, New York, 1989, 1994

UNICEF/UNIFEM, "Planning and Afghan Women," Report from the Workshop, 21-23 August, 1989

United Nations, *Compendium of Statistics and Indicators on the Situation of Women*, 1986, New York, 1989

United Nations, *1989 World Survey on the Role of Women in Development*, New York, 1989

United Nations, "Population Studies No. 109/Add. 1," *Adolescent Reproductive Behavior*, Vol. II, New York, 1989

United Nations, Draft Report on "Women and Social Trends," 1970–1990, Mimeo, New York, 1990

United Nations, *The World's Women, Trends and Statistics*, 1970–1990, New York, 1991

United Nations Commission on the Status of Women, "Report on the Thirty-Third Session, Economic and Social Council, Supplement No. 9," New York

Waldron, Ingrid, "World Health Statistics," *Quarterly Report*, 40:3, 1987, pp. 194–213, WHO, Geneva, 1987

Ware, Helen, *Women, Demography and Development*, Development Studies Centre Demography Teaching Notes 3, The Australian National University, Canberra, 1981

WHO, "World Health Statistics," *Quarterly Report*, Vol. 40, 1987, pp. 194–213

WHO, "Nutrition: Sex Biases in Nutritional Status of Children 0–4 Years," *Weekly Epidemiological Record*, No. 21, 20th May, 1988

WHO, "Youth and Reproductive Health," in *The Health of Youth: Facts for Action*, Geneva, 1989

Wilensky, H., "Women's Work: Economic Growth, Ideology, Structure," *Industrial Relations*, 7 (3):235-248, 1968

Williamson, N., *Sons or Daughters: A Cross-Cultural Survey of Parental Preferences*, Sage, Beverly Hills, 1976

Wolf, Margery, *Women and the Family in Rural Taiwan*, Stanford University Press, Palo Alto, CA, 1972

World Bank, "School Enrollment in Indonesia," by D. Cherinchovsky and O.A. Meesok, Staff Working Paper No. 746, Washington, DC, 1985

World Bank, WHO and UNFPA, "Preventing the Tragedy of Maternal Deaths, A Report on the International Safe Motherhood Conference," Nairobi, Kenya, February, 1987

World Bank, *World Development Report 1988*, Washington, DC, 1988

World Bank, *World Development Report 1990*, Washington, DC, 1990

World Bank, *Gender and Poverty in India*, Washington, DC, 1991

Worldwatch Institute, *Worldwatch Paper* 97, "The Global Politics of Abortion," by Jodi L. Jacobson, Washington, DC, July, 1990

Worldwatch Institute, *World Watch*, Vol. 2, No. 2, March–April, 1989

Young, K., "Introduction," in UNESCO, "Women's Concerns and Planning: a methodological approach for their integration into local, regional and national planning," *Socioeconomic Studies* 13, 1986, pp. 9–20

Young, K., ed., *Women and Economic Development: Local, Regional and National Planning Strategies*, Berg Publishers, Ltd., Oxford, New York, 1988

Zachariah, Mathew, "Letter to the Editor," *Comparative Education Review*, November 1992: 550–554

Appendix I

Matrix of Gender Discrimination in Childhood

Public Policy	Discriminatory Growth Cycle (Age Group)	Family Policy
•No control over genetic interference for sex selection •Inadequate monitoring and enforcement of anti-feticide and anti-femicide laws	**Age Group 0 Outcome** •Almost exclusively, planned abortion affects female fetuses	•Religious and sexual rituals to enhance the conception of a male child •Abortion or feticide if female fetus is detected
•No gender-wise monitoring of mortality, morbidity patterns, causes, health and nutritional care, curative care, etc. •Inefficient registration systems for recording sex-related mortality and related data •No policy or incentives to tackle "son preference" •No defined medical, psychological or social science guidelines to enable "gender-free" childrearing and parenting	**Age Group 0-1 Outcomes** •Even with greater biological resilience, higher mortality of girls than boys •Beginning of lower life expectancy •Beginning of gendered identity	•"Son preference" resulting in: Less enthusiasm for girl child; occasional hostile or criminal response to her birth and presence •Shorter breast feeding; quicker and inadequate weaning; denial of high protein foods •Delayed or no medical treatment of girls •No registration of deaths of female children

•No policy commitment to preschool care and learning anywhere near the level of public policy support extended to primary and upper levels of education •No gender exclusive program provisions	**Age Group 2-5** **Outcomes** •Two to four times as much nutritional anemia among girls as among boys •Greater vulnerability to diseases and mortality •Development of gendered conception of self	(In addition to the above-stated factors:) •Discriminatory socialization and disciplining •Excision, circumcision and other harmful health practices
•No official recognition of the female child's Fundamental Right to Childhood •No instrumental support to enforce universal education for girls (through female teachers, exclusive schools, closely located schools, flexible school timing, relevant content and teaching methods) •No policy on reorientation of gender roles and socialization, or on reevaluation of productive and non-productive labor •No policy or enforcement mechanisms to detect and address child abuse (sexual and physical); child overwork; child neglect or abandonment; child	**Age Group 6-10** **Outcomes** •Heavy burden of surrogate motherhood and womanhood, especially without additional dietary and other care, damages the growth process causing lower weight, height, motor and mental ability; self-inflicted eating disorders cause growth damage in girls from affluent countries and cultures •Lower educability affects life preparation and opportunities •Greater risks to life from accidents at home arising from unsupervised surrogacy •Further stamping of gendered behaviors and expectations	•Denial of Right to Childhood through the girl's induction into household, farm, and urban occupational labor; no enrollment, intermittent school-going, or early withdrawal •No increase in allocation of family's food and other resources and no compensatory upgrading in her status on account of surrogate motherhood and womanhood •Intra-family allocation of food, labor, amenities and status, as well as issues of discipline and socialization are outside the purview of the State

marriage; sale of child as bonded labor or for trafficking, begging and other purposes; and traumas associated with homelessness and street living •No preferential targets for supportive instruments (such as transportation, fuel, fodder, water and sanitation) to assist girls to be freed for attending school and to pursue other activities	•Life-long impact of early or forced sexuality and/or sexual and physical abuse	
•No gender specific health care, educational and apprenticeship learning programs •No 'medical science' of adolescent health and emotional care •Inadequate formulation and enforcement of policy and legislation to combat early marriage, dowry, bride selling or burning, purdah, excision and other malpractices, including sexual and physical abuse by relatives and strangers •No policy commitment to family planning education of adolescent boys and girls; no effort to	**Age Group 11-14 Outcomes** •Growth catch-up opportunity lost •Adverse permanent consequences by way of smaller physical and pelvic size, delayed menarche, and reduced mental and bodily functioning •Further damage to perceived self-worth because of parents' vindictive approach to puberty •Permanent effects of cultural repression and social prisonization •Restricted mobility and access to public spaces and amenities diminish her personal autonomy and life chances	•Marriage is the only development option contemplated for and offered to the girl •Prevalence of purdah and other means of achieving social seclusion of girls •Punishing adolescence by equating it to sexuality and immorality (denial of girlhood linked to denial of girl's sexuality) •No psychosocial or other support to the growing girl •Insufficient personal and public role models for occupation and life outside domesticity

target boys in the discourse and treatment of teen pregnancy •No policy to regulate child labor conditions and entitlements in the household and in unregulated, informal sectors of the economy (which is where the girl child is principally employed)	•Further definition in gendered identity •Inadequate preparation for career options, and goals outside of marriage	
•No public policy on reduced fertility, maternal deaths, and morbidity focusing on this age group •No nutrition, health, learning and employment generation programs for girls bound and chained to households •No recovery mechanisms to restore them to schooling and productivity, or to tackle issues of self-esteem and survival •Inefficient monitoring, and lax legal provisions and mechanisms to cope with crimes of violence (both within the family and outside) against girls •No targeted policies or provisions for	**Age Group 15-19** **Outcomes** •Marriage and fertility become the only available option •A long reproductive span covering 16-18 years poses great risk to her own and to her progeny's life •Intergenerational transfer of nutritional depletion •Continued state of neglect and alienation even after marriage; no real welcome or gender equity in the nuptial home; bride burning and dowry deaths in extreme contexts •Lack of skills for improved earning or learning reinforce the cycle of disadvantage for her and for her offsprings	•No parental support to girl after her marriage; no further responsibility for her safety or well-being •No legitimacy for the bride in the nuptial home; no obligation to honor the daughter-in-law's rights and privileges •Seclusion of married girls and total restriction on their mobility •Intragender oppression syndrome, caused by incompatibility with mother-in-laws; in extreme contexts, causing death or grave injury to the girl •Wife battering and abuse; over-working; no monetary allowance; no

widowed, deserted, separated, single girls; or for disabled girls who are either unable to marry or are renounced after marriage on account of their disability; no provisions for street, homeless, and runaway girls	•Drop in self-esteem and occupational aspirations even among girls in developed countries •Reinforced gendered identity and role perpetuate the cycle of patriarchy	permission or encouragement to pursue learning and earning activities; domestic violence rampant across nations and societies •In many contexts, no provision for alimony, child support, or for rights of widowed, and disabled married girls

Notes:

1. The matrix assumes an overflow of causes, as well as outcomes between various stages of the discriminatory growth cycle.
2. "No" policy or mechanism refers to "none or not enough" articulation of policy and instruments.

APPENDIX II

THE CONVENTION ON THE RIGHTS OF THE CHILD

Adopted by the General Assembly of the United Nations on 20 November 1989*

PREAMBLE

The States Parties to the present Convention,

Considering that in accordance with the principles proclaimed in the Charter of the United Nations, recognition of the inherent dignity and of the equal and inalienable rights of all members of the human family is the foundation of freedom, justice and peace in the world,

Bearing in mind that the peoples of the United Nations have, in the Charter, reaffirmed their faith in fundamental human rights and in the dignity and worth of the human person, and have determined to promote social progress and better standards of life in larger freedom,

Recognizing that the United Nations has, in the Universal Declaration of Human Rights and in the International Covenants on Human Rights, proclaimed and agreed that everyone is entitled to all the rights and freedoms set forth therein, without distinction of any kind, such as race, color, sex, language, religion, political or other opinion, national or social origin, property, birth or other status,

Recalling that, in the Universal Declaration of Human Rights, the United Nations has proclaimed that childhood is entitled to special care and assistance,

---

*The Convention came into force on 2 September 1990, after 20 States had ratified or acceded to it. (This is the unofficial summary of main provisions. Those interested in the full text of this document are directed to contact the United Nations or a research library.)

Convinced that the family, as the fundamental group of society and the natural environment for the growth and well-being of all its members and particularly children, should be afforded the necessary protection and assistance so that it can fully assume its responsibilities within the community,

Recognizing that the child, for the full and harmonious development of his or her personality, should grow up in a family environment, in an atmosphere of happiness, love and understanding,

Considering that the child should be fully prepared to live an individual life in society, and brought up in the spirit of the ideals proclaimed in the Charter of the United Nations, and in particular in the spirit of peace, dignity, tolerance, freedom, equality and solidarity,

Bearing in mind that the need to extend particular care to the child has been stated in the Geneva Declaration of the Rights of the Child of 1924 and in the Declaration of the Rights of the Child adopted by the United Nations on 20 November 1959 and recognized in the Universal Declaration of Human Rights, in the International Covenant on Civil and Political Rights (in particular in articles 23 and 24), in the International Covenant on Economic, Social and Cultural Rights (in particular in article 10) and in the statutes and relevant instruments of specialized agencies and international organizations concerned with the welfare of children,

Bearing in mind that, as indicated in the Declaration of the Rights of the Child, 'the child, by reason of his physical and mental immaturity, needs special safeguards and care, including appropriate legal protection, before as well as after birth,"

Recalling the provisions of the Declaration on Social and Legal Principles relating to the Protection and Welfare of Children, with Special Reference to Foster Placement and Adoption Nationally and Internationally; the United Nations Standard Minimum Rules for the Administration of Juvenile Justice ("The Beijing Rules"); and the Declaration on the Protection of Women and Children in Emergency and Armed Conflict,

Recognizing that, in all countries in the world, there are children living in exceptionally difficult conditions, and that such children need special consideration,

Taking account of the importance of the traditions and cultural values of each people for the protection and harmonious development of the child,

Recognizing the importance of international cooperation for improving the living conditions of children in every country, in particular in the developing countries.

Have agreed as follows:

Summary of Articles

Part I

Article 1. Definition of a child

A child is recognized as a person under 18, unless national laws recognize the age of maturity earlier.

Article 2. Non-discrimination

All rights apply to all children without exception. It is the State's obligation to protect children from any form of discrimination and to take positive action to promote their rights.

Article 3. Best Interests of the child

All actions concerning the child shall take full account of his or her best interests. The State shall provide the child with adequate care when parents, or others charged with that responsibility, fail to do so.

Article 4. Implementation of rights

The State must do all it can to implement the rights contained in the Convention.

Article 5. Parental guidance and the child's evolving capacities

The State must respect the rights and responsibilities of parents and the extended family to provide guidance for the child which is appropriate to her or his evolving capacities.

Article 6. Survival and development

Every child has the inherent right to life, and the State has an obligation to ensure the child's survival and development.

Article 7. Name and nationality

The child has the right to a name at birth. The child also has the right to acquire a nationality and, as far as possible, to know his or her parents and be cared for by them.

Article 8. Preservation of Identity

The State has an obligation to protect, and if necessary, re-establish basic aspects of the child's identity. This includes name, nationality and family ties.

Article 9. Separation from parents

The child has a right to live with his or her parents unless this is deemed to be incompatible with the child 's best interests. The child also has the right to maintain contact with both parents if separated from one or both.

Article 10. Family reunification

Children and their parents have the right to leave any country and to enter their own for purposes of reunion or the maintenance of the child-parent relationship.

Article 11. Illicit transfer and non-return

The State has an obligation to prevent and remedy the kidnapping or retention of children abroad by a parent or third party.

Article 12. The child's opinion

The child has the right to express his or her opinion freely and to have that opinion taken into account in any matter or procedure affecting the child.

Article 13. Freedom of expression

The child has the right to express his or her views, obtain information, make ideas or information known, regardless of frontiers.

Article 14. Freedom of thought, conscience and religion

The State shall respect the child's right to freedom of thought, conscience and religion, subject to appropriate parental guidance.

Article 15. Freedom of association

Children have a right to meet with others, and to join or form associations.

Article 16. Protection of privacy

Children have the right to protection from interference with privacy, family, home and correspondence and from libel or slander.

Article 17. Access to appropriate information

The State shall ensure the accessibility to children of information and material from a diversity of sources, and it shall encourage the mass media to disseminate information which is of social and cultural benefit to the child, and take steps to protect him or her from harmful materials.

Article 18. Parental responsibilities

Parents have joint primary responsibility for raising the child, and the State shall support them in this. The State shall provide appropriate assistance to parents in child-raising.

Article 19. Protection from abuse and neglect

The State shall protect the child from all forms of maltreatment by parents or others responsible for the care of the child and establish appropriate social programs for the prevention of abuse and the treatment of victims.

Article 20. Protection of a child without family

The State is obliged to provide special protection for a child deprived of the family environment and to ensure that appropriate alternative family care or institutional placement is available in such cases. Efforts to meet this obligation shall pay due regard to the child's cultural background.

Article 21. Adoption

In countries where adoption is recognized and/or allowed, it shall only be carried out in the best interests of the child, and then only with the authorization of competent authorities, and safeguards for the child.

Article 22. Refugee children

Special protection shall be granted to a refugee child or to a child seeking refugee status. It is the State's obligation to cooperate with competent organizations which provide such protection and assistance.

Article 23. Disabled children

A disabled child has the right to special care, education and training to help him or her enjoy a full and decent life in dignity and achieve the greatest degree of self-reliance and social integration possible.

Article 24. Health and health services

The child has a right to the highest standard of health and medical care attainable. States shall place special emphasis on the provision of primary and preventive health care, public health education and the reduction of infant mortality. They shall encourage international cooperation in this regard and strive to see that no child is deprived of access to effective health services.

Article 25. Periodic review of placement

A child who is placed by the State for reasons of care, protection or treatment is entitled to have that placement evaluated regularly.

Article 26. Social security

The child has the right to benefit from social security including social insurance.

Article 27. Standard of living

Every child has the right to a standard of living adequate for his or her physical, mental, spiritual, moral and social development. Parents have the primary responsibility to ensure that the child has an adequate standard of living. The State's duty is to ensure that this responsibility can be fulfilled, and is. State responsibility can include material assistance to parents and their children.

Article 28. Education

The child has a right to education, and the State's duty is to ensure that primary education is free and compulsory, to encourage different forms of secondary education accessible to every child and to make higher education available to all on the basis of capacity. School discipline shall be consistent with the child's rights and dignity. The State shall engage in international cooperation to implement this right.

Article 29. Aims of education

Education shall aim at developing the child's personality, talents and mental and physical abilities to the fullest extent. Education shall prepare the child for an active adult life in a free society and foster respect for the child's parents, his or her own cultural identity language and values, and for the cultural background and values of others.

Article 30. Children of minorities or indigenous populations

Children of minority communities and indigenous populations have the right to enjoy their own culture and to practice their own religion and language.

Article 31. Leisure, recreation and cultural activities

The child has the right to leisure, play and participation in cultural and artistic activities.

Article 32. Child labor

The child has the right to be protected from work that threatens his or her health, education or development The State shall set minimum ages for employment and regulate working conditions.

Article 33. Drug abuse

Children have the right to protection from the use of narcotic and psychotropic drugs, and from being involved in their production or distribution.

Article 34. Sexual Exploitation

The State shall protect children from sexual exploitation and abuse, including prostitution and involvement in pornography.

Article 35. Sale, trafficking and abduction

It is the State's obligation to make every effort to prevent the sale, trafficking and abduction of children.

Article 36. Other forms of exploitation

The child has the right to protection from all forms of exploitation prejudicial to any aspects of the child's welfare not covered in articles 32, 33, 34, and 35.

Article 37. Torture and deprivation of liberty

No child shall be subjected to torture, cruel treatment or punishment, unlawful arrest or deprivation of liberty. Both capital punishment and life imprisonment without the possibility of release are prohibited for offenses committed by persons below 18 years. Any child deprived of liberty shall be separated from adults unless it is considered in the child's best interests not to do so. A child who is detained shall have legal and other assistance as well as contact with the family.

Article 38. Armed conflicts

States Parties shall take all feasible measures to ensure that children under 15 years of age have no direct part in hostilities. No child below 15 shall be recruited into the armed forces. States shall also ensure the protection and care of children who are affected by armed conflict as described in relevant international law.

Article 39. Rehabilitative care

The State has an obligation to ensure that child victims of armed conflicts, torture, neglect, maltreatment or exploitation receive appropriate treatment for their recovery and social reintegration.

Article 40. Administration of juvenile justice

A child in conflict with the law has the right to treatment which promotes the child 's sense of dignity and worth, takes the child's age into account and aims at his or her reintegration into society. The child is entitled to basic guarantees as well as legal or other assistance for his or her defense. Judicial proceedings and institutional placements shall be avoided wherever possible.

Article 41. Respect for higher standards

Wherever standards set in applicable national and international law relevant to the rights of the child are higher than those in this Convention, the higher standard shall always apply.

Implementation of the provisions

Part II

The provisions of articles 42 - 54 notably foresee:

(i) the State's obligation to make the rights contained in this Convention widely known to both adults and children.

(ii) the setting up of a Committee on the Rights of the child composed of ten experts, which will consider reports that States Parties to the Convention are to submit two years after ratification and every five years thereafter. The Convention enters into force—and the Committee would therefore be set up— once 20 countries have ratified.

(iii) States Parties are to make their reports widely available to the general public.

(iv) The Committee may propose that special studies be undertaken on specific issues relating to the rights of the child, and may make its evaluations known to each State Party concerned as well as to the U.N. General Assembly.

(v) In order to "foster the effective implementation of the Convention and to encourage international cooperation," the specialized agencies of the U.N. (such as the ILO, WHO, and UNESCO) and UNICEF would be able to attend the meetings of the Committee. Together with any other body recognized as "competent," including NGOs in consultative status with the U.N. and U.N. organs such as the UNHCR, they can submit pertinent information to the Committee and be asked to advise on the optimal implementation of the Convention.

Appendix III

Convention on the Elimination of All Forms of Discrimination Against Women

On 18 December 1979, The Convention on the Elimination of All Forms of Discrimination against Women was adopted by the General Assembly. It became an international treaty on 3 September 1981 after the twentieth country had ratified it.

Bringing the female half of humanity into the focus of human rights concerns, the Convention establishes not only an international bill of rights for women but also an agenda for action by countries to guarantee those rights.

Governments are committed to:

- creating conditions within which women can exercise and employ basic rights and freedoms.

- affirmative action for women until parity with men is achieved.

- abolishing all forms of slavery and prostitution of women.

- securing women's rights to vote, stand for election and hold public or political office.

- providing equal opportunity for women to represent their countries internationally.

- allowing women the right to change or retain their nationality and that of their children, regardless of marital status.

- ensuring girls' and women's equal access to quality education in all subjects and at all levels, including continuing and vocational programs for women.

- ensuring equal employment opportunities, promotion, vocational training, job security benefits and equal pay for work of equal value. In addition, they must ensure that women who are married, pregnant or have children have the right to work and the right to maternity leave and other benefits; they must also ensure that child care is available and that pregnant women are protected from work that may be hazardous to their health.

- providing adequate health services, including family planning where necessary, and pre-natal and post-natal care, including nutrition for pregnant and lactating mothers.

- ensuring access to financial credit and family benefits, and the right to participate in recreational cultural and athletic activities.

- giving special attention to all the provisions of the Convention to women living in rural areas.

- ensuring equal rights to choose a spouse, name or occupation, marry and divorce; own, buy, sell and administer property; share parenting, regardless of marital status; and choose the number and spacing of their children, including adoption or guardianship. In addition, governments are committed to establishing a minimum age for marriage and to ensuring that all marriages are entered into freely, by mutual consent.

Source: U.N., *The World's Women: Trends and Statistics 1970-1990,* U.N., New York, 1991, p. 115.

Appendix IV

Nairobi Forward-Looking Strategies for the Advancement of Women

The Nairobi Forward-Looking Strategies for the Advancement of Women were adopted by the World Conference to Review and Appraise the Achievements of the United Nations Decade for Women: Equality, Development and Peace, held in Nairobi, Kenya, 15–26 July 1985,[1] and endorsed by the General Assembly in its resolution 40/108 on 13 December 1985. They call for:

Social equality[2]

- the elimination of all forms of discrimination against women

- equal rights under the law

- equal rights to marriage and divorce

- the establishment, in every country, of a high-level governmental body to monitor and implement progress towards equity.

Women's autonomy and power[3]

- the right of all women—irrespective of marital status—to buy, sell, own and administer property and other resources independently

- the protection of women's rights to land, credit, training, investment and income as an integral part of all agrarian reform and agricultural development

- the equal involvement of women, at every stage and level of development

- the promotion of women to positions of power at every level within all political and legislative bodies in order to achieve parity with men

- measures to promote equal distribution of productive resources and reduce mass poverty among women, particularly in times of economic recession.

Recognition of women's unpaid work[4]

- recognition of the extent and value of women's unpaid work, inside and outside the home

- inclusion of women's paid and unpaid work in national accounts and economic statistics

- the sharing of domestic responsibilities

- the development of services, to reduce women's child-care and domestic workload, including introduction of incentives to encourage employers to provide child-care facilities for working parents

- the establishment of flexible working hours to encourage the sharing of child-care and domestic work between parents.

Advances in women's paid work[5]

- equal employment opportunities

- equal pay for work of equal value

- recognition of the extent and value of women's work in the informal sector

- measures to encourage women to work in male-dominated occupations and vice versa, in order to desegregate the work place

- preferential treatment in hiring of women so long as they are a disproportionate share of the unemployed

- adequate social security and unemployment benefits.

Health services and family planning[6]

- equal access to health services

- adequate health facilities for mothers and children

- every woman's right to decide on the number and spacing of her children, and access to family planning for every woman

- discouragement of child-bearing at too early an age.

Better educational opportunities[7]

- equal access to education and training

- efforts to have more girls study subjects usually selected by boys, and vice versa, in order to desegregate curricula

- efforts to ensure that girls don't drop out of school

- the provision of adult education for women.

Promotion of peace[8]

- the involvement of women in promoting peace and disarmament.

Minimum targets for the year 2000[9]

- enforcement of laws guaranteeing implementation of women's equality

- an increase in the life expectancy of women to at least 65 years in all countries

- the reduction of maternal mortality

- the elimination of women's illiteracy

- the expansion of employment opportunities.

Notes

1 See Report of the Conference to Review and Appraise the Achievements of the United Nations Decade for Women: Equality, Development and Peace (United Nations publication, Sales No. E. 85, IV, 10).
2 Ibid., paras. 43, 54, 74, 57
3 Ibid., paras. 74, 62, 86, 111, 119
4 Ibid., paras. 59, 120, 59, 228, 136 and 228
5 Ibid., paras. 54, 137, 59 and 120, 137, 133 and 138, 144 and 145, 140
6 Ibid., paras. 54, 155, 156, 158
7 Ibid., paras. 54 and 189, 171, 165
8 Ibid., paras. 240
9 Ibid., paras. 35, 155, 35, 132

Source: U.N., *The World's Women: Trends and Statistics, 1970-90,* U.N., New York, 1991, pp. 113-14

Maternal and Child Health Books Available From
THIRD PARTY PUBLISHING COMPANY

Code	Titles and Authors	Calif. residents (inc. taxes)	Other U.S.A. states	Int'l cost (includes shipping)
0408	The Burden of Girlhood: A Global Inquiry into the Status of Girls — **Neera Kuckreja Sohoni**	$21.95	$19.95	$24.95
0416	Maternal and Child Health Practices, 4th Ed.— **Wallace/Nelson/Sweeney**	42.95	39.95	49.95
0343	Principles and Practices of Student Health (3 vol. set) — **Wallace/Patrick/Parcel/Igoe**	54.95	49.95	59.95
A102	The National Adolescent Student Health Survey — **ASHA/AAHE/SOPHE**	21.95	19.95	24.95
0432	Health Care of Women and Children in Developing Countries, 2nd Ed. — **Wallace/Giri/Serrano**	42.95	39.95	49.95
0424	Quantitative Problem Solving in Maternal, Child, and Adolescent Health — **Gould**	21.95	19.95	24.95
0467	Prenatal Care for Hispanic Women — **Wallace et al.**	21.95	19.95	24.95
0386	Report of Infant Mortality Study in San Diego County — **Wallace et al.**	21.95	19.95	24.95

Order From
THIRD PARTY PUBLISHING COMPANY
P.O. Box 13306, Montclair Station
Oakland, California 94661-0306, U.S.A.
Telephone 510/339-2323
Fax 510/339-6729
(U.S. institutional purchase orders accepted. International orders, and orders from U.S. individuals, must be prepaid in U.S. dollars by check, money order, or VISA/MasterCard credit card.)